Schubert and His Vienna

Schubert
and His Vienna

Charles Osborne

ALFRED A. KNOPF ∞ NEW YORK

1985

THIS IS A BORZOI BOOK
PUBLISHED BY ALFRED A. KNOPF, INC.

Library of Congress Cataloging-in-Publication Data

Osborne, Charles, 1927–   Schubert & his Vienna.

Includes index.
1. Schubert, Franz, 1797–1828.   2. Composers—
Austria—Biography.   3. Vienna (Austria)—Intellectual life.
I. Title.   II. Title: Schubert and his Vienna.
ML410.S3087   1985   780'.92'4   [B]   85-40350   ISBN 0-394-54111-1

Manufactured in the United States of America

First American Edition

To
Rudolf Serkin,
most Schubertian of musicians

Contents

Illustrations

Unless otherwise indicated, the illustrations are reproduced by kind permission of the Historisches Museum der Stadt Wien.

Preface

Of all the great composers, surely none has reached a wider audience than Franz Schubert, the melodies of whose 'Serenade', 'Ave Maria', 'Hark! hark! the lark at heaven's gate sings' and other songs and instrumental pieces are recognized by millions who may not realize that several other tunes they have known since childhood were also written by this most accessible of the Viennese classical composers, and incidentally the only one actually to have been born in Vienna.

Schubert is a composer of more than one mood and more than one level of experience. It would be wrong to suggest that all of him is to be found in the engaging and lyrical melodies of his most popular songs, for much of his chamber music is, in its way, as profound as that of Beethoven. But I know of no composer whom it is easier to begin to know and to love. My own introduction to Schubert was, as it happens, not through any of the well-known songs. As a child, I was taken to a chamber music recital whose programme consisted of quartets by Mozart, Beethoven and Schubert. For many years now, I have known and loved many of the quartets of all three composers, but on that evening I found most of the music, all of which I was hearing for the first time, somewhat daunting – that is, until the last movement of the Schubert quartet. It was the E flat major Quartet, D.87, which Schubert wrote at the age of sixteen. I know it now as a delightful work, but then I sat and let the pleasant but strange music flow over me, until it reached what I now know to be the second subject of the final allegro, which was a tune so natural, so cheerful and so friendly, that I smiled in sheer delight. I got to know other pieces by Schubert, and soon found that he could move me to tears as well. Nearly fifty years later, I am still making discoveries about him.

It is in order to share my feelings about a composer who since my childhood has been very dear to me that I have written this life of Schubert. This volume is not a musicological treatise, nor does it contain detailed musical analysis with examples or excerpts from works by the composer. It is an attempt to tell the story of Schubert's life, against a background of the city that he so greatly loved. It is a book, therefore, not for the specialist, but for the general music lover, or indeed for anyone who enjoys reading about past times and the lives of great men. Because the music of Schubert grew so naturally from his Viennese background, and because the influence of Vienna is so readily discernible in his more sociable pieces, I have chosen to alternate chapters of pure biography with chapters on various aspects of life in Vienna in the first quarter of the nineteenth century, and on Schubert's circle of friends.

I have attempted to describe Schubert's major works in non-technical language, and also to appraise many of his minor works, including the highly engaging waltzes and other dance music, as well as the music that he composed for the church. I have tried to write what might be described as a 'popular' as opposed to an academic biography, without, I hope, resorting to the romantic and over-wrought prose too often associated with such an approach.

An important feature of this book is the extent to which it makes use of the words of Schubert himself, and his contemporaries. In particular, Schubert's extant letters and diaries are quoted in full (mostly in the author's translation), with the exception only of a few short notes whose content is insubstantial or insignificant. The composer is given ample opportunity to speak for himself. Certain misconceptions regarding his popularity during his lifetime are corrected, and new light is thrown on various aspects of his personal life.

No one writing on Schubert in the twentieth century can fail to be heavily indebted to the eminent Austrian bibliographer Otto Erich Deutsch (1883–1967), the leading authority on Schubert, upon whose volume *Schubert: A Documentary Biography*, which contains virtually all the existing documents relating to the composer, I have drawn frequently and gratefully.

Charles Osborne
London, January 1985

CHAPTER ONE

1797–1814
A Youth's Calling

The world into which Franz Schubert was born in 1797 was a revolutionary world. Across the Atlantic the American colonies had recently gained their freedom and a New World was in the process of creation, while, nearer home, on the other side of the Alps Europe was still shuddering from the aftermath of the French Revolution. But Schubert was born in Vienna, the capital city of an Austria which had been, as yet, not directly affected by revolution. A largely Protestant Germany had suffered violent repercussions from the French upheaval, but these were hardly felt at all across the border in the multilingual empire of Catholic Austria. The country was rich and fertile, living was cheap and, although social inequality was rife, comparatively few appeared positively to be harmed by it. Church, monarchy and civil service kept the Empire in good order, an Empire whose cities included Prague and Budapest as well as the great capital, Vienna.

Although Schubert's Vienna was not to remain untouched by the shadow, or indeed the substance, of Napoleon, the year of the composer's birth was a relatively peaceful one. The Vienna in which Schubert (the only one of the great Viennese classical composers actually to have been born there) grew up was Europe's capital of music. It was the city of Haydn, Gluck, Mozart, Beethoven and a host of lesser names. Even today, long after Vienna's Empire has crumbled, the visitor to the city who is at all sensitive to music can hear the sounds of the past all around him, and can almost feel music in the fabric of the houses and palaces where so many masterpieces were first performed. The music of Vienna, like its cuisine and its literature, was created from a number of sources, for Vienna was a melting-pot of nations and races. Various minorities, Czech, Moravian, Polish,

Slovakian, Croatian, Slovenian, Hungarian, Italian, South German, and of course Jewish, made up the Viennese character. (Vienna, until the twentieth-century *Anschluss*, was the most Jewish city in Europe: a fact of huge importance in its development as the city of music.)

The half-century from 1770 to 1830 in Vienna is generally regarded as one of the world's greatest artistic periods, along with Periclean Athens, Elizabethan England, and both Paris and Vienna at the end of the nineteenth and the beginning of the twentieth century. Gluck, Haydn, Mozart, Beethoven and Schubert have been revealed by time as the great glories of Vienna's classical period, but a host of minor composers were also active during those years in Vienna, among them Reutter, Monn, Wagenseil, Albrechtsberger, Pleyel, Czerny, Dittersdorf, Mysliweczek, Franz Benda, Georg Benda, Stamitz, Koželuch, Wanhall, Salieri and Cimarosa.

Though the Vienna into which Schubert was born was a city as yet untouched by revolution, it was not one unaffected by war. The Empress Maria Theresia had died in 1780, to be succeeded by her son Josef II, who consolidated the progress towards unification made by his mother. After the death of Josef in 1790, his brother Leopold and, two years later, his nephew Franz succeeded him, and the Habsburg dynasty, which had lasted since the thirteenth century, found itself under threat from Napoleon.

In April 1792 France declared war against Austria. Fighting on two fronts, through Germany and Italy, Austria was eventually forced to concede victory in Italy to Napoleon, who had entered Milan in May 1796 and had proceeded to conquer the whole of the Austrian territory of Lombardy. While the battles were still being fought, a corps of volunteers from Vienna left in the autumn of 1796 to join the army in Italy. In their honour, Beethoven wrote a 'Song of Farewell to the Citizens of Vienna'. Some weeks later, the Austrian Government commissioned from Haydn a national anthem, 'Gott erhalte Franz den Kaiser' (God Save the Emperor Franz), which was sung in all Austrian theatres for the first time on 12 February 1797, twelve days after the birth of Schubert. (It continued to be the Austrian national hymn until Germany annexed the tune with new words: 'Deutschland, Deutschland über alles.')

On 2 February the Viennese volunteer corps was forced to surrender to the French in Mantua, and Napoleon was able to march into Austria. More volunteers were called for, and on Easter Monday in Vienna a new corps marched out from the inner city to do battle with the enemy. The music to which they marched included a new song by Beethoven, 'Kriegslied der Österreicher' (War Song of the Austrians). But by then the war was over, and the new corps was not called upon to fight. A peace treaty was negotiated with Napoleon under the terms of which the Habsburg Empire lost its Belgian province of Flanders, and its Austrian territory of Lombardy, but received the territory (including the city) of Venice, as well as Istria and Dalmatia.

The name 'Schubert' means 'shoemaker'. The composer's family can be traced back as far as the early seventeenth century to one Kaspar Schubert, of Waltersdorf in the north of Moravia. Kaspar's second son, Christoph, became a farmer in the neighbouring village of Neudorf, and Hans, the youngest of Christoph's nine children, was the great-grandfather of the composer. It was this generation of the family which seems to have advanced from the status of peasant-farmer to that of small landowner. Among Hans's numerous children was Karl, Franz Schubert's grandfather, who married Susanna Mück in 1754, and later bought his father-in-law's farm land. Karl, a respected citizen of Neudorf, was for a time a minor official. Of his thirteen children, only four survived to adulthood, among them the eldest child, Karl, who became a farmer, and a younger son, Franz Theodor Florian Schubert, the father of the composer.

Karl tired of the land while still in his twenties, made his way to Vienna, and became a schoolmaster in the suburb of Leopoldstadt. In 1783, his younger brother Franz, now twenty years of age, followed him to Vienna and became Karl's assistant. Two years later, Franz married Elisabeth Vietz, a domestic servant in the suburb of Liechtental. (Brother Karl, after the death of his first wife in 1792, married Elisabeth Vietz's younger sister, Maria Magdalena.)

Franz Schubert was the twelfth of the fourteen children born to his parents, Franz and Elisabeth Schubert, and one of the five to survive infancy. Soon after his marriage, Franz Schubert senior had become master of a school in the Himmelpfortgrund district of Vienna, to the north-west of the city. In June 1786 he moved into a house, number 72, in the High Street, named *Zum roten Krebsen* (The Red Crab). Later, when the street was renamed and the houses renumbered, it became Nussdorferstrasse 54. It still stands, and today houses the

Schubert Museum, the most frequently visited Schubert memorial site. Here Franz Peter Schubert was born, at 1.30 p.m. on 31 January 1797. The parish Register of Births gives the family religion as Catholic.

In Schubert's time, the house was divided into sixteen separate small apartments, each consisting of one room and kitchen. When Franz was born, his parents occupied two of these apartments. Four years later, the family moved to a somewhat larger house in the nearby Säulengasse, which also still stands (though today it is the Schubert Garage).

Himmelpfortgrund was part of the suburb of Liechtental, which, at the beginning of the nineteenth century, was still almost rural in character. A short distance away, the Vienna Woods began, and the outlines of Vienna's domestic hills, the Kahlenberg and the Leopoldsberg, could be seen. The house in the Säulengasse was both the Schubert family residence and the school-house, where Franz's father was responsible for more than two hundred day-pupils. It was here, at the age of six, that young Franz was enrolled in one of his father's classes.

Music played an important part in the life of the Schubert family, as it did in the lives of most middle-class Viennese families of the time. Franz Schubert senior was a good enough musician to be able to teach young Franz to play the violin, and Franz's eldest brother, Ignaz, gave him his first lessons on the piano. Michael Holzer, the organist and choir-master of the Liechtental parish church, who taught Franz the organ, singing and the rudiments of composition, said of his young pupil, 'Whenever I wished to impart something new to him, he always knew it already. I often looked at him in silent wonder.' Music, it seemed, came almost as naturally to the child as breathing. According to Ferdinand, the second of his three elder brothers, by his eleventh year Franz was the first soprano in the parish church, played violin solos from the organ loft of the church, and had already begun to compose 'small songs, string quartets and pianoforte pieces'.

In 1808, when Franz was eleven, his parents responded to an announcement in the *Wiener Zeitung* of 28 May that there were vacancies for two boy choristers in the Imperial and Royal Court Chapel. Applicants for the two posts were 'to present themselves on 30 September at 3 p.m. at the Imperial and Royal City Seminary, Universitätsplatz 796, and to undergo an examination, as regards both

4

the progress made by them in their studies and such knowledge as they may have already gained in music, and to bring their school certificates with them'. The boys were also required to have passed their tenth birthdays, to be suitable to enter the Latin class, and to show evidence that they were past the danger of smallpox.

Young Franz passed the examination with flying colours, and became one of three boys admitted to the Court Chapel Choir in the autumn of 1808. Two of the judges were Antonio Salieri, Music Director to the Austrian court, who is remembered today mainly for his rivalry to Mozart, and Dr Franz Innocenz Lang, headmaster of the seminary at which the boys of the Chapel Choir received their general as well as their musical education. Their verdicts have been recorded. Salieri's is in Italian, the only language he spoke with ease although he had been resident in Vienna for more than forty years: 'Fra gli soprani gli migliori sono Francesco Schubert e Francesco Müllner' (Among the sopranos the best are Franz Schubert and Franz Müllner). Dr Lang concurred: 'The two sopranos Schubert and Müllner also excel all the others in elementary knowledge.'

The Court Chapel Choir had been founded in 1498 and, although there is no longer an imperial Austrian court, the choir still exists today, providing music for the Sunday services in the old court chapel of the Hofburg in Vienna. Its sopranos and altos are members of the Vienna Boys' Choir (Wiener Sängerknaben), its tenors and basses are drawn from the chorus of the State Opera, and its instrumentalists from the Vienna Philharmonic Orchestra.

The Imperial and Royal City Seminary (Kaiserlich-königliches Stadtkonvikt) was, when Schubert entered it in 1808, a relatively new institution. It had been founded in 1803 by the Emperor Franz to replace an earlier Jesuit seminary which had been dissolved, and it served not only as a school for the choirboys but also as a preparatory establishment for students of the university. The school was housed in the old university building, opposite the new hall and next to the Jesuit church, in that area of the old city between the cathedral (the Stephansdom) and the Danube Canal.

Becoming a member of the Court Chapel Choir and thus a student at the seminary meant that the young Schubert was assured of the finest musical and general education that the city of Vienna could offer. Although the majority of the 130 boarders were not music students, there was sufficient musical talent amongst them for one of them, a twenty-year-old law student named Josef von Spaun, to form a student orchestra which soon acquired an enviable reputation. Spaun, who played second violin in the orchestra, was a good eight years older than Schubert, but became one of the boy's firmest friends.

From his very first term, Schubert did remarkably well at the seminary. A report issued in his second term shows him to have received good marks in Singing, Violin and Pianoforte. In the student orchestra he played in the second violins. His musical studies were in the hands of Wenzel Ruzicka (1758–1823), a minor composer who was court organist and played the viola in the Burgtheater orchestra. Ruzicka said of Schubert, 'This one has learned it from God.'

The orchestra rehearsed a short programme, consisting of a symphony and an overture, on most evenings. Soon Schubert had moved to the first violins, and in a short time he was leading the orchestra whenever Ruzicka was absent. For a time in the summer of 1809, orchestral practice was interrupted. Vienna was occupied by the French, and Napoleon was in residence at Schönbrunn. During the bombardment which preceded the occupation, the seminary building was pierced by a howitzer shell on the evening of 11 May. An event which may have affected Schubert more deeply was the death of Haydn on 31 May.

By 1811 Schubert was being singled out for praise for 'the excellent progress he has shown in all subjects'. He had already begun to compose pieces which impressed his teachers: a fantasy for piano duet (D.1) in April 1810; a string quartet (D.2c) and an overture for string quintet (D.8) in the following year, and on 30 March 1811, his first surviving song, 'Hagars Klage' (Hagar's Lament, D.5), for soprano voice and piano.

For someone who was to become the greatest of all composers of Lieder, or German-language songs, 'Hagar's Lament' might seem an inauspicious beginning. The Old Testament story of Hagar and her child left to perish in the wilderness is told in limping and sentimental verses by a minor poet, Clemens August Schücking, and the fourteen-year-old Schubert has turned them into not so much a song as a miniature operatic scena. Fifteen pages long and taking about seventeen minutes to perform, 'Hagar's Lament' is composed in the style of Johann Rudolf Zumsteeg (1760–1802), a composer of songs who was generally admired at the time, but whose music is now thought to be mainly of historical importance. According to Josef von

Spaun, the young Schubert could 'revel in [Zumsteeg's] songs for days on end'. 'Hagar's Lament' is a remarkably mature piece for a boy of fourteen to have composed, but it could have been written by any competent adult composer of the period. The individual genius of Schubert is not to be heard in it, though the song is said to have aroused the interest of Salieri, with whom Schubert took lessons twice a week after he had completed his elementary studies under Ruzicka.

It was in 1811 that Schubert heard his first operas. He was taken twice to the Kärntnertor theatre by his friend Josef von Spaun, to performances of operas by Josef Weigl (1766–1846): *Das Waisenhaus* (The Orphanage) and *Die Schweizerfamilie* (The Swiss Family). Schubert was extremely fortunate to have lived as a child in Vienna, and to have been able to hear such a profusion of performances of music by the great classical composers, from Handel to Gluck, Haydn, Mozart and Beethoven. The experience could have been overwhelming to the point of being inhibitory had it not been allied to the musical education he was receiving at the seminary.

On 28 May 1812, Schubert's mother died. A curious allegorical tale, 'My Dream', which Schubert wrote when he was twenty-five (see pp. 88–9), has led some writers on the composer to believe that, at the time of his mother's death, he had been banished from the family house for some offence or other, and was allowed to return home only for his mother's funeral. This is highly unlikely. He was, after all, only fifteen, was still a boarder at the seminary, and would have lived at home only during the holidays.

In July, Schubert's voice began to break. A note in his own hand at the end of the alto part of a Mass by Peter Winter reads, 'Schubert Franz crowed for the last time, 26 July 1812.' The following day he began to compose a trio for piano, violin and cello and a month later had completed the opening Allegro (D.28), at which point he appears to have abandoned the work. The Allegro, a remarkable piece for a fifteen-year-old to have composed, is tuneful and engaging.

Schubert had already begun to compose church music, having completed a 'Salve Regina' (D.27) at the end of June. Although he could no longer sing as an alto in the Chapel Choir, he was able to continue his education at the seminary, and remained there for a further year. The earliest surviving letter by Schubert dates from this time. Written on 24 November 1812, it is addressed to one of his brothers, probably Ferdinand:

7

Let me say straight out what is on my mind, and come to the point without my usual beating about the bush. For some time now I've been thinking about my life here, and have decided that, although on the whole it's reasonably good, there is still room for improvement here and there. You know from your own experience that there are times when you feel like a roll or a few apples, and especially if, after a moderate-sized lunch, all you have to look forward to is a miserable supper eight and a half hours later. This persistent longing is becoming more and more frequent, and I must do something about it, willy nilly. The few *Groschen* that father allows me are all gone in the first few days, so what am I to do for the rest of the time? 'Whosoever believeth on him shall not be ashamed' (Matthew, Chapter 3, verse 4). I thought so too. How would it be if you were to let me have a few *Kreutzer* each month? You wouldn't notice it, and I, in my cell here, would be content. As I said, I rely upon the words of the Apostle Matthew, where he says: 'He that hath two coats, let him give one to the poor.' In the meantime, I hope that you will lend an ear to the voice that calls unceasingly on you to remember

> your loving, poor, hopeful, and once
> again poor brother,
> Franz.

Franz's letter is a mixture of cheek and charm, and it probably produced some additional pocket money from his brother, despite the inaccuracy of the biblical quotations: the first is not from Matthew, but from Romans 10:11, and the second is a paraphrase not of Matthew, but of Luke 3:11: 'He that hath two coats, let him impart to him that hath none.'

In April 1813 Schubert's father married for the second time. His bride, Anna Kleyenböck, the twenty-nine-year-old daughter of a Viennese silk manufacturer, made a kindly stepmother to the children, and later on several occasions helped Franz out of her housekeeping money. Meanwhile, with his monthly allowance slightly augmented, the now sixteen-year-old youth continued to learn and to compose. He had become a proficient pianist, and had come to love the instrument. Fond of dancing, he composed in 1813 three minuets for orchestra, and thirty for the piano.

Schubert also, at the end of October, completed his First Symphony (D.82), an elegant, somewhat Haydnesque piece which, though it may lack individuality, is yet an attractive work, composed with skill and assurance. Despite the fact that the world it inhabits is that of the late eighteenth century, a theme in its first movement bears a more than fleeting resemblance to Beethoven's famous 'Eroica' theme. (Beethoven in 1813 had already composed eight of his nine symphonies.) The serenity of the symphony's slow movement and the gaiety of its finale are qualities which Schubert shared with the city of his birth. Nor did he lack the melancholy underside of that hedonistic surface, which is as typically Viennese as the high spirits (though this appears in the First Symphony as no more than a certain wistfulness in the third movement). The symphony, written for the student orchestra at the seminary, is nevertheless no mere student exercise, and can still be listened to with pleasure today.

Schubert was soon to become so prolific a composer that he had little energy to spare for other forms of creative endeavour. He did, however, occasionally write verse, for which he had no more aptitude than one would expect to find in the average well-educated person. Schubert's earliest surviving poem, which he wrote in May 1813, is entitled 'Time'. The first of its four stanzas reads:

> Unrelenting does it fly,
> Once departed, never tarrying.
> Thee, fair comrade of our days,
> To our grave we shall be carrying.

It was early in 1813 that Josef von Spaun took the sixteen-year-old Schubert to hear a performance of Gluck's opera *Iphigénie en Tauride*, and introduced him to the young poet Theodor Körner, whom they encountered at the theatre. (Körner was to die in battle against the French some months later, at the age of twenty-two.) The three of them dined together after the opera at the 'Hunter's Horn' in the Dorotheergasse, just off the Graben, and enthused about the singers they had heard: Anna Milder-Hauptmann as Iphigenia and Johann Michael Vogl as Orestes. In later years, Schubert was to set several of Körner's poems to music.

In October 1813 Schubert was offered a grant from an endowment fund to allow him to continue his studies at the seminary but, possibly at his father's urging, he did not accept the offer. Instead, he left the school, returned home to live, and attended as a day-student a training college for primary-school teachers which was situated in the inner town in the Annagasse. One sometimes reads that Schubert decided to become a school teacher in order to avoid conscription into the army. That this may have been one of his reasons is possible, even though as

9

a fully grown adult he was only 5 feet 1½ inches and thus under the minimum height for military service. After all, at the age of sixteen he had presumably not reached his full height. But it is more likely that he agreed to take up the profession of schoolmaster because this was what his father wanted him to do.

Schubert had begun to compose string quartets in 1811 at the age of fourteen. By now he had written nine quartets, concise in form and classical in style, reminiscent of Haydn and early Beethoven. The String Quartet in E flat (D.87), which he wrote in November 1813, is the earliest in which the young composer's own musical personality begins to assert itself. Its first movement owes something to Mozart and its second, a scherzo, even more to Beethoven, but the adagio is deeply felt and personal, while in the final allegro a wholly Schubertian lyricism is clearly heard in the delightful second subject.

Between leaving the seminary and beginning to attend the teachers' training college, Schubert began to compose the first of his several operas. (A year or so earlier, he had begun to write, as an exercise for his teacher, Salieri, an opera entitled *Der Spiegelritter* [The Looking-Glass Knight, D.11] to a nonsensical libretto by the popular sentimental dramatist August von Kotzebue [1761–1819], but had abandoned it before the end of Act I. The seven numbers that he completed fall easily upon the ear.) Throughout his short life Schubert continued to write operas, though he never achieved any real success with them. This first completed attempt, *Des Teufels Lustschloss* (The Devil's Pleasure Castle, D.84), again with a text by Kotzebue, was a *Singspiel* – a work whose spoken dialogue is interspersed with musical numbers. On the title-page of his manuscript the young composer proudly noted, 'Pupil of Herr Salieri, First Court Music Director in Vienna.' In May 1814 he showed the completed work to Salieri, whose comments led him to revise the first and third acts. By October the revision was complete. However, although it contained much delightful music, the opera failed to attract the interest of any management, and was not performed until many years after the composer's death.

Another of Schubert's close friends at the seminary was Albert Stadler, who, three years Franz's senior, became a civil servant and lived on into his nineties. Many years after Schubert's death, Stadler set down his reminiscences of the composer. They include a vivid word-picture of the young Schubert in the throes of composition:

To see and hear him play his own pianoforte compositions was a real pleasure. A beautiful touch, a quiet hand, clear, neat playing, full of insight and feeling. He still belonged to the old school of good pianoforte players, whose fingers had not yet begun to attack the poor keys like birds of prey. It was interesting to see him compose, for very rarely did he use the pianoforte while doing it. He often said that would interrupt his train of thought. Quietly, and hardly disturbed at all by the chatter or noise of his fellow-students, which was unavoidable at the seminary, he would sit at his little writing-table, bent closely over the sheet of music-paper and a book of poems (for he was very short-sighted), chewing his pen, sometimes drumming with his fingers on the table as if trying out a passage, and writing easily and fluently, with few corrections, as if it had to be like that and not otherwise.

After he had left the seminary, Schubert frequently returned there on Sundays and holidays to visit Stadler, Anton Holzapfel, and other former school friends. When, on Sundays, the students had to attend the afternoon service in the University church, they would leave Schubert alone with a few pages of manuscript paper and any volume of poems which happened to be at hand. They would return an hour later, usually to find that he had composed a song, which, as often as not, he would present to one of his friends.

Another friend at the seminary, Franz Eckel (who was to become a Doctor of Medicine), also left a description of Schubert:

Schubert lived as a youth for the most part in an inner meditative life. Even with his intimate friends, amongst whom at that time Anton Holzapfel and myself were numbered, for we read and sang his first songs composed at the City Seminary almost before the ink was dry on the paper, he used few words. He was almost entirely uncommunicative except in matters which concerned his divine muse to whom he dedicated his brief but complete life, and whose favourite he was.

Anton Holzapfel (1792–1868), who became a municipal councillor in Vienna, was five years older than Schubert. He, too, wrote down his recollections of Schubert, thirty years after the composer's death. (These, and many other biographical notes by Schubert's friends, were collected in 1858 by one Ferdinand Luib [b. 1811], who planned, but did not complete, a biography of the composer.) Although he was a fellow-pupil of Schubert's at the seminary, Holzapfel was in a senior year:

When I got to know him better, he was in the fourth grammar class, a short, stocky boy, with a friendly, round face and strongly marked features. He was not a particular favourite with the clerical teachers, but he did not cause them any particular trouble through excessive liveliness. He proved to possess one of those quiet, deep natures which, judged by the standards of superficial book-learning, may appear to have little talent. Even then, he was mentally far in advance of his years, as was proved by a long poem of his, written at that time, which I kept, but have since lost. It was in the style of Klopstock's Odes, hardly understood by us pupils, but whose theme was the omnipotence of God in all creation.

By the autumn of 1814, having assimilated all that could be taught to him at the seminary and the training college, the seventeen-year-old Schubert, short, his stockiness verging on plumpness, his short-sightedness already corrected by the steel-rimmed spectacles he is seen wearing in all the familiar portraits, began to teach in his father's school. He continued, however, to take lessons with Salieri for another two years, and he began to compose music in every moment that he could spare. Music, it seemed, simply flowed from him, or through him. Sketches for a string quartet, songs, dances for the piano, and music for the church were among his compositions in 1814. Between 5 and 13 September he wrote the String Quartet in B flat (D.112), noting proudly on his score that the first movement had taken him only four and a half hours. The Quartet is a mellifluous work, the voice of Schubert making itself heard between amiable echoes of Beethoven and Haydn.

Early in the year, for some family occasion or other, he had turned another composer's trio for flute, violin and guitar into a quartet (D.96) by adding a cello part. His manuscript was found in 1918, and published as a guitar quartet by Schubert. The work is a charming piece of Biedermeier domestic music, and not unworthy of the youthful Schubert who never lost his ability to compose pieces of amiable unimportance as well as works of great genius. It was, however, identified some years after its publication as an arrangement of a piece by Wenzel Thomas Matiegka (1773–1830), a minor Austrian composer who flourished in Vienna at the beginning of the nineteenth century, and who specialized in music for the guitar.

It was already becoming clear to Schubert that his greatest gift was for song. By the time of his death at the age of thirty-one, he had written more than six hundred songs, and so many of them of such beauty and power that he sometimes seems to us today to have been the fount of all song. His literary taste was uncertain, and he set some extremely bad poems to music. But he also set a great many of the masterpieces of German poetry, poems by Goethe, Heine and Schiller. There were simply not enough great poems in existence to soak up all the music that Franz Schubert carried within him.

Many of Schubert's earliest songs are similar in style to his first effort, 'Hagar's Lament': long and rambling settings of graveyard fantasies for which the schoolboy Franz obviously had a taste. But as early as 'Der Jüngling am Bache' (The Youth at the Brook, D.30), a setting of Schiller's poem which he composed at the age of twelve, eighteen months after 'Hagars Klage', an engaging and typically Schubertian charm asserts itself. Then, in October 1814, the seventeen-year-old composer wrote the first of his masterpieces, a song of sheer genius, 'Gretchen am Spinnrade' (D.118), a setting of the poem 'Gretchen at the Spinning-Wheel', from Goethe's *Faust*. In the play, the virgin Gretchen has succumbed to the charms of Faust. She sits at her spinning-wheel, her disconnected thoughts only of him. The poem, simple in expression and form, matching the girl's artlessness, is touching in its portrayal of lost innocence. Schubert responded to the poem and the situation with an intuitive flash of emphatic genius, and created a song which has so delicately yet firmly etched Gretchen's words into music that one would have to be determinedly wilful to imagine them sung to any other melody. At the same stroke, Schubert freed the piano part, the erstwhile mere accompaniment, once and for all from subservience to the voice. In his piano the treadle of the wheel is heard, transformed into musical image.

Schubert wrote 'Gretchen am Spinnrade' quickly, in the white heat of inspiration, on the afternoon of 19 October 1814. Three days earlier, on the 16th, his first completed Mass was performed in the Liechtental parish church. Schubert had worked on the Mass from mid-May until near the end of July, and to have it performed in their local church was considered by the entire family to be a great honour. They and their friends helped to swell the congregation on that autumn day, and the Schubert family must have felt proud of what seemed to them to be Franz's first real public achievement. What they heard was not a work of profound religious feeling, but a light, graceful, almost Haydnesque setting of the liturgical Catholic Mass. And this is what they would have expected to hear. The everyday church music of the time possessed the cheerful, almost secular complacence of Austrian baroque-rococo church architecture, and what Schubert had produced was, naturally, modelled on the kind of music he had been singing for four years as a member of the Court Chapel Choir.

Schubert's Mass No. 1 in F major (D.105) is scored for soprano, alto, tenor and bass soloists, chorus and orchestra. In the Liechtental performance, the soprano solos were sung by a young woman of Schubert's acquaintance named Therese Grob. The Grob family were friends of the Schuberts, and were popular in the neighbourhood because of their musical evenings. Frau Grob was a middle-aged widow who owned a silk-weaving business in Liechtental, and her two children, both musically gifted, were Therese, who possessed a good high-soprano voice, and Heinrich, who played the piano, violin and cello.

When she sang in the seventeen-year-old composer's Mass, Therese was only fourteen, but was already considered to be the finest amateur soprano in the district. Schubert was a frequent visitor at the Grob house, admired Therese's voice and her musical understanding, and was encouraged by her to concentrate on writing songs. In the year following the performance of the Mass, he managed to compose 150 songs despite the long hours he must have had to devote to his duties as a school teacher. Many of these songs were first performed at the Grob house by Therese and the composer.

The performance of Schubert's Mass in the Liechtental church, directed by Schubert himself, and with his brother Ferdinand playing the organ, was the first occasion on which a work by the young composer was heard in public. The performance was repeated ten days later, not in the suburb of Liechtental but in the church of St Augustine (the Augustinerkirche) in the city, and again under Schubert's direction. This time the work was heard by a fashionable audience which must have included a number of foreigners who were in Vienna for the Congress of 1814–15. Schubert's father was so proud of his son's success with the Mass that he presented him with a five-octave piano from the Konrad Graf workshop.

Schubert and Therese Grob were close friends for six years, and there can be no doubt that he fell in love with her. Indeed, he declared later that he would have married Therese had he not been kept in poverty by his art. But it is probable that he never revealed to her the depth of his feeling. Therese was a plain, amiable girl who, in 1820, married a master-baker. From that time on, Schubert ceased visiting the Grobs. According to one of his friends, Anselm Hüttenbrenner (1794–1868), Schubert never recovered from his disappointment over Therese Grob:

During a walk I took with Schubert in the country in 1821, I asked him if he had ever been in love. As he was so cold and unresponsive towards the fair sex, I had begun to think that he disliked women. 'Oh, no,' he replied. 'I loved someone very dearly, and she loved me in return. She was somewhat younger than I, and in a Mass which I composed she sang the soprano solos magnificently and with deep feeling. She was not beautiful, and her face was pock-marked, but she was so good-hearted. For three years, I hoped to marry her. But I could find no decent situation much to the sorrow of both of us. Finally she married someone else at her mother's urging. I still love her, and since then no one else has pleased me better or as much. It seems she was just not meant for me.'

Hüttenbrenner elsewhere writes: 'From the time I got to know Schubert he did not have even the suspicion of a love affair. Towards the fair sex he was boorish and, consequently, not exactly gallant. He neglected his appearance, and especially his teeth, smelled strongly of tobacco, and had none of the qualifications of a suitor . . . he had a dominating aversion for the daughters of Eve.'

Whether or not he was averse to the daughters of Eve, it is true that the circle of friends which grew around Schubert was essentially masculine. He formed deep and romantic (though, as far as is known, non-sexual) attachments with his male friends, and only rarely sought the company of women. His passion was for friendship, and he was fortunate to find affection and understanding in a few close associates.

Two of Schubert's closest friends were Johann Mayrhofer and Franz von Schober, both of whom he met through the earliest of his friends from the seminary days, Josef von Spaun. Like Spaun, Mayrhofer and Schober were law students, and like almost everyone in the Schubert circle they dabbled in writing verse. Mayrhofer was, in fact, a gifted though somewhat gloomy poet, who entered the Austrian civil service, became increasingly a prey to melancholia, and committed suicide in 1836. In 1814, however, he was a twenty-six-year-old law student who wrote poetry. On 7 December 1814 Spaun gave Schubert a copy of a Mayrhofer poem, 'Am See' (By the Lake), which Schubert set to music on the spot. (The song, D.124, begins promisingly with an engaging and gentle melody, but then subsides into nondescript quasi-recitative.) A few days later Spaun took Mayrhofer to meet Schubert, and the two became good friends. Over the years, Schubert was to set more than a hundred of Mayrhofer's poems to music; there are more Schubert settings of Mayrhofer than of any other poet except Goethe.

Mayrhofer was nearly ten years older than Schubert. Franz von Schober was Schubert's age, and he did not wait for his friend Spaun to introduce him to Schubert: he sought out the young composer in his school-house. He had got to know some of Schubert's songs, through Spaun, and he instantly recognized their composer's enormous talent. It was Schober who fired Schubert with at least a certain degree of ambition, making him no longer satisfied to remain a suburban school teacher for ever. And it was Schober of whom, in time, Schubert came to be even fonder than of his other close friends, despite Schober's somewhat undisciplined character and propensity to dilettantism.

By the end of 1814, Schubert had set five more poems by Goethe, to follow 'Gretchen am Spinnrade'. They include the melancholy 'Schäfers Klagelied' (Shepherd's Lament, D.121), a song which a few years later was to achieve popularity, and 'Nachtgesang' (Night Song, D.119), a tender serenade for which Schubert provided a sensitive and graceful melody. On 10 December he began his Second Symphony (in B flat major), on which he worked intermittently until the following March, when, soon after he had completed it, the symphony was given its first performance by the seminary's student orchestra. This Second Symphony (D.125) adds to the freshness of its predecessor a certain expansiveness. The young composer's engaging shyness permeates its slow movement, a theme with variations, and his genial love of the dance bursts forth in the robust minuet and contrastingly graceful trio of the third movement, leading to a final movement which is positively Beethovenian in its rhythmic energy.

CHAPTER TWO

The Congress of Vienna

In 1805, when Schubert was a child of eight, Beethoven's opera *Leonore* was given its first performance at the Theater an der Wien. It was a failure, was withdrawn by the composer and, recast in two acts instead of three, was presented again the following year. Again it was withdrawn. Later, Beethoven undertook a thorough revision of the score, and, with a change of title to *Fidelio*, the opera was staged again on 23 May 1814, at the Kärntnertor theatre. Franz Schubert, now seventeen, was in the audience on that occasion: Moritz von Schwind, who did not know Schubert until later, claimed that the young composer had sold his school-books in order to get the money to attend the performance. This time, the opera was a triumph. Beethoven's hymn to freedom and loyalty had touched the Viennese, who themselves had now, after years of oppression and deprivation, won through to what seemed likely to be a lasting peace.

In June 1814, the Emperor Franz I entered Vienna, having signed the Peace of Paris. Napoleon was in exile on the island of Elba, and a congress was about to convene in Vienna, its purpose being to settle the affairs of Europe on a lasting basis of legitimate monarchy and firm government. The Congress of Vienna, which met between September 1814 and June 1815, was one of the most brilliant international assemblies of modern times. It was attended by a majority of the rulers of Europe, as well as a host of lesser potentates, ministers, diplomats and civil servants of high rank. Entertainment on a lavish scale was offered by the Emperor Franz, and between the official meetings there was much unofficial intrigue. To the citizens of Vienna, the Congress was an excuse for an extended carnival-time of gaiety and celebration.

The major negotiating countries represented in Vienna at the Congress were, on the one side, the principal members of the grand alliance (Austria, Prussia, Great Britain and Russia) and, on the other, the defeated France. The chief negotiators were: for Austria, Prince Metternich; for Prussia, Prince Carl August Hardenberg and Baron Wilhelm von Humboldt; for Great Britain, Viscount Castlereagh and the Duke of Wellington; for Russia, Tsar Alexander I accompanied by several advisers; for France, Charles de Talleyrand.

The principal decisions were made by the four major allied powers, the other members of the grand alliance (Spain, Portugal and Sweden) being allowed to participate only in the treatment of fairly obvious or unobjectionable subjects. Countless minor delegations flocked to Vienna. For example, some thirty-two German royal personages arrived, most of whom had brought with them their wives, mistresses or loving friends, and their Secretaries of State. There were two delegations from Naples, one representing the legitimate Bourbon dynasty, and the other the interests of Joachim Murat, the innkeeper's son whom Napoleon had made King of Naples. The Pope was represented, and so was the Sultan of Turkey. Several unofficial deputations had also arrived in Vienna: the Jews of Frankfurt had sent representatives to look after the special interests of Jewry, the German Catholics did likewise, and a gentleman named Cotta, from Augsburg, arrived to represent the publishing trade. There was a full supporting cast of international eccentrics, each with his own peculiar axe to grind.

Serious problems of accommodation and maintenance were created by the prolonged stay in Vienna of so large a number of foreign visitors. A programme of lavish entertainment for them was devised by the Austrian authorities: a programme whose immense cost had to be borne by the Austrian exchequer and thus the Austrian public. As Harold Nicolson expressed it in his book *The Congress of Vienna* (1946): 'At any international gathering it is bound to happen that some of the attendant staffs find time hangs heavy on their hands, whereas others are demonstrably overworked. The proportion established at Vienna between the employed and the unemployed was an ill-balanced proportion; the repute of the Congress has suffered accordingly.'

The same point was made more succinctly by Charles-Joseph, Prince de Ligne, a marshal of both Austria and Russia who, when asked how the Congress was going, punningly replied: 'Le congrès ne marche pas, il danse.' Apparently, Ligne made his remark in

September 1814, before the Congress had officially opened, and repeated it on every possible occasion until 13 December, when he died of influenza, contracted, it is said, by his having waited too long on a street corner in his eightieth year 'for an amatory assignation'.

The noble intent of the Congress was soon obscured. Though it might still appear to the outside world that a number of European heads of state were conferring to secure a lasting peace on the continent, in Vienna itself the citizenry, somewhat bemused at finding their beloved city thrust on to the harshly lit stage of world affairs, watched what seemed to them, from the gossip which circulated daily, to be the unedifying spectacle of a small number of great countries adopting a bullying stance towards a large number of small countries. Unable to form well-grounded opinions from the confusion of rumours, the Viennese quickly decided simply to enjoy the spectacle of the Congress, its lavish receptions, its festivities graced with the illustrious presences of the most famous political and social personalities, and its scandals concerning the private lives of these eminent individuals.

Rumour had always spread quickly in Vienna. Now, with so much more material to work upon, it assumed the proportions of a veritable epidemic. What a certain distinguished foreigner did in his bedroom at night, and with whom, would be known immediately to his valet, transmitted next morning to a chambermaid, immediately passed on to a groom, who informed his fiancée, who made it known to her father, whose cousin was either a journalist who would give the story a wide circulation or a coffee-house habitué who would give it even wider circulation. Vienna had always taken an obsessive interest in the doings of its domestic celebrities, its actors and actresses, opera singers, and members of the royal family. Now it was able to extend that interest to the private affairs of other nations' royalty. The aristocracy, as well as the bourgeoisie, enjoyed whatever gossip they could get hold of, and repeated it with great enthusiasm.

Information of all kinds, official and unofficial, serious and frivolous, was of interest not only to the citizens but also to the Viennese police. Baron Hager, the Austrian Police President, had organized a police network which benefited from the city's propensity for gossip. That gossip was carefully noted, sifted and used. In addition to the local police, there were scores of police agents from other countries who had been brought in, ostensibly as diplomats or advisers to the various countries' delegations. Also, the Viennese cafés were full of people exchanging information, revealing the contents of secret documents perused, letters opened and copied, conversations overheard. The Viennese police were forced to recruit a large number of part-time spies, from all strata of society, to keep them informed about the questionable activities of so many distinguished foreigners. Dukes and duchesses, chambermaids and porters, all were enthusiastically recruited.

A police report was put before the Emperor Franz himself each morning. These files still exist, and from them it is possible to discover much about the personal habits and idiosyncrasies of, for instance, the King of Prussia, the Tsar, or the Duke of Baden.

Some of the reports to be found in the Austrian imperial archives have to be read to be disbelieved: 'The King of Prussia this morning visited the Archduke Charles. In the evening he went out in civilian clothes with a round hat pulled down over his eyes. He had not returned at 10 p.m. The Tsar of Russia went out at 7 p.m. with one of his aides-de-camp. It is believed he went to visit the Princess Thurn und Taxis. Every morning a large block of ice is brought to the Tsar with which he washes his face and hands.'

Most of the diplomatic couriers were in the pay of the Austrians, and all letters were opened and transcribed as a matter of course. As this fact was generally known at the time, thanks to Viennese *Schlamperei* (or slovenliness), very little useful information was gathered in this way, but frank communication between the delegations and their Governments was effectively hampered.

One of Baron Hager's anonymous correspondents, in a letter of 9 October 1814, gave a fascinating description of the atmosphere prevailing at the time in the higher echelons of society:

I have heard much talk from Prince Starhemberg about the spying that goes on between courts and missions and in society. It is said that 'courts and missions are very busy spying on one another'. This is very natural and easily explained. It is certain that, when they depart, these foreign rulers will have a thorough knowledge of our own court. However, society espionage amongst the Viennese themselves, that is, espionage within society, is becoming intolerable. Ferdinand Pálffy belongs to the secret police, while Countess Esterházy-Roisin and Mlle Chapuis are spies for old Princess Metternich, who instructs and encourages them. Prince Kaunitz, Franz Pálffy, Friedrich Fürstenberg and Ferdinand Pálffy all offered their services to the rulers at present in Vienna. Prince Metternich has already questioned me on this subject, and informed me that all my conversations were known. I replied that the Prince ought to help me by finding me a position, and that I would then sing his praises without qualification. I am, in fact, under an obligation to him on account of my lottery, but what I can neither accept nor forgive him for are these Binders, Paul Esterházys and the like with whom he closets himself and whom he confides in. This is what Prince Starhemberg said to me.

The British, of course, were adept at keeping close counsel. Not only had they brought even their own chambermaids from England, but they also were careful to make no use of Austrian messengers. 'It is quite impossible to intercept anything,' Baron Hager was told. 'The Lord [Castlereagh] sends everything by his own couriers, and his secretaries collect and burn all papers. On the 2nd [October 1814] they sent couriers to Munich, Brussels and Naples, and during the night they were burning papers until two in the morning.' An agent attempted to discover from a Mr Parr, one of the British delegation's secretaries, how his colleagues spent their leisure time in Vienna. He was told: 'Since they are on holiday, they spend the day sight-seeing in the city and the surrounding countryside. In the evening they generally visit young Countess Rzewuska, who gives agreeable receptions, and then they go off with girls and get drunk on Hungarian wine.'

Going off with girls and getting drunk were certainly among the more popular pastimes during the Congress, and the elegantly malicious Viennese observed, in particular, the debaucheries of their royal visitors with huge enjoyment. Many were the satires and pamphlets circulating about the town concerning the sexual tastes of foreign monarchs, dukes or princes. As well as amusement, there was profit to be derived from their amorous activities: a certain Herr Mayer showed great enterprise by selling to foreign nobility a remedy against venereal disease.

Lord Castlereagh, who led the British delegation, was the unfortunate British Minister of War and Foreign Secretary to whom uncomplimentary references are to be found in the works of two of the leading British poets of the day, Shelley and Byron. In Byron's *Don Juan* he is 'the intellectual eunuch Castlereagh', while two lines in Shelley's *The Mask of Anarchy* stigmatize simultaneously his character and his bearing:

I met Murder on the way –
He had a mask like Castlereagh.

Talleyrand's passion for music endeared him to the Viennese. He had brought with him from France not only several diplomats but also an Austrian composer and pianist, Sigismond Neukomm, whose task it was to play the piano to Talleyrand while he was working at his desk. (Neukomm, originally from Salzburg, had lived in Paris since 1809. A pupil of Haydn, he was a respected composer: his C minor Requiem was performed in Vienna on 21 January 1815, before the distinguished international company assembled for the Congress.) Neukomm confided to his friends that, when he was playing the piano, often for hours on end, while Talleyrand was seated at his desk, he doubted whether the statesman heard much of the music, which he seemed to need merely as a kind of sympathetic background noise while he pursued his own thoughts.

Probably the most popular of the foreign rulers present in Vienna for the Congress was the Russian Tsar, Alexander I, because of the countless opportunities he gave the local populace to gossip about him. Alexander's sexual encounters with a wide social range of women from princesses to prostitutes during the time he was in Vienna were talked of throughout the town. But even the Tsar's more innocent, if unseemly, exploits caused an inordinate amount of outrage. At a dinner party, the Tsar and an Austrian countess argued as to whether men or women spent more time over their toilette. To settle the question, they left the room together to undress and dress again. The Countess won the argument, and the Tsar not only lost but, as a result, was denounced by the Papal Nuncio: 'This is the kind of man by whom the world is governed! The gossip-mongers of the Congress will add this choice incident to the other shameful and shocking stories about this prince of coxcombs, and posterity one day will learn how the palace of the Emperors served as a brothel for the Tsar of Russia.'

The producer and principal performer of the theatrical spectacle (which the Congress of Vienna appears primarily to have been) was Prince Clement Wenceslaus Lothaire Nepomucène Metternich, who at the time of the Congress was in his early forties. At the age of thirty-six he had been appointed Minister for Foreign Affairs by the Emperor Franz, and he continued to hold this post in the Austrian Government until the revolution of 1848, when he and his wife escaped to England. Metternich believed in a united Europe, a confederation of states each under absolute monarchist rule but with common interests. Although predominantly reactionary, he was far-sighted enough to write that 'we must always consider the *society* of states as the essential condition of the modern world. The great axioms of political science proceed from the knowledge of the true political interests of *all* states; it is on these general interests that the guarantee of their existence is based.'

It was by organizing and directing the amusements of his foreign guests at the Congress that Metternich was able to maintain his control over them, and it was by his ingenuity in negotiation that he succeeded, if not in bringing a united Europe into being, then at least in postponing the revolution for thirty years or more. During that time he continued to work to maintain Austrian security through a continental balance of power and the suppression of nationalistic and liberal forces.

While some of the politicians and civil servants laboured in conference and committee, others enjoyed themselves. The Congress may not have danced, but the rest of Vienna did. Music and the dance flourished, as always. The Viennese waltz had already supplanted the more stately minuet, and it was to the waltzes of Michael Pamer, whose orchestra played in the new dance halls, that the middle-class Viennese danced in such numbers. Vienna's dance halls ranged from the huge, glittering palaces of the aristocracy to the low-ceilinged suburban halls where the working classes disported themselves. The most popular establishment with the middle classes was the *Apollosaal*, which had been opened in January 1808, on the occasion of the wedding of the Emperor Franz. On its opening night, more than four thousand people crowded into the *Apollosaal*, which consisted of five enormous ballrooms and four large drawing rooms. 'Marvellous greenery and flowers abounded everywhere,' wrote Heinrich Kralik, a Viennese historian, 'amid waterfalls and grottos and a lake with real swans in it. Garlands, flowering shrubs turned the place even in winter into a veritable garden, the whole being reminiscent of the luxury of ancient Rome.' The *Apollosaal*'s chief rival was the *Mondscheinsaal*, or Moonlight Hall, where, according to another Viennese writer, Heinrich Laube,

it was the fashion to be a dashing dancer, and the man had to whirl his partner from one end of the hall to the other with the greatest possible speed.

If one round of the immense hall had been considered sufficient one might have allowed this bacchantic dance [the waltz] to pass. But the circuit had to be made six to eight times at top speed without pause. Each couple endeavoured to top the performance of the others, and it was no rare occurrence for apoplexy of the lungs to put an end to such madness.

The Viennese passion was, however, not only for the dance but for the art, indeed the very spirit, of music. More than twenty years after the Congress, the German composer Robert Schumann visited Vienna and entered in his diary a description of the city of music which epitomizes its atmosphere and its appeal:

Vienna and the spire of St Stephen's Cathedral, its lovely women and its luxury, Vienna enfolded by the winding Danube, which flows through a plain slowly rising towards ever higher mountains, Vienna which calls to mind the great masters of music, must be a fertile field for the musician's imagination. Often, when I looked down upon it from the hilltops, it occurred to me how frequently the eyes of Beethoven must have gazed upon the distant Alpine chain, how Mozart may have dreamily followed the flow of the Danube, and how Papa Haydn may have peered up to St Stephen's tower, shaking his head at such dizzying height. Put together the pictures of the Danube, St Stephen's and the far mountain ranges, cover them with the faint scent of Catholic incense and you have a portrait of Vienna. And when the charming landscape comes wholly alive for us, strings may be heard that otherwise might never have sounded within us. At the touch of Schubert's symphony and the clear blossoming life in it, the city rises more clearly than ever before us, and most plainly I can see again how such works can be born in just such a setting.

During the time of the Congress, Vienna's greatest living composer, Ludwig van Beethoven, was at his most active, after a period of silence and inactivity. To celebrate the Duke of Wellington's defeat of Napoleon at the Battle of Vitoria in Spain on 21 June 1813, Beethoven had composed a work entitled 'Wellington's Victory', or 'The Battle of Vitoria' (which came to be known as the 'Battle' Symphony). At its first performance in Vienna in December 1813, the city's leading musicians performed: Hummel and Salieri played the drums and the cannonades called for in Beethoven's score; Schuppanzigh led the violins; and Spohr, Mayseder and several others participated. Beethoven's Seventh Symphony was given its first performance at the same concert, and both works were enthusiastically received, a contemporary newspaper noting that the 'applause rose to the point of ecstasy'.

Beethoven suddenly attained an unprecedentedly high level of national popularity, and was thus encouraged into a period of intense productivity. Throughout 1814, he composed a number of vocal and choral occasional works in support or celebration of the Allied campaign against Napoleon. Though hardly to be numbered amongst his masterpieces, they include several compositions which became immediately popular in Vienna. Beethoven had become the leading patriotic composer of his country.

For the Congress, Beethoven composed two new works: 'Chor auf die verbündeten Fürsten' (Chorus to the Allied Princes), and a cantata, 'Der glorreiche Augenblick' (The Glorious Moment). The cantata was performed at a concert in the *Redoutensaal* (ballroom) of the Hofburg, on 29 November 1814, an occasion which was one of the highlights of the Congress festivities. Virtually all of the visiting monarchs were present along with their entourages, and the programme also included the 'Battle' Symphony, 'Wellington's Victory', first heard the previous year.

During the Congress period, Beethoven was presented by his patrons Count Andreas Razumovsky (the Russian Ambassador) and Archduke Rudolf to most of the assembled royal visitors, and received from them not only compliments but also sums of money. The Tsarina granted him an audience and, presented by Beethoven with his Polonaise for piano, opus 89, responded with a gift of 50 ducats. The composer, who had been renowned for his brusque dismissal of courtly etiquette, noted in his diary, 'It is certain that one writes most prettily when one writes for the public, also that one writes rapidly', and inserted the following extraordinary announcement in a Viennese newspaper:

A WORD TO HIS ADMIRERS

How often, in your chagrin that his depth was not sufficiently appreciated, have you said that Beethoven composes only for posterity! You have, no doubt, now been convinced of your error, even if only since the general enthusiasm aroused by his immortal opera *Fidelio*; and also that the present finds kindred souls and sympathetic hearts for that which is great and beautiful without withholding its just privileges from the future.

It was at a concert given on 25 January 1815 to celebrate the Tsarina of Russia's birthday that Beethoven appeared in public as a pianist for the last time. His deafness, already embarrassingly apparent, was becoming much worse.

There was one personage of royal blood in Vienna who did not participate in the gay social life of the Congress. This was the Emperor Franz's daughter, the Princess Marie Louise, who had been married to Napoleon. She had returned to Vienna with her young son, the King of Rome, who was half a Bonaparte and half a Habsburg, and later to be known as the Duke of Reichstadt. Marie Louise's somewhat awkward position as the wife of the French leader whose downfall had brought the Congress into being made it inappropriate for her to appear in public, as did the presence in Vienna of Napoleon's son and heir.

If Napoleon was responsible for the birth of the Congress, he was equally responsible for its speedy end, an end which Metternich was to recall in his memoirs:

On the night of 6–7 March [1815], there had been a meeting in my rooms of the plenipotentiaries of the Five Powers. This meeting had lasted until three in the morning. I had forbidden my valet to disturb my rest if courtiers arrived at a late hour in the night. In spite of this prohibition, the man brought me, at about six in the morning, an express despatch marked 'Urgent'. Upon the envelope I read the words, 'From the Imperial and Royal Consulate General at Genoa'. As I had only been in bed for about two hours I laid the despatch, without opening it, upon the table beside my bed. I tried to go to sleep. But having once been disturbed I was unable to rest again. At about 7.30 I decided to open the envelope. It contained only the following six lines: 'The English commissioner Campbell has just entered the harbour enquiring whether anyone had seen Napoleon at Genoa, in view of the fact that he had disappeared from the island of Elba. The answer being in the negative, the English frigate without further delay put to sea.'

I dressed myself in a flash, and before 8 a.m. I was with my Emperor. He read the above-mentioned despatch. He then, with that perfect calm which never deserted him on great occasions, said to me: 'Napoleon appears anxious to run great risks; that is his business. Our business is to give to the world that repose which he has troubled all these years. Go at once and find the Tsar of Russia and the King of Prussia. Tell them that I am prepared to order my armies once again to take the road to France. I have no doubt that the two sovereigns will join me in my march.'

At 8.15 I was with Tsar Alexander, who used the same language as the Emperor Franz. At 8.30 King Friedrich Wilhelm III gave me a similar assurance. By 9 o'clock I had returned home. I had already summoned Field Marshal Prince Schwarzenberg to come to my house. At 10, the ministers of the Four Powers had gathered at my invitation in my study. At the same hour, aides-de-camp were flying in all directions carrying to the several army corps, who were retiring, their new orders. In this way, war was decided upon in less than an hour.

Napoleon's Waterloo came only one hundred days later. The new map of Europe which had been drawn at the Congress of Vienna survived, in the main, until 1914, despite a series of revolutions and wars. However, the Congress itself, whose deliberations might otherwise have proceeded at a leisurely pace for several more months, came abruptly to an end. The talking had ceased, and so had the dancing.

CHAPTER THREE

1815–1821
Master of Song

Although his responsibilities as a school teacher occupied most of his mornings, Schubert managed during the year 1815 to compose no fewer than 189 works, ranging in scope from songs to symphonies. For the first three months of the year he was engrossed in his Second Symphony, which he completed towards the end of March, but it was to opera that his thoughts most frequently turned, due in no small measure to the inspiration he had derived from Beethoven's *Fidelio* the previous year. As soon as he realized that his first attempt at a work for the stage, *Des Teufels Lustschloss*, was not going to be taken up by any theatre, he embarked upon other operatic projects, completing four more operas during the year.

The first of these, *Der vierjährige Posten* (The Four-Year Sentry, D.190), was a one-act light opera which he composed in eleven days in May. His music, consisting of an overture and eight separate numbers (one aria, one duet, one trio, one quartet, and the other four numbers ensembles of one kind or another), is both fluent and tuneful, but isolated numbers separated by long stretches of dialogue hardly make a successful opera unless the musical pieces are inherently dramatic in form. Schubert's were not; nor, for that matter, was Theodor Körner's libretto, an over-extended joke about a young soldier who, in order to avoid punishment, pretends to have remained on sentry duty for four years, waiting for someone to relieve him. *Der vierjährige Posten* did not reach the stage until 1896, more than a half-century after its composer's death, and then only in an arrangement which replaced the spoken dialogue with accompanied recitative and incorporated music from other forgotten stage works by Schubert. It is still very seldom performed, and is probably best heard in concert form or on records.

The composition of the String Quartet in G minor (D.173) occupied Schubert from 25 March to 1 April. Like most of his early quartets, it is a model of formal construction using the language of the Viennese classical tradition, but with Schubertian individuality breaking through, in this instance, in the lyrical andantino.

Between 24 May and 19 July, Schubert composed his Third Symphony in D major (D.200), a work of rococo charm like its two predecessors, with a slow movement, an allegretto, of a delicacy and enchantment which clearly anticipate the mature Schubert of the later symphonies. While he was at work on the symphony, he also composed his next one-act opera or *Singspiel*, *Fernando* (D.220), to a libretto written by Albert Stadler, a friend and ex-fellow-pupil of the seminary. Stadler's libretto is an overwrought and melodramatic account of the misfortunes and highly unlikely adventures of a family in the Pyrenees which the author himself described years later as a piece 'which I wrote for him, not without a youthful display of curses and floods of tears'. Schubert composed seven musical numbers for *Fernando*, among them a gentle bass aria for the father, a delightful and original soprano aria for the mother, and a touching duet when the two parents are reunited, but the separate numbers again do not add up to form an integrated whole. This is the least successful of Schubert's teenage attempts to write for the stage, and that it was not produced until the opera company at Magdeburg tried it out in 1918 is hardly surprising.

Schubert's next operatic project, which he commenced on 26 July, was somewhat more ambitious. This was a setting of *Claudine von Villa Bella*, a satirical play by Goethe which the great poet had written in 1776 at the age of twenty-seven. For the first time Schubert had an excellent libretto to work on, albeit one which had already been used several times by other composers (among them Johann André, 1778; Claus Schall, 1787; Ignaz von Beecke, 1780; Johann Friedrich Reichardt, 1789; Johann Christoph Kienlen, 1810; and Traugott Eberwein, 1815).

The chance that one of Schubert's operas might be staged was slight, for operas were usually commissioned by theatres, whereas Schubert, not yet eighteen and not known to theatre impresarios, waited for no commission but simply composed when it pleased him to do so. The fate of his *Claudine von Villa Bella* (D.239), however, was one worse than neglect. The manuscript somehow made its way into the hands of Schubert's friend Josef Hüttenbrenner (brother of Anselm), perhaps in 1822 when Hüttenbrenner was attempting to interest Viennese theatre managements in Schubert's operas; and years later, in 1848, Hüttenbrenner's servants used Acts II and III by mistake to light fires. All that survives is Act I, which consists of an overture and seven numbers, two of which are known out of context because they were included in a complete edition of Schubert's songs, with their orchestral accompaniments arranged for piano. One of these is the delightful 'Liebe schwärmt auf allen Wegen' (Love Roves Down Every Road), the sixth number in the opera and sung by the heroine, Claudine. The other, less satisfactory out of context, though a pleasant enough little song, is No. 3, 'Hin und wieder fliegen die Pfeile' (Hither and Thither the Arrows Fly), which is sung by Lucinda, the other principal character. Occasional concert perform-ances of the overture and surviving numbers frustratingly suggest that the complete *Claudine von Villa Bella* might well have proved the one Schubert opera capable of holding a place in the permanent repertory of opera houses.

The last of Schubert's four 1815 operas is the two-act *Die Freunde von Salamanka* (The Friends from Salamanca, D.326), which he began on 18 November and completed on New Year's Eve. This time, the libretto was provided by the composer's friend Johann Mayrhofer. Mayrhofer's dialogue has been lost, but his plot is easily reconstructed from the musical numbers and turns out to be a cheerfully complicated romantic comedy in which two friends plan the mock abduction and rescue of an heiress. With new dialogue (by Günther Ziegler), the work was staged for the first time in 1928 in Halle. Schubert's music (an overture and eighteen numbers) is unfailingly attractive, though again essentially undramatic. The duet 'Gelagert unter'm hellen Dach' (Lying under the Bright Roof), sung in the opera by Diego (tenor) and Laura (soprano), is quite superfluous to the dramatic action, but it begins with one of the composer's loveliest and most 'Schubertian' tunes. He salvaged it nearly ten years later, when it became the theme of the 'Andante con variazioni' movement of his Octet. Other parts of Act II of *Die Freunde von Salamanka* were plundered by Schubert when he came to compose the opera *Fierrabras* in 1823.

It was in this year, 1815, that the eighteen-year-old Schubert composed most prolifically, working every day on one or more large-scale pieces, and turning aside to produce songs, which seemed to spring spontaneously from his reading of the poems which he set. Numerous dances for piano date from this year, as well as his first two piano sonatas, and the well-made String Quartet in G minor (D.173), a charming and melodious work composed in seven days at the end of March.

Schubert's piano sonatas fall into three distinct groups: the first twelve sonatas, some of them left incomplete, composed between 1815 and 1819; a later group of five, written at various times between 1823 and 1826; and the final three masterpieces, all of which he composed in the last weeks of his life. Those five of the early and middle sonatas which Schubert left in an unfinished state have been completed by the Viennese pianist and scholar Paul Badura-Skoda, who has made a most convincing case for the method he has adopted. In all instances but one, Schubert had completed the unfinished movement up to the point of recapitulation of its opening theme. Most of Schubert's recapitulations are virtually literal transpositions of the musical material as first heard in the exposition. For the most part, Badura-Skoda was able, therefore, to complete the movement without having to invent more than a few bars, here and there. The Piano Sonata No. 1 in E (D.157) is a delightful work, conventional in form but fresh in musical invention. The Sonata No. 2 in C (D.279), equally enjoyable, lacked a final movement, which Schubert probably wrote but which was subsequently lost. An allegretto in C (D.346), dating from these months, is, Badura-Skoda suggests, the missing last movement. It certainly makes a fitting conclusion to the sonata.

Schubert also composed much choral music during the year, including two Masses. One of these, the Mass No. 2 in G (D.167), composed in March and performed in the Liechtental parish church the following month, is the most interesting of his early settings of the Mass, a work of lyrical beauty and dramatic power with a prominent soprano part which was obviously written with Therese Grob in mind as soloist. The Mass No. 3 in B flat (D.324), composed in November, is a gracious, melodic and lyrical work.

Most impressive of all Schubert's achievements in 1815 are the songs he composed: their quantity as well as their quality. This was the year in which he set thirty of Goethe's poems, and in doing so created some of his finest and most popular songs. Germany's greatest poet more often than not inspired the young Austrian composer to rare and exalted heights. 'Am Flusse' (By the River, D.160), Goethe's hurt and bitter little poem about derided love, drew a powerfully compressed song of deep feeling from the composer, whose thoughts may have turned to Therese Grob as he wrote it; but 'Nähe des Geliebten' (Nearness of the Beloved, D.162) is gentler, an even more beautiful song about an all-pervading love.

The challenge of matching the verse of the greatest living poet drew from Schubert some of his most superb music, a proof, surely, that he was not, as is often claimed, impervious to the literary merit of his poets. Fine feelings occasionally inspired him to great things, but fine words invariably did. 'Meeres Stille' (Silence of the Sea, D.216), in which Goethe depicts a becalmed, serene landscape which is beautiful in itself but dangerous for the seaman, is carried over into music which magically renders stillness and silence audible. Similar in its brevity and calm, and even more moving by virtue of the controlled yearning of its melody, is 'Wanderers Nachtlied 1' (Wayfarer's Night Song 1, D.224), a setting of Goethe's quiet sigh of world-weariness.

Schubert was frequently able to compose a number of supremely beautiful songs in one day. On 19 August, for example, he produced five Goethe songs which are among his finest: 'Der Rattenfänger' (The Rat-Catcher, D.255), 'Der Schatzgräber' (The Treasure-Hunter, D.256), 'Bundeslied' (Song of Union, D.258), 'An den Mond' (To the Moon, D.259) and 'Heidenröslein' (Hedge-Rose, D.257). The popular 'Heidenröslein' displays to perfection Schubert's extraordinary gift of apparently spontaneous melody. Its tune, now jaunty, now sad, is so right and inevitable that one feels it must have sprung, ready-made, from the soil in which the rose itself grew.

Schubert also composed in 1815 a number of songs based on poems by Schiller, among them 'An die Freude' (To Joy, D.189), a setting of that same poem which Beethoven was to use eight years later for the 'Ode to Joy' choral finale of his Ninth Symphony. Schubert's tune is actually more joyful, less thumping than Beethoven's theme. It is written for solo voice, with unison chorus, but is equally effective without the chorus. 'Amalia' (D.195), an extended recitative and arietta whose words are the heroine's song in Schiller's play *Die Räuber* (The Brigands), is one of the most attractive of these Schiller settings of 1815.

Schubert would occasionally concentrate entirely on one poet for several weeks on end. In the autumn of 1815, he turned his attention to Friedrich Gottlieb Klopstock (1724–1803). Klopstock's reputation had been made with his huge religious epic, *Messias* (Messiah), but some of his finest writing is to be found in his poems and unrhymed odes. Though a variable and uneven poet, he is one of the most important forerunners of the *Sturm und Drang* (Storm and Stress) period in German literature. Nine of Schubert's thirteen Klopstock songs were composed in the autumn of 1815, and of these the finest is undoubtedly 'Dem Unendlichen' (To the Eternal One, D.291). The poem is one of Klopstock's more impressive pietistic outbursts, and Schubert has matched the religious ecstasy of the poem with a vocal line of majestic nobility. Although the piano part looks conventional on the page, it adroitly follows the changing emphases of the words. 'Dem Unendlichen' is a fine example of Schubert in his exalted vein.

There is, of course, a price to be paid for facility, and that price is occasional failure. There are times when Schubert appears not to have been very deeply touched by a poem, and one wonders why he bothered to set it. But there are also many virtually unknown Schubert songs which are as attractive as the popular favourites; many which remain neglected simply because Schubert composed more than six hundred songs, and no one can know them all. Some are unaccountably neglected by singers, others are shamefully not even mentioned in the standard books on Schubert's songs. Two fugitive songs of 1815 are 'Das Bild' (The Portrait, D.155) and 'Mein Gruss an den Mai' (My Greeting to the Month of May, D.305). 'Das Bild' is an especial delight. To a poem on the portrait of a girl, by an unidentified poet, the young composer has added a graceful though quirky little melody.

It is, however, the settings of Goethe which make 1815 such an important Schubert year. It was in this rich year that the composer first grappled with the poems in Goethe's strange novel, *Wilhelm Meisters Lehrjahre* (Wilhelm Meister's Apprenticeship), which had been published in 1795–6. The poems are songs sung by a mysterious character, the Harper, and by Mignon, the Italian waif who turns out to be the Harper's child, offspring of an incestuous love. Mignon's 'Kennst du das Land, wo die Zitronen blühn' (Do you know the land where the lemon trees blossom, D.321) is the most famous lyrical poem not only in Goethe but in all German literature, a poem whose resonances extend far beyond its apparent meaning in the context of the novel. It is a poem which speaks of a northerner's yearning for the south, of a child's desire for a dream world, of an adult's despairing cry

33

after a vanished golden childhood. It has the truth, relevance and beauty of great poetry, and is so complete in itself that one sees both how and why composers were lured into setting it, and how and why they were likely to fail. Schubert's setting is not insensitive, and indeed it is an attractive song, but it does not match Goethe's imaginative sweep, any more than that poet could have found words to parallel the sound of Schubert's great C major Quintet of 1828.

If he failed with 'Kennst du das Land' (where Hugo Wolf was to succeed memorably more than seventy years later), Schubert succeeded gloriously with his final two Goethe songs of 1815, 'Rastlose Liebe' (Restless Love, D.138) and 'Erlkönig' (Erl King, D.328). Goethe's tempestuous young lyric, 'Rastlose Liebe', affected Schubert immediately and vividly, wringing from him a song different from anything he had previously attempted. The composer's violent depth of feeling provides the perfect musical response to Goethe's exultant cry of urgent young love. Of the composition of 'Erlkönig', Josef von Spaun left a valuable account:

One afternoon I went with Mayrhofer to see Schubert, who was then living with his father on the Himmelpfortgrund; we found Schubert all aglow, reading 'Erlkönig' aloud from the book. He paced up and down several times with the book, suddenly he sat down and in no time at all (just as quickly as one can write) there was the glorious ballad finished on the paper. We ran with it to the seminary, for there was no pianoforte at Schubert's, and there, on the very same evening, 'Erlkönig' was sung and enthusiastically received. The old organist, Ruzicka [Schubert's old teacher] then sat down and, with the greatest interest, played it through himself in all its sections, but without the voice, and was most moved by the composition. When some people wished to point out a dissonance which recurred several times, Ruzicka explained, sounding it on the piano, how it was necessary here, in order to correspond with the words, how beautiful it was on the contrary, and how happily it was resolved.

How those notes of Schubert's must have seared the pages. They still do, long after the minor ninths at the words 'Mein Vater' (My father) have ceased to sound dissonant to any ears. Schubert's 'Erlkönig' challenges and equals Goethe's, whereas a setting by the song composer Loewe three years later does no more than adequately accompany the poem. At the seminary that day in 1815, Schubert's song was performed three times in succession. After the first time the composer, who was at the piano, simplified the accompaniment, which was too difficult for him to play, remarking, 'The triplets are too difficult for me; you need to be a virtuoso to play them.'

It was six years before 'Erlkönig' was to achieve individual publication in its own right as Schubert's opus 1. We have seen just how much had been composed prior to that opus 1. Now, however, having achieved such an astonishing maturity at the age of eighteen, Schubert did not, in the conventional sense of the word, develop throughout the remaining thirteen years of his brief life. He was already, at eighteen, a master of song, and ready to embark upon his finest creative period, while barely out of his adolescence. It was as though nature, knowing that he had not been allotted a full complement of years, chose to accelerate the creative process.

In the autumn of 1815, Schubert composed a splendid 'Magnificat' (D.486) for soloists, choir, orchestra and organ, its jubilant outer movements flanking a reflective central section.

There is no doubt that Schubert found the duties of the classroom irksome, and after his initial meeting with Franz von Schober his dissatisfaction with life as a suburban schoolmaster in Vienna must have become more intense, for Schober continually encouraged him to break the confining fetters of bourgeois conformity and mediocrity. It was in a mood of desperation, combined with a certain spirit of adventure, that Schubert answered an advertisement which appeared in the *Wiener Zeitung* in February 1816, calling for applications for the post of music master at a training school for elementary teachers at Laibach (now Ljubljana in Yugoslavia), about 65 kilometres northeast of Trieste. Schubert applied, somewhat belatedly, in April, having been encouraged to do so by Salieri, who provided a testimonial supporting his application. Salieri's recommendation made Schubert a strong candidate, but in September the Laibach authorities assigned the position to a local musician, Franz Sokol.

It was in April 1816 that Josef von Spaun took it upon himself to send a collection of Schubert's songs in manuscript copies to Goethe, with an accompanying letter in which he commended the young composer to the elderly and distinguished poet, adding that 'the artist now wishes to be allowed to dedicate [these songs] most submissively to Your Excellency to whose glorious poetry he is indebted not only for the origin of a great part of them but also, in all essentials, for his development into a German song-writer'.

The specimen book of songs was returned, but without any reply from Goethe.

In March and April, Schubert produced three pleasant and un-demanding sonatas for violin and piano (D.384, 385 and 408), and in April he composed his Fourth Symphony (D.417), to which he gave the title 'Tragic', probably because of its slow and weighty intro-duction. The symphony's second movement, an andante, is by no means tragic but is a poetically lyrical outpouring of sound, and one of Schubert's most beautiful slow movements.

Schubert began to keep a diary in June 1816. He probably did not keep it up for long, and the only pages that have been preserved relate to June and September of that year. The first entry, dated 13 June, was written after he had heard the violinist Martin Schlesinger and other musicians playing a Mozart string quintet:

All my life I shall remember this fine, clear, lovely day. I still hear softly, as from afar, the magic strains of Mozart's music. With what unbelievable vigour, and yet again how gently, did Schlesinger's masterly playing impress it deep, deep into the heart. Thus does the mind retain these lovely impressions, which neither time nor circumstance can efface. They influence for good our entire existence. In the darkness of this life they point to a bright, clear and distant future, for which we hope with confidence. O Mozart, immortal Mozart, how many, how infinitely many inspiring perceptions of a finer and better life have you brought to our souls! – This quintet is, so to speak, one of the greatest of his lesser works. – I too had to make an appearance on this occasion. I played a set of variations by Beethoven, and sang [my settings of] Goethe's 'Restless Love' and Schiller's 'Amalia'. Unanimous applause for the former, less for the latter. I too think my 'Restless Love' better than 'Amalia', but I cannot deny that the essential musicality of Goethe's poetic genius was largely responsible for the applause. I also made the acquaintance of Mme Jenny, an extraordinarily brilliant pianist, though her playing appears to be somewhat lacking in genuine expression.

Schubert can have had very little time, at this period of his life, for country walks or strolls in the Vienna Woods. In addition to his work at the school-house, he was giving music lessons to supplement his income, and whatever time remained was devoted to composition. When he did manage to take a little time off to walk in the country, the event was noteworthy enough to be recorded in his diary, on 14 June:

I went for an evening walk, which I had not done for several months. There is hardly anything more agreeable than to get out into the green countryside at the end of a hot summer's day: and for this purpose the fields between Währing and Döbling seem to have been specially created. In the mysterious twilight and with my brother Karl for company, I felt so happy and contented. 'How beautiful,' I thought, and exclaimed aloud, standing still with enchantment. The churchyard close by reminded us of our dear mother. Thus, talking of sad and intimate matters, we came to the point where the road to Döbling divides. And, as though from heaven itself, I heard the sound of a familiar voice, issuing from a coach which had halted. I looked up – and there was Weinmüller, who, as he alighted, greeted us in his hearty and honest way. In an instant our conversation turned to the subject of outward cordiality in people's voices and language. How many people attempt in vain to reveal their real feelings in open and heartfelt language, while others make efforts which merely turn themselves into laughing-stocks. One realizes that this is not something one acquires, but a natural gift.

The following day, Schubert visited an exhibition of paintings mounted by the Academy of Fine Arts at St Anna's, a gallery which had formerly been a Jesuit monastery. The only picture to impress him was a portrait of the Virgin and Child by the Austrian painter Josef Abel (b. 1764). In his diary he wrote:

It is quite common to be disappointed in one's expectations. This happened to me when I saw the exhibition of Austrian paintings held at St Anna's. Among all the pictures a Madonna and Child by Abel appealed to me most. The velvet cloak of a prince disappointed me completely. For the rest, I admit that it is necessary to see such things several times and at leisure, if one is to discover the proper expression and receive the correct impression.

Two fascinating and little-known works which Schubert composed in 1816 are the Rondo in A major for violin and strings (D.438), which he wrote in June, and the Adagio and Rondo in F major for piano and strings (D.487), which followed in October. Although 'Adagio' is not mentioned in the title of the first work, both are in effect miniature truncated concertos consisting of an adagio and rondo, shorn of an opening allegro, and both are delightful essays in a late-eighteenth-century rococo style. Schubert was never to compose real concertos, perhaps because the element of virtuosity implied in the pitting of soloist against orchestra was alien to him.

On Sunday, 16 June 1816, the fiftieth anniversary of the arrival of Salieri in Vienna was celebrated. The day began with a service in the Minoritenkirche, after which the Lord High Chamberlain, in the name of the Emperor, presented the composer with the civil gold

medal of honour. Salieri then conducted High Mass in the Court
Chapel with music of his own. The celebrations continued throughout the day, and in the evening a concert arranged by his pupils took
place at Salieri's home. Schubert's contribution to this was a short
male-voice trio (D.441), with piano accompaniment, for which he
wrote not only the music, which is no more than quite pleasant, but
also the text, a piece of doggerel which begins: 'Gütigster, Bester,
Weisester, Grösster!' (Kindest, best, wisest, greatest of men!).
Schubert noted the event in his diary:

It must be beautiful and inspiring for a musician to see all his pupils
gathered around him, each one striving to give of his best for his master's
jubilee, and to hear in all their compositions the pure expression of nature,
free from all that eccentricity which is common among most composers
nowadays, and which is due almost wholly to one of the greatest German
musicians; that eccentricity which confuses and confounds the tragic and the
comic, the sacred and the profane, the pleasant and the unpleasant, heroic
strains and mere howling; which engenders in people feelings not of love but
of madness; which incites them to scornful laughter instead of lifting up their
thoughts to God. To see these extravagances excluded from the circle of his
pupils and instead to look upon the pure source of nature must give the
greatest satisfaction to a musican who, following in the steps of Gluck, seeks
his inspiration in nature alone in spite of the unnatural tendencies of our
present age.

Having spent fifty years in Vienna, and nearly as long in the Emperor's
service, Herr Salieri celebrated his jubilee, was awarded a gold medal by His
Majesty, and held a big gathering of his pupils, male and female. The works
written for the occasion by his composition students were performed in the
order in which they had studied with him. The performance also included a
chorus and an oratorio, 'Jesu al Limbo', both by Salieri. The oratorio is
modelled closely on Gluck. The occasion was of interest to everybody.

The great German musician whom Schubert accuses of fostering
eccentricity is clearly Beethoven. Schubert, before he was much older,
was to venerate Beethoven completely. At this stage of his life,
however, he was understandably still under the influence of Salieri,
who would have shared the conventional, conservative view of the
great German composer who had adopted Vienna as his home.

The day after the Salieri celebrations, Schubert noted proudly in his
diary: 'Today I composed for money for the first time.' He had
written a cantata, *Prometheus* (D.451), for the name-day of
Professor Watteroth, a professor of law, and he conducted its

performance in the garden of Watteroth's house on 12 July. His fee was 100 Viennese florins, or about £8.50. There were, at this time, two currencies in Austria: Assimilated Currency, based on the Convention concluded in 1753 between a number of German-speaking states, and Viennese Currency, a system of paper money used in Austria from 1811 to 1854. Five florins of Viennese Currency were worth only two of Assimilated Currency. This led to the Viennese Currency ('Wiener Währung') becoming known as W.W. or 'Weh! Weh!' ('Woe! Woe!').

In May 1816 Schubert's friend Josef von Spaun took lodgings with Josef Witteczek in a house in the Erdberggasse, where their rooms soon became the scene of those domestic musical evenings devoted to the music of Schubert which came to be known as Schubertiads. A generation earlier in Vienna, the music of Mozart was frequently to be heard, but mainly in the homes of the aristocracy. Now music was being taken up by the bourgeoisie as well. A middle-class home was not complete without a piano, and usually more than one member of the family was a reasonably proficient musician. The music written for aristocratic houses had included symphonies and pieces for chamber music ensembles: the middle classes could rarely maintain their own orchestras, and the music which they tended to cultivate was more likely to be written for the piano, or for piano and one other instrument, or, of course, for voice and piano. Schubert became a prolific provider of dances for the piano as well as a composer of songs. At the Schubertiads, he would often sing as well. His friends described his voice as 'weak but very agreeable'. He could sing baritone or tenor as well as, when necessary, soprano or alto: in other words, he had a typical composer's voice.

In the summer, Schubert composed his Piano Sonata No. 3 in E (D.459), sometimes known as 'Fünf Klavierstücke' as its five movements were at one time thought to be five separate piano pieces. More expansive in style than the first two sonatas, it reveals Schubert to be developing rapidly as a composer for the piano.

Among the other piano pieces composed by Schubert in 1816 was a wistful little waltz (D.365, No. 2), which soon became extremely popular among the composer's friends and which, when it was published in 1821 (as opus 9, No. 2), with a number of other 'original dances for the pianoforte' by Schubert, was burdened with the title 'Trauerwalzer' (Mourning Waltz), much to Schubert's amusement. 'What fool would compose a "mourning" waltz?' he is reputed to have said. Oddly enough, when it was republished in 1826 it was as the 'Sehnsucht' or 'yearning' waltz, and misattributed to Beethoven. The 'Trauerwalzer' became known in countless arrangements, and eventually found its way into the twentieth-century operetta *Das Dreimäderlhaus*, or *Lilac Time* (see p. 67).

The music which Schubert composed for the church in 1816 includes his Mass No. 4 in C (D.452), a serene and warm-hearted piece like its predecessors, and several shorter pieces, among which is an affecting 'Salve Regina' for unaccompanied chorus (D.386): affecting, that is, if one's modern sensibilities are not shocked by nineteenth-century sentimentality being found a place in religious music. The light-hearted 'Tantum ergo' for soprano, chorus, orchestra and organ (D.460) is a test of one's responses in these matters. The more devout will prefer, or will at least object less strongly to, another setting of the 'Tantum ergo' for four soloists, chorus and orchestra (D.461). Both were composed in August 1816. In September, Schubert began a string trio (D.471) but composed only the opening movement, a generously melodic allegro and the beginning of an andante before breaking off.

Schubert's diary entry for 8 September 1816, a series of superficial philosophical musings, would appear to have been influenced by the melancholy nature of his friend Mayrhofer:

Man resembles a ball, the plaything of chance and passion.

This sentence seems to me to be extraordinarily true.

I have often read it said that the world is like a stage on which every man plays a part. Praise and blame are awarded in the next world. – But just as rôles on the stage are assigned, so are our parts assigned to us, and which of us can say whether he has played his well or badly? – It is a bad producer who gives his actors rôles they are unable to play. Negligence is unthinkable with us, for no actor has been dismissed from this world theatre because he spoke his lines badly. If he is given a suitable rôle he will play it well. Whether or not he is applauded will depend upon how the audience, in its various moods, is disposed towards him. Up above, praise and blame depend solely upon the world's producer. Thus public censure is suspended.

A man's natural disposition and education determine his mind and his heart. The heart is the ruler, though the mind should be. Take people as they are, not as they ought to be.

Moments of bliss relieve the sadness of this life. Up above, these blissful moments will become perpetual joy, while even happier moments will turn into visions of even more blessed worlds, and so on.

Happy is he who finds a faithful friend. Happier still is he who finds a faithful friend in his wife.

Nowadays, to a single man matrimony is a terrifying thought. He sees in it only dreariness or crude sensuality. Monarchs of today, you see this and are silent! Or do you not see it? If so, O God, veil our minds and our senses in darkness; yet one day draw back the veil again without lasting harm.

Man bears misfortune without complaining, but finds it therefore the harder to bear. – Why then did God endow us with compassion?

A light head, a light heart. Too light a head, however, usually conceals too heavy a heart.

City politeness and human sincerity are the complete antithesis of each other.

The wise man's greatest unhappiness and the fool's greatest happiness are grounded in convention.

The noble-minded man experiences, in misfortune as in prosperity, the full measure of both prosperity and misfortune.

I can't think of anything more now. Tomorrow I shall certainly think of something else. Why is that? Is my mind duller today than tomorrow because I have eaten well and am sleepy? – Why does the mind not go on thinking when the body is asleep? It goes off, wandering, no doubt? – For surely it cannot sleep, too?

> What are these thoughts?
> I hear folks say.
> They cannot be proven,
> Try as we may.
> And so good night
> Till morning's sight.

Johann Mayrhofer wrote a poem, 'Geheimnis' (Secret), in 1816, and dedicated it to Schubert. 'Tell us your secret,' the poet asks. 'Tell us who taught you to sing so tenderly and sweetly.' Schubert's art is praised in four stanzas which, when he was shown them in October, he unblushingly set to music. The result is a song (D.491) which, though quite charming, is not one of Schubert's most spontaneous.

It was in the autumn that Schubert composed his next symphony (No. 5 in B flat, D.485), which he completed on 3 October. Scored for a small orchestra, without trumpets or drums, the symphony was first performed at one of the musical evenings in the house of Otto Hatwig in the Schottenhof. The orchestra, an amateur group which had grown out of the Schubert family's string quartet, was conducted by Hatwig, who was a violinist at the Burgtheater. Schubert himself played the viola. The Fifth Symphony, a delightful work, is the most Mozartian of these early Schubert symphonies, and also the most popular of them.

Schubert's songs of 1816 include several which magically improve upon the poetic material he chose to set. Ludwig Hölty, an eighteenth-century poet who died of consumption at the age of twenty-eight, had first been set by Schubert the previous year. In 1816 the composer returned to Hölty, setting a further thirteen poems. While he was not a great or even a consistently good poet, Hölty had a quality which not only appealed to Schubert but also inspired him to some of his best essays in that delicate, more often than not pathetic vein which came so easily to him. Many of these songs, neglected by singers, are worth studying and singing: for example, 'Auf den Tod einer Nachtigall' (On the Death of a Nightingale, D.201), 'Die frühe Liebe' (Young Love, D.430), and 'Der Leidende' (The Sufferer, D.432). One of them, the delightful 'Seligkeit' (Bliss, D.433), is already deservedly popular with concert audiences.

A Schubertian poet encountered for the first – and last – time in 1816 is Johann Georg Jacobi, from whose verses Schubert fashioned seven songs, all but one of them pleasant but inconsequential. The exception is 'Litanei' (Litany, D.343), one of the masterpieces of German Lieder. 'Litanei' is not so much a prayer for the souls of the dead as a song of consolation to those who mourn them, and Schubert's calm and noble melody is indeed sweetly consoling in its effect.

Great settings of the three Harper's songs from Goethe's *Wilhelm Meister* belong to this year: 'Wer sich der Einsamkeit ergibt' (He who gives way to solitude, D.478), 'Wer nie sein Brot mit Tränen ass' (He who never ate his bread with tears, D.480), and 'An die Türen will ich schleichen' (I will creep to the doors, D.479). These three songs of the Harper, sorrow distilled into music, defy description in words and do not always render up their secrets easily in performance. But, sung by an artist whose technique is secure enough to allow him to do no more than merely enunciate the words sensitively and clearly, they can be almost unbearably moving to hear. Schubert the composer of great depths of feeling coexisted happily with Schubert the cosy provider of Biedermeier delights.

Another Goethe-Schubert masterpiece of 1816 is 'An Schwager

Kronos' (To Coachdriver Chronos, D.369). The young Goethe's wildly imaginative address to Time, which he sees as a reckless coachdriver rushing him on towards death, is superb poetry. Once one has heard Schubert's exhilarated and carefree setting, it is difficult to contemplate the poem deprived of his music.

The text of one of Schubert's most famous songs, 'Der Wanderer' (The Wanderer, D.489), is by a very minor poet indeed, one Georg Philipp Schmidt von Lübeck (1766–1849), and Schubert is said to have come across the poem in an almanac. Schmidt von Lübeck's poem is, however, almost the perfect expression of the romantic *Sehnsucht* and *Weltschmerz* which were such prominent features of the *Sturm und Drang* movement. The wanderer has come from far away. To him the sun seems cold, the flowers faded. He continually hears the whisper 'Where?' and seeks in vain the land which speaks his own language. A ghostly voice tells him 'There, where you are not, there is where your happiness resides'. It is a poem of splendid, if theatrical, gesture, and Schubert responded to it by composing a scena, but not too elaborate a one, and by providing a slightly self-pitying but none the less beautiful tune for the lines 'Ich wandle still, bin wenig froh,/Und immer fragt der Seufzer: wo?' (I walk in silence, am seldom merry, and always the whisper asks: where?). The adagio melody to the words 'Die Sonne dünkt mich hier so kalt' (The sun here seems so cold to me) was used again by Schubert six years later in his 'Wanderer' Fantasy for piano (D.760). This song of 1816 was enthusiastically taken up by Viennese domestic amateurs and soon became, after 'Erlkönig', Schubert's most popular song. Some critics today make the mistake of despising it for its sentimentality.

Would that there had been a literary genius in Schubert's amiable band of Viennese friends. Johann Mayrhofer's poems are rather poor, but they brought forth a few fine songs by Schubert, some of them classical in subject and in manner, some curiously Wagnerian, and a few of them nature pieces that would have been even better than they are had not the gloom of Mayrhofer's sentiment occasionally toppled over into absurdity. 'Lied eines Schiffers an die Dioskuren' (Boatman's Song to the Dioscuri, D.360) stands out from the other 1816 Mayrhofer songs, a noble hymn to his guiding stars sung by a boatman.

Among the settings of another not very interesting poet, Matthias Claudius, is the famous 'Wiegenlied', or lullaby, 'Schlafe, schlafe,

43

holder, süsser Knabe' (Sleep, sleep, my sweet precious child, D.498). And, although the poems of Schubert's friend Franz von Schober are distinctly weak, they brought into being some charming songs, including (in 1816) 'Am Bach im Frühling' (By the Brook in Spring, D.361), and (in 1817) one which is held dear by all lovers of Schubert, 'An die Musik' (To Music, D.547), in which Schubert offers his thanks to the art of music itself. This is one of his most deeply felt songs, its melody natural and graceful, its chordal accompaniment simple and deeply affecting: a very beautiful prayer of gratitude to the art which sustained Schubert.

Franz von Schober had returned to Vienna in the autumn of 1816, after a visit of some months' duration to his birthplace in Sweden. He now persuaded Schubert to break away from the profession of teaching, and also from the parental home. By December, Schubert was living with Schober and Schober's mother in a house in the Landskrongasse in the inner city, where he was to remain for several months. Schober's hope was that, freed from having to teach, Schubert would be able to devote himself wholeheartedly to com-position, and live by selling his works to publishers and theatre managements. Schubert would pay a small amount for his board and lodging, but only when he was able to do so.

To Schubert's father and his brothers, the twenty-year-old Franz's action in leaving home must have seemed precipitate and foolhardy, but to the young composer it represented a move in the only direction he felt equipped to take, towards personal and artistic freedom. He was confident enough to assume that, in time, he would be able to live by his music, but also young enough not to consider the consequences if it should transpire that he could not.

The masterpieces of song now began to appear with increasing frequency. In March 1817, the month of 'An die Musik', Goethe's great poem 'Ganymed' was taken in by the composer and breathed out again upon rapturous phrases (D.544). The 1817 Mayrhofer songs include the finest of them, 'Memnon' (D.541). Under the guise of writing about the world of the past, the poet produced in 'Memnon' an unbearably painful cry from the heart which Schubert translated into music which is at once noble and moving.

'Der Tod und das Mädchen' (Death and the Maiden, D.531) is justly celebrated, a song whose simplicity masks a resonance and depth which even Schubert achieved only rarely. The 'Death' theme from this song was used again by the composer in his D minor String Quartet (D.810) of 1826. An equally fine pendant to 'Der Tod und das Mädchen', from which it quotes, is 'Der Jüngling und der Tod' (The Youth and Death, D.545), its poem by Josef von Spaun.

Later in 1817 came the popular and engaging 'Die Forelle' (The Trout, D.550), written to a poem by C. F. D. Schubart which recounts the minor tragedy of the trout who, for all his nimble darting and splashing, was finally no match for the cunning angler. Schubart's poem had a final stanza, which Schubert did not set, pointing the moral that girls should avoid fishy young men! The song flows charmingly along, and it requires no great imagination on the listener's part to see the trout as it is depicted in the accompaniment, alternately flashing and gliding through the stream. Two years later, Schubert used the principal tune of 'Die Forelle' as the theme for the variations in the fourth movement of his A major Piano Quintet (D.667).

In the autumn, Schubert composed the greatest of his Schiller settings, 'Gruppe aus dem Tartarus' (Group from Tartarus, D.583), in which he gave tumultuous musical life to the poet's wild vision of hell and damnation. Again and again, when one considers Schubert's vast output of song, one is struck most of all by the intense breadth of his range. The adjective 'Schubertian' has come unfairly to denote certain of his qualities only: his charm, his gentleness, his Biedermeier *Gemütlichkeit*; but, as the later symphonies and piano sonatas remind one, he was not merely a composer of graceful trifles. Many of the early songs already mentioned have shown evidence of his power and depth: a juxtaposition of the charming 'Die Forelle' and the tormented 'Gruppe aus dem Tartarus' makes the point strongly.

It was in April 1817 that Schubert's friends persuaded him to send a copy of 'Erlkönig' to the famous Leipzig firm of music publishers, Breitkopf & Härtel. As the only Franz Schubert known to Breitkopf & Härtel was Franz Anton Schubert, a forty-nine-year-old Dresden composer and double-bass player in the Dresden orchestra, the publishers sent a copy of the manuscript to him for confirmation. He replied indignantly, in a letter of 18 April:

With the greatest astonishment I beg to state that this cantana [*sic*] was never composed by me. I shall retain the same in my possession in order to learn, if possible, who has so impertinently sent you that sort of rubbish, and also to discover the fellow who has thus misused my name.

The publishers returned Franz Peter Schubert's manuscript to him in Vienna without comment.

In February or March, Schober had introduced Schubert to the famous opera singer Johann Michael Vogl (1768–1840), who was destined to play an important part in popularizing Schubert's songs. Vogl, who was already approaching fifty, had been the Vienna Court Opera's leading baritone for twenty-two years, a greatly admired Orestes in Gluck's *Iphigénie en Tauride* and Count Almaviva in Mozart's *Le Nozze di Figaro*. He had also created the role of Pizarro in the 1814 première of Beethoven's *Fidelio* at the Theater an der Wien.

At their first meeting, Schubert showed Vogl a number of his songs. After the baritone had looked through them, he said to the young composer: 'There is much fine stuff in these songs, but you are not enough of an actor, not enough of a charlatan. You waste many of your fine thoughts instead of developing them.' Despite his initial cynical appraisal, however, Vogl became an advocate of Schubert's songs after he had examined more of them, and in time he was to prove a warm friend of the composer.

Vogl was a man of wide culture. He had studied law before adopting music as a profession, and was fluent in several classical and modern languages. His own performances of Schubert Lieder were described by many as unforgettable because of his superb declamation. The evidence of some of the songs which Schubert composed expressly for Vogl suggests that the singer must have possessed a high baritone voice with an extension into the tenor range. Performances of Schubert's songs by Vogl accompanied by the composer quickly became a popular feature of the Schubertiad evenings, and the two musicians were greatly in demand in a number of Viennese salons. At first, Vogl was inclined to use Schubert's songs simply as opportunities to display his vocal art, but, as the relationship between the two men became closer, so Vogl's understanding of Schubert as a composer grew and deepened. (He and Schubert continued to perform together throughout the composer's lifetime, and Vogl was to give his final performance of *Winterreise* some years after Schubert's death. Then over seventy, and within a year of his own death, the aged singer, suffering with gout, invited a number of his friends to a party at which he sang Schubert's great song-cycle in a voice which, though weak, had retained its sweetness. More than one survivor from the days of the Schubertiads was moved to tears that evening by Vogl's interpretative artistry.)

In addition to the songs he composed during 1817, Schubert also concentrated, between May and August, upon the composition of six sonatas for the piano. These sonatas are the work of a young artist who was still developing, for Schubert curiously achieved maturity as a composer of songs much earlier than as a composer of instrumental and orchestral music; nevertheless, the 1817 piano sonatas constitute a distinguished group of works for the piano, somewhat Beethovenian in mood and manner, but with many distinct traces of Schubert's creative personality. The Sonata No. 4 in A minor (D.537) is an inward-looking, restrained piece, with a beautiful slow movement; No. 5 in A flat (D.557) oddly casts a backward glance at the less personal, almost Haydn-like world of the 1815 sonatas; and No. 6 in E minor (D.566; its fourth movement, a Rondo, is catalogued as D.506) is an unjustly neglected work of impressive stature and a distinctive Schubertian personality. The Sonata No. 7 in E flat (D.568), much better known, has a particularly enchanting first movement and, like No. 9 in B (D.575), is a spacious and well-constructed work.

Perhaps the most interesting of these 1817 sonatas is No. 8 in F sharp minor, which has to be numbered D.571/604/570, for it has been re-assembled by Paul Badura-Skoda. The manuscript is of an incomplete first movement (D.571) which has been completed by Badura-Skoda, who, giving convincing musicological reasons for having done so, has identified a Scherzo and Allegro (D.570) as the third and fourth movements of the sonata, and an Andante (D.604) as the missing slow movement. The result is a delightful, graceful and cohesive example of Schubert's now rapidly developing sonata style.

By the autumn, Schubert was home again, for he had been obliged to give up his room at Schober's to his friend's brother, a lieutenant in the army who was expected home from France. (As it happened, Schober's ailing brother died before he reached Vienna.) Before the end of the year, Schubert composed a sweetly melodic sonata for violin and piano in A major (D.574) and a string trio in B flat (D.581). The trio is a charming work, predominantly Haydnish in style, though with occasional Schubertian touches. In November, he composed two overtures 'in the Italian style' (D.590 and 591), which are exuberant imitations of Rossini, whose operas were then immensely popular in Vienna.

On Christmas Eve, 1817, Schubert's father was transferred to a better post as master of a school in Rossau, a district near Liechtental but a little closer to the inner city. When the Schubert family moved to its new home early in the new year, Franz moved with them.

In 1818, Lanner and Strauss were just beginning their careers, the waltz was in its infancy, and Franz Schubert was living at home again with his father, stepmother and family, in their new house in the Rossau district. In February Franz made his first appearance in print as a composer when his song, 'Am Erlafsee' (On Lake Erlaf, D.586), was published. This setting of a poem by Johann Mayrhofer appeared as a supplement to a Viennese periodical with the unwieldy title of *Mahlerisches Taschenbuch für Freunde interessanter Gegenden, Natur- und Kunst-Merkwürdigkeiten der Oesterreichischen Monarchie* (Picturesque Pocket Book for Lovers of the Country, and Natural and Artistic Objects of Interest of the Austrian Monarchy). By now, Schubert had written about 350 songs, but 'Am Erlafsee' was the first to be printed in any form.

The following month, another work became the first by Schubert to be performed at a public concert. This was an overture, one of the two (D.590 and 591) which Schubert had written the previous autumn 'in the Italian style'. Described in a newspaper advertisement as 'An entirely new overture by Herr Franz Schubert', it was included in a miscellaneous programme performed by a group of musicians engaged by Eduard Jaëll, a violinist in the orchestra at the Theater an der Wien. The concert took place on 1 March in the hall of the hotel *Der römische Kaiser* (The Roman Emperor), and Schubert's composition was given a favourable notice in the *Theaterzeitung* on 14 March:

The second part began with a wondrously lovely overture by a young composer, Herr Franz Schubert, a pupil of the famous Salieri. He has learned already how to touch and move all hearts to emotion. Although the theme is simple enough, a wealth of the most astonishing and agreeable ideas developed from it, worked out with vigour and skill. It is to be wished that this artist will quite soon delight us with a new gift.

The overture was also reviewed in a Dresden newspaper, this being the first foreign criticism of any work by Schubert. Meanwhile, during the winter of 1817–18, the young composer had been working on another symphony, his sixth (D.589), which he completed in February. This symphony in C (known as the 'little' C major, to distinguish it from the later 'Great' C major) is a charming and light-hearted work, though perhaps melodically less fresh and inventive than some of the earlier symphonies. The scherzo is clearly modelled on Beethoven and specifically on his First Symphony.

Schubert's friendship with Anselm Hüttenbrenner, a fellow-pupil with Salieri, had deepened, and he had also become friendly with Anselm's younger brother, Josef. At midnight on 21 February 1818, at Anselm's lodgings, where he occasionally spent the night, the twenty-one-year-old Schubert finished copying out for Josef a song, 'Die Forelle' (The Trout), which he had composed the previous year. Not entirely sober, for he had been drinking Hungarian red wine the entire evening, he picked up the ink-well by mistake instead of the drying-sand, and made a huge blot over the manuscript before he realized his error. But he sent the song, accompanied by a letter:

Dearest Friend,
I am exceedingly pleased that you like my songs. As a proof of sincerest friendship, I am sending you another, which I have just written down at midnight, at Anselm Hüttenbrenner's. I wish that we could pledge our friendship in a glass of punch. Vale.
Just now, in my haste to sprinkle sand over the thing, half-drunk with sleep I took up the ink-well and poured it all over. What a disaster!

On 1 March one of Schubert's two 'Italian style' overtures was played in public, this time in an arrangement for two pianos, eight hands (D.597). The concert was again at the *Römischer Kaiser*, and the four pianists were Schubert himself, Anselm Hüttenbrenner, and the sisters Therese and Babette Kunz. This time the reviewer of the *Theaterzeitung* wrote that he regarded it as his duty to draw special attention to the young artist, Herr Schubert:

Profound feeling, disciplined yet spontaneous force, and appealing charm mark his every work, large and small. Once practice, that mother of all human perfection, has done her own work with him, his compositions will without a doubt find their favoured place among the productions of the day.

No longer receiving a salary as a schoolmaster, and earning next to nothing as a composer, Schubert decided to give music lessons in order to live. In the spring of 1818, Johann Karl Unger, the father of the singer Caroline Unger, introduced the composer to Count Johann Karl Esterházy von Galánta, recommending him as a music teacher for the count's two daughters. Schubert was duly engaged, and spent the summer with the Esterházy family at their summer residence, a castle at Zseliz (then in Hungary, now in Czechoslovakia), about 100 miles east of Vienna. His duties consisted in giving musical instruction to the two young countesses, Marie, aged sixteen, and Caroline, aged thirteen, both of whom sang and played the piano. He was also required to participate in the musical performances which were given from time to time in the castle.

From Zseliz on 3 August Schubert wrote a letter addressed to Franz von Schober and his other friends:

Dearest and best friends,

How could I possibly forget you – you who mean everything to me? Spaun, Schober, Mayrhofer, Senn, how are you all? I am in the best of health. I live and compose like a god, as though indeed nothing else in the world were possible.

Mayrhofer's 'Einsamkeit' [Solitude, D.620] is finished, and I believe it to be the best thing I have done, for I felt without a care when writing it. I hope that you are all happy and in the best of health, as I am. Thank God I am really alive at last! It was high time, otherwise I should have become merely another frustrated musician. Would Schober please pay my respects to Herr Vogl, to whom I shall soon take the liberty of writing. If you get a chance, ask him if he would consider singing one of my songs – whichever he likes – at the Kunzes' concert in November. Greetings to everyone you can think of. My humblest respects to your mother and sister, Schober. Write to me soon, all of you, for every word from you is precious to me.

To his brother Ferdinand, on 24 August, he wrote:

It is half-past eleven at night, and your German Requiem [D.621] is finished. It made me rather sad, believe me, for I put my whole soul into its composition. Add the finishing touches wherever they are lacking: for instance fill in the text under the staves, and the musical signs above it. If you want to make some repeats, do so, without writing to Zseliz to consult me about it. Things are not going well with you: I wish I could change with you, so that you could be happy for once. You would then find all heavy burdens cast from your shoulders. Dear brother, I wish this for you with all my heart – Oh, my foot has gone to sleep now, which is very annoying. If the silly thing could write, it wouldn't fall asleep –

Good morning, little brother! I fell asleep, as well as my foot, and am now continuing this letter at 8 a.m. on the 25th. In exchange for your request, I have one, too: give my love to my dear parents, brothers and sisters, friends and acquaintances, not forgetting Karl in particular. Did he not mention me in his letter? – Stir up my friends in town to write to me, or get someone to give them a sharp kick as a reminder. Tell mother that my laundry is very well looked after, and that her maternal care greatly touches me. (But if you could send me some more clothes, I should be extremely glad to have some more handkerchiefs, scarves and stockings. Also, I badly need two pairs of cashmere trousers. Hart could take the measurements from anything of mine he likes. I should send the money for them at once.) I received during July, inclusive of travelling expenses, 200 florins.

It is already beginning to get cold here, but we shall not set out for Vienna before the middle of November. Next month I hope to go for a few weeks to Freistadtl, the property of Count Erdödy, the uncle of my Count. The country around there is said to be exceptionally pretty. I hope also to get to Pest, for it is not far from Pócs-Megyer, where we are going for the vintage. I should be extremely glad if I were able to meet the administrator Daigele there. But above all I am looking forward to the vintage festivities, for I have heard such nice things about them. The harvest here is very interesting too. The corn is not put into barns as in Austria. Instead they make enormous stacks, which they call *Tristen*, in the fields. These stacks are often some eighty to a hundred yards long and 100 to 120 feet high. They are built with such skill that the rain runs off them without doing any damage. Oats and such-like are buried underground.

Well and happy as I am here, and kind as the people are, I am counting the days to the moment when the cry goes forward, 'To Vienna! To Vienna!' Indeed, beloved Vienna, you hold in your narrow compass the dearest and most precious things in my life, and nothing but the heavenly sight of them again will put an end to my longing. Once again, please do not forget my wish mentioned above.

Heartiest greetings to my Aunt Schubert and her daughter.

I remain, with love to all, your true and faithful Franz. A thousand greetings to your good wife, and dear little Resi.

(The German Requiem [*Deutsches Requiem*, D.621] mentioned at the beginning of the letter was written by Schubert for his brother Ferdinand, who dabbled in composition. Ferdinand, with Franz's permission, passed it off as his own work at a performance in Vienna in September, and also used it in December 1819, at his examination in musical theory. In 1826, the German Requiem was published under Ferdinand's name, and it was not until 1928 that it was republished as a work by Franz Schubert.)

The days at Zseliz were spent happily. Schubert enjoyed giving piano tuition and instruction in musical theory to the two girls, and found himself coaching the Count and Countess as well, for both were enthusiastic amateur singers, the Countess a contralto and the Count a bass. Schubert wrote vocal exercises for them, and accompanied them in performances of arias and songs, including several of his own. He composed pianoforte duets for the daughters to play, part-songs for impromptu musical evenings at the castle, and must often have improvised music for dancing at parties or balls.

Towards the end of the summer, another letter was despatched to the Schubertian circle of friends. Dated 8 September 1818, it was addressed to 'Dear Schober, dear Spaun, dear Mayrhofer, dear Senn, dear Streinsberg, dear Waiss, dear Weidlich':

How infinitely happy the letters from you, separately and together, make me is beyond my powers of expression. I was attending a cattle auction when they handed to me your nice, fat letter. As I broke it open, I caught sight of Schober's name and a loud cry of joy burst from me. I read it through in a neighbouring room, laughing to myself all the time with childish pleasure. It was as though I were embracing all of my dear friends personally. But now I must answer you all in the proper order.

Dear Schobert,
I see that we shall have to stick to this alteration of your name. Well then, dear Schobert, your letter was very precious to me and delightful from beginning to end, and especially the last page. Yes, indeed, the last page sent me into transports of delight. You are a splendid fellow (in Swedish, of course) and, believe me, my friend, you will not fail, for your understanding of art is the finest and sincerest imaginable. That you should look upon this change as a small one pleases me very much, for, after all, you have had one foot in our pandemonium for a long time. That the management of the Opera House in Vienna should be so stupid as to produce the finest operas when I am not there makes me pretty furious. Here in Zseliz I have to rely entirely upon myself. I am obliged to be composer, author, audience, and goodness knows what else. There is not a soul here with any real feeling for music, except, perhaps, now and then, the Countess (unless I am mistaken). So I am all alone with my beloved art, and have to hide her in my room, in my pianoforte, and in my own heart. Although this is often very depressing, on the other hand it inspires me to greater things. Do not be afraid, then, that I shall stay away any longer than is absolutely necessary. Several new songs have come into being during this time, and I hope very successful ones. That the bird of Greece [Vogl] should be fluttering his wings in Upper Austria does not surprise me at all, since it is his native country and he is on holiday. I wish I were with him. I should certainly know how to make good use of my time. But that

you, by nature a sensible fellow, should think that my brother is wandering about there alone, with neither guide nor companion, does surprise me very much. Firstly, because an artist likes best of all to be left to himself; secondly, because there are too many beautiful districts in Upper Austria for him not to be able to find the loveliest; and thirdly, because he has a very pleasant acquaintance in Herr Forstmeyer in Linz. He certainly knows, therefore, what he is up to.

If you could manage a greeting to Max, when his melancholia has improved, I should be infinitely glad. And since you will shortly be seeing your mother and sister, please give them my kindest regards. It is possible that this letter will not reach you in Vienna in time, for I only received yours at the beginning of September, just when you were due to leave. I shall have it sent on to you. By the way, I am very glad that, for you, Frau Milder is irreplaceable. I feel the same about her. She sings more beautifully than anyone else – and trills worst of all.

Now a description for everybody:

Our castle here is by no means one of the largest, but it is very attractively built, and surrounded by a lovely garden. I live in the estate agent's house. It is fairly quiet, except for some forty geese which at times set up such a cackling that one cannot hear oneself speak. All the people around me are thoroughly kind-hearted. It must be rare for a nobleman's house to be run as smoothly as this one. The agent, a Slavonian, is a good fellow, and very much fancies his own former musical talents. He can still blow two German dances on the flute with great virtuosity. His son, a student of philosophy, has just arrived here on his holidays, and I hope I shall get on well with him. His wife is a lady. The steward is perfectly fitted to his job: a man of extraordinary perspicacity in whatever concerns his own purse and pocket. The doctor, a really able man, is only twenty-four but as full of ailments as an old lady. It's all very unnatural. The surgeon, whom I like best of all, is a venerable old man of seventy-five, always happy and serene. May God grant so fortunate an old age to everyone! The magistrate is an unassuming and pleasant man. One of the Count's companions, a cheerful old bachelor and a capable musician, often comes to see me. The chef, the lady's maid, the chambermaid, the lodge-keeper, etc. and coachmen are all good people. The chef is something of a rake; the lady's maid thirty years old; the chambermaid very pretty and often in my company; the children's nurse a nice old body; the lodge-keeper my rival. The two coachmen are better suited to the stables than to human society. The Count is rather a rough sort of man, the Countess haughty but more sensitive, and the little Countesses are nice children. So far I have been spared any invitation to dine with the family. I can think of nothing more to tell you now. I need hardly say to all of you, who know me, that with my naturally frank disposition I get on quite well with all these people.

Dear Spaun, I was truly most heartily glad to know that you are able at last to build palaces for junior court officials to run about in. I suppose you mean a vocal quartet. Remember me to Herr Gahy.

Dear Mayrhofer, you cannot be longing for November much more than I am. Stop being ill, or at least give up taking medicine, and the rest will come of itself.

Hans Senn, kindly read as above.

Friend Streinsberg appears to be dead by now: he is therefore excused from writing. Friend Weidlich may tack his name on to someone else's letter.

The good Waiss remembers me with gratitude, and is thus an excellent man.

And now, dear friends, good-bye. Write to me very soon. My best and favourite form of entertainment is to read your letters through a dozen times.

Greetings to my dear parents, and please tell them how much I long for a letter from them.

With enduring love,
Your faithful friend,
Franz Schubert.

(Of the recipients of the letter, Schober, Spaun and Mayrhofer were to remain faithful members of the Schubert circle. Streinsberg was another of Schubert's schoolfellows at the seminary, as was Waiss. Weidlich was an acquaintance from Kremsmünster. Schober had apparently been about to depart to his family home in Sweden, but in fact remained in Vienna. He had now given up the law, and was attempting to become a landscape painter. All his life he remained a dilettante. Vogl is called 'the bird of Greece' because of his love of classical Greece, and perhaps also because of his roles in operas such as Gluck's *Iphigénie en Tauride* and Cherubini's *Médée*; and 'Vogel' is the German word for 'bird'. 'Herr Forstmeyer in Linz' was Leopold Forstmayer, a government official and friend of Karl Schubert.)

One of the works composed at Zseliz was the Piano Sonata in F minor (D.625 and 505), whose not quite complete first movement has been completed by Paul Badura-Skoda. An earlier piano sonata, composed in April, the Sonata in C major (D.612 and 613), has its first and last movements completed by Badura-Skoda. Both sonatas are fluent and engaging works.

In mid-October, Ferdinand Schubert wrote a long letter to his brother Franz, in which he referred to having passed off the German Requiem as his own, and gave news of performances of works by Franz in Baden and Vienna. On 29 October Franz replied from Zseliz:

The sin of appropriation was already forgiven you in my first letter. You had no reason, therefore, except perhaps your tender conscience, for putting off writing so long. So my German Requiem pleased you, you wept during the performance of it, and perhaps at the same passage over which I wept myself. Dear brother, that is the highest reward possible for this gift of mine: do not let me hear you speak of any other.

If I did not get to know the people around me here better from day to day, I might be just as contented as I was at the beginning. But I see now that, with the exception of a couple of really good-hearted girls, I have nothing in common with any of them. I long for Vienna more and more each day. We shall set out in the middle of November. Loving greetings and kisses to those dear little creatures, Pepi and Marie, and also to our excellent parents. My friends in town are very neglectful. Now that Schober's wish [to be a landscape painter] is no longer a secret, I breathe again.

The musical events left me pretty cold. I am only amazed at the blind and wrong-headed zeal of my somewhat clumsy friend Doppler, whose friendship does me more harm than good. As for me, I shall never turn my inmost feelings to personal or political account: I come straight out with what is in me, and that's that.

By all means have my pianoforte moved over to you. I shall be delighted. The only thing that worries me is that you should imagine your letters to be disagreeable to me. It is dreadful to think such a thing of your brother, and still more to write it. What I do dislike is that you are always talking about payments, rewards and thanks, and that between brothers. Shame on you! Kiss your dear wife and your little Resi for me. Goodbye!

Ignaz and Resi, I was so pleased to get letters from you both. You, Ignaz, are still the same old man of iron. Your implacable hatred of the whole tribe of clerical bigwigs does you credit. But you have no notion what the local priesthood here is like: as bigoted as mucky old cattle, as stupid as jackasses, and as boorish as buffaloes. You may hear sermons here in comparison with which our much venerated Father Nepomucene is nothing. They fling from the pulpit such epithets as 'Blackguards', 'Rabble', etc., oh, it's really something lovely. Or they bring up a skull into the pulpit with them, and say: 'Look at this, you pock-marked mugs! That's what you will be like, one of these days.' Or else: 'See that lad! There he goes, taking a slut into the tavern. They dance the whole night through, then fall into bed together, tight, and soon there'll be three of them', etc., etc.

I wonder if you thought of me during the festivities. So you often think of me, dear Resi. How charming! I send ninety-nine kisses each to the Hollpeins, husband and wife, to Resi, and Heinrich, and Karl, and to his godfather and the godfather's future wife. Whether or not I have thought of you will be answered soon in person by

Franz.

55

(Pepe and Marie were Schubert's half-sisters, and Resi was Ferdinand's first child, Therese, born in 1816. The other 'dear Resi' is Schubert's sister, Therese. The third Resi ['Resi and Heinrich and Karl'] is Therese Grob. Heinrich was her brother, and Karl the youngest son of the Hollpeins, who lived next door to the Grobs. Schubert's brother Ignaz, in contrast to their father, who was a religious man, was a freethinker with a low opinion of the clergy. Schubert himself was conventionally rather than devoutly religious.)

In November 1818, the Esterházys returned to Vienna, and Schubert accompanied them. His father wanted him to return not only to the family home but also to the profession of teaching, but Schubert was determined to live life on his own terms. Too poor to rent a room on his own, he took refuge with friends. He shared rooms in the Wipplingerstrasse with his friend Mayrhofer, and continued throughout the winter to give music lessons to the Esterházy daughters. Since he lived cheaply, he was able to subsist on the fees from these and perhaps from other lessons as well.

Back in Vienna and able to visit theatres after his comparatively inactive summer in the Hungarian countryside, Schubert began to think seriously again about composing for the theatre as a means of livelihood. As soon as he had settled down in his new lodgings with Mayrhofer, he began work on the music for a one-act operetta, *Die Zwillingsbrüder* (The Twin Brothers, D.647), which he completed during January.

The libretto of *Die Zwillingsbrüder* had been adapted by Georg von Hofmann from a French farce, *Les Deux Valentins*. Hofmann, to whom Schubert had been introduced by Vogl, was the general secretary of the Kärntnertor theatre, and it was the hope of both men that their operetta would be staged at the Kärntnertor. It consists of an overture and ten numbers (three arias, two duets, one trio, one quartet, one quintet and two choruses) separated by dialogue. Schubert's score, from his engagingly Mozartian overture to the final happy chorus, is quite charming, and the two duets for the young lovers are especially engaging. However, the management of the Kärntnertor theatre appeared to be in no hurry to stage the work. Rossini was still the current rage in Vienna, and it was a Rossini première, that of *Otello*, which caused the staging of *Die Zwillingsbrüder* to be delayed.

On 8 January a second performance of Schubert's cantata,

Prometheus (written in 1816 and first performed then), was given in the house of Ignaz von Sonnleithner, the father of Schubert's friend Leopold. Sonnleithner regularly held domestic concerts in his house, and on this occasion sang the part of Prometheus himself. Schubert's name was becoming more widely known in Viennese musical circles, and this may well have been why he refused an invitation from the Esterházys to travel again with them to Hungary for the summer, preferring to remain available in Vienna.

On 28 February, at a concert in the *Römischer Kaiser* hotel, a Schubert song was sung for the first time on a public occasion, as distinct from a private musical soirée. The song was 'Schäfers Klagelied' (Shepherd's Lament, D.121), and it was sung by Franz Jäger, a tenor from the Theater an der Wien. 'A beautiful composition sung most feelingly in Herr Jäger's enchanting voice,' said the *Theaterzeitung*, while a Berlin journal, the *Gesellschafter*, found Schubert's song to be the most enjoyable piece on the programme, and added, 'We look forward, indeed, to a larger work by this promising artist which is now being prepared for our delectation.' This refers probably to *Die Zwillingsbrüder*.

Anselm Hüttenbrenner had been living in Graz since the previous autumn, and had composed two symphonies. Schubert wrote to him on 21 January:

Dear old friend,
Are you still alive? When I consider how long it is since you went away, and since you have written, and how faithlessly you have abandoned us, I feel really obliged to ask.

The last hope of your return has now flickered out. What on earth keeps you bound hand and foot in that accursed Graz? Have you fallen under some spell that holds you in terrible fetters and makes you forget all the rest of the world? I had, indeed, a presentiment when I kissed you good-bye that you would not soon return.

You have composed two symphonies: that is good. You let us see nothing of them: that is not good. You should really let your old friend hear something of you now and again.

What has become of all those supremely happy hours that we once spent together? Perhaps you do not think of them any more. But I do, and so often. You will have heard that otherwise everything is going very well with me.

I wish the same to you, with all my heart.
Be my friend always and do not forget
Your
Schubert.

Hüttenbrenner must have eventually replied, for Schubert continued the correspondence on 19 May:

Dear Friend,

A rogue, that's what you are, and no mistake. It will probably be ten years before you see Vienna again. First one girl and then another turns your head. Well then, may the devil take all girls, if you allow them to bewitch you in this manner. For heaven's sake, get married, and then there will be an end to it.

Of course you may say, like Caesar, that you'd rather be first in Graz than second in Vienna. But be that as it may. I am really in a raging fury because you are not here. The above proverb applies even more to Cornet than to you. God give him joy of it! I shall end by coming to Graz too, and becoming your rival.

There is little news here. If one hears anything good, it is sure to be old. Rossini's *Otello* was given here recently. Apart from Radicchi, it was all very well done. It is a far better, that is to say more characteristic, opera than *Tancredi*. His extraordinary creative genius is undeniable. The orchestration is at times highly original, and occasionally the vocal parts too, except for the usual Italian galloping and several reminiscences of *Tancredi*. In spite of Vogl, it is difficult to outmanoeuvre such rabble as Weigl, Treitschke, etc. So, instead of my operetta, they stage other wretched stuff that makes your hair stand on end.

Catel's *Semiramis* is to be given soon, with absolutely glorious music. Herr Stümer, a tenor from Berlin, who has already sung in several operas, is to appear in it here. His voice is rather weak, with no low tones, and continual falsetto in the upper register.

I cannot think of anything else now. Keep on at your composition, and let us see something of it.

(The two men derided by Schubert are the composer Josef Weigl, active as a conductor of opera in Vienna, and Georg Friedrich Treitschke, producer and house librettist at the Kärntnertor theatre. *Semiramis*, an opera by the French composer Charles-Simon Catel, had been seen in Vienna at the Theater an der Wien in 1806. It was revived at the Kärntnertor in May 1819, with the Berlin tenor Heinrich Stümer in the role of Arsoz. He was to create the role of Max in Weber's *Der Freischütz* in Berlin in 1821.)

Michael Vogl, the singer, liked to spend the summer vacation in his native town of Steyr in Upper Austria. In 1819, he invited Schubert to go with him, and at the beginning of July the two friends left Vienna for the attractive old town at the confluence of the Steyr and the Enns rivers, about ninety miles west of Vienna. In Steyr, Schubert lodged at the house of Dr Albert Schellmann, an expert in mining law. On 13 July, he wrote to his brother Ferdinand:

I trust that this letter will find you in Vienna, and that you are well. I am really writing to ask you to send me, as soon as possible, the *Stabat Mater* which we want to perform here. So far I am very well, except that the weather is persistently unfavourable. Yesterday, the 12th, a violent thunderstorm broke over Steyr, and the lightning struck and killed a girl, and paralysed two men in the arm. At the house where I am lodging there are eight girls, nearly all pretty. So you see, one is kept busy. The daughter of Herr von K[oller], at whose place Vogl and I have our meals every day, is very pretty, is a good pianist, and is learning to sing several of my songs. . . . Whatever you do, don't forget the *Stabat Mater*. P.S. The country around Steyr is inconceivably lovely.

(The *Stabat Mater* to which Schubert refers was probably the one he wrote in 1816, to a German text by Klopstock [D.383]. He may have intended to have it performed in the Steyr parish church. Josef von Koller, with whom Schubert and Vogl took their meals, was an iron merchant who lived in the central square of the city. One evening, an impromptu quartet performance of Schubert's 'Erlkönig' was given at Koller's house with the composer singing the role of the father, Koller's daughter Josefine the child, Vogl the Erl King, and Albert Stadler playing the pianoforte part.)

Josefine von Koller was herself an accomplished pianist, and it was probably for her that Schubert composed his graceful A Major Piano Sonata (D.664). In Steyr, Schubert also made the acquaintance of Sylvester Paumgartner, a mining official and amateur wind player and cellist, who arranged concerts at his house. Paumgartner admired Schubert's song 'The Trout', and commissioned a piano quintet from the composer, stipulating that one movement should consist of variations on the principal tune of 'The Trout'. Schubert began to sketch the composition at Steyr, but did not complete his 'Trout' Quintet until after his return to Vienna.

In August, Schubert paid a short visit to Linz. There, on 19 August, he wrote to Mayrhofer:

If you are as well as I am, you must be in the best of health. I am in Linz at present, and have been at the Spauns' house where I met Kenner, Kreil and Forstmayer, got to know Spaun's mother, and also Ottenwalt, to whom I sang his 'Lullaby' ['Wiegenlied', D.579], in my own setting. I enjoyed myself very much in Steyr, and mean to do so again. The country there is heavenly, and around Linz it is lovely too. We, that is Vogl and I, are to go to Salzburg in a few days. How I look forward to [it]. . . . We celebrated Vogl's birthday with a cantata [D.666] for which Stadler wrote the words and I the music, and it was a great success. Now goodbye, until the middle of September.

(The ten-minute-long 'Cantata for the Birthday of the Singer Michael Vogl', written for soprano, tenor and bass, with piano accompaniment, is pleasant but undistinguished. 'Wiegenlied' is not the widely known 'Lullaby' [D.498], which was composed the previous year.)

On his return to Vienna in September, Schubert worked on his Piano Quintet, the 'Trout' (D.667), for Sylvester Paumgartner. This, one of the composer's most famous and most popular works, is scored for piano, violin, viola, cello and double-bass. Paumgartner apparently told Schubert that what he wanted was something like Hummel's Piano Quintet, so Schubert obligingly took Hummel's work as his model. His finished composition, however, soared imaginatively beyond Hummel's pleasant little imitation of early Beethoven, in its wealth of melody, its high spirits and charm, and its delightful evocation of the landscape around Steyr, which clearly inspired the composer. A German critic once referred to the Steyr countryside as a 'secret collaborator' in the composition of the quintet. Indeed it was, as were the composer's own sociability and the good-humoured companionship of his fellow musicians. Sylvester Paumgartner is said to have been a merely adequate cellist, but he, too, deserves some credit for having helped this sunny masterpiece into existence.

The first performance of the 'Trout' Quintet was given by Paumgartner and a group of fellow musicians in Steyr at the end of 1819, after which the composition completely disappeared for ten years. Schubert does not seem to have realized that he had composed a work which would rank with the greatest chamber music works of Mozart and Beethoven. It was only in 1829, after the composer's death, when Ferdinand Schubert sold it to the publisher Josef Czerny, that the quintet became known beyond the town of Steyr. In advertising its publication, Czerny announced:

This quintet having already been performed in several circles at the publisher's instigation, and declared to be a masterpiece by the connoisseurs present, we deem it our duty to draw the musical public's attention to this latest work by the unforgettable composer.

The lakes, the valleys and hills of the romantic Upper Austrian countryside are happily mirrored in the 'Trout' Quintet's foaming melodies. Schubert was to rise to greater heights in his later chamber music pieces, but he would never surpass the charm of this enchanting, youthful effusion.

A picture of Schubert's life in Vienna in 1819 is given by Hüttenbrenner:

While Schubert and Mayrhofer were living together in Wipplingerstrasse, the former every day at 6 o'clock in the morning would seat himself at his writing-desk and compose without a break until one in the afternoon, smoking a few small pipes. If I came to see him in the morning, he would play to me what he had already written, and would want to hear my opinion. If I especially praised any song, he would say: 'Yes, that was a good poem, and when one has something good the music comes easily, melodies just flow into one, so that it is a real joy. With a bad poem, everything sticks. One can make a martyr of oneself over it, but only the driest stuff comes forth. I have often rejected dozens of poems that have been pressed upon me.'

We have already seen evidence of power in many of Schubert's songs. In October 1819 he tackled Goethe's poem 'Prometheus'. This great monologue of defiance is an extract from an unfinished drama, and in it Goethe uses the classical Greek myth to make an essentially modern utterance. His Prometheus speaks with the voice of eighteenth-century rationalism: 'Ich kenne nichts Ärmeres/Unter der Sonn', als euch, Götter!' (I know nothing more pitiable under the sun than you, Gods!) Schubert seems to have been totally gripped by Goethe's proud monologue, which he set (D.674) as a dramatic scena of such force that one is convinced he could, in different circumstances, have become an opera composer of Wagnerian stature.

One type of composition of which Schubert was an extremely prolific creator is the part-song for male voices. Part-singing had been eagerly taken up in Vienna, and amateur male-voice choirs proliferated throughout the city. Music publishers were therefore continually looking for compositions suitable for such groups. Haydn, Mozart and Beethoven all contributed to the repertoire, but no one composed more for these choirs than Schubert, who produced nearly a hundred part-songs for male voices. His early works in this genre include such grisly effusions as the 'Totengräberlied' (Gravedigger's Song, D.38) of 1813 and 'Der Geistertanz' (Dance of the Spirits, D.494) of 1816. More typical of the adult Schubert is 'Das Dörfchen' (The Little

Village, D.598), composed in 1818, and first performed on 19 November 1819, at Ignaz Sonnleithner's, a few days after Schubert's return from Upper Austria. It was sung as a quartet by four members of the Schubert circle, the tenors Josef Barth and Johann Umlauff, and the basses Josef Götz and Wenzel Nejebse. (Barth and Götz were professional singers, and members of the Court Chapel Choir.) 'Das Dörfchen' became immensely popular in Viennese musical circles, even before its publication in 1822.

It was in 1819 that Schubert composed the finest of his part-songs, a setting of one of his favourite Goethe poems, 'Nur wer die Sehnsucht kennt' (Only he who knows yearning, D.656), better known through the English translation of Tchaikovsky's setting as 'None but the Lonely Heart'. Schubert had already composed three different settings of the poem as a solo song before arriving at this definitive and masterly version for male voices in which the warmth and colour of his harmonies perfectly catch the poem's mood of romantic despair. He was, however, to return twice again to the poem in 1826.

The beginning of 1820 found Schubert at work on a religious piece, *Lazarus* (D.689), a cantata for solo voices, mixed chorus and orchestra. He was still working on it in March when, rather startlingly, he managed to get himself arrested. He was in the rooms of a friend, the young Tyrolese poet Johann Senn, when the police arrived to examine and confiscate some of Senn's papers concerning a student organization which was suspected of illegal political activity. The police report of the incident claims that Senn used offensive language, asserted that he 'did not care a hang about the police' and that 'the Government was too stupid to be able to penetrate into his secrets'. It also states that his four friends who were present, among them Schubert, 'chimed in against the authorized official in the same tone, inveighing against him with insulting and opprobrious language'. They were all arrested. Schubert and most of the others appear to have been released almost immediately, but Senn remained under detention, was later tried, and was deported to the Tyrol.

Lazarus, which Schubert never completed, perhaps because he was upset and disturbed by the police incident and by the deportation of Senn, would certainly have numbered among the composer's most important works. Intended to be in three acts, it has survived in substantial fragments. The music for Act I and most of Act II was recovered in the middle of the nineteenth century and later published, revealing the work to be a remarkable fusion of melody and recitative: evidence more compelling than the stage works that Schubert could have become a master of operatic composition.

On 14 June 1820, *Die Zwillingsbrüder* finally reached the stage. It was given in the Kärntnertor theatre, with Vogl in the dual role of the twins, Franz and Friedrich. Described as a 'Farce with Songs in One Act', it occupied the first half of a double bill, the second half of which consisted of a comic ballet. At the première, Schubert sat in the gallery with Anselm Hüttenbrenner, and apparently could not be induced to exchange his old frock-coat for Anselm's evening tail-coat, in order to take a curtain-call. At the close of the performance, in answer to applause, Vogl stepped forward and said: 'Schubert is not present: I thank you in his name.' In the gallery, Schubert smilingly listened to Vogl's speech, and then went off with his friends to Lenkay's wine-shop in the Liliengasse, near St Stephen's Cathedral, where the composer's success was toasted in a few pints of cheap Hungarian wine.

The success of *Die Zwillingsbrüder* was, however, at best moderate. A spectator in the theatre, Josef Karl Rosenbaum, wrote in his diary that 'the operetta has nothing to recommend it, yet Schubert's friends made a lot of noise while the opposition hissed'. The critic of the Vienna edition of the *Allgemeine Musikalische Zeitung* wrote a long and considered review, which was the first detailed criticism Schubert had ever received in print:

Herr Schubert . . . has so far been known to us only by a few meritorious romances. His opera, which he allowed to appear modestly under the title of 'farce', was talked about as early as the end of 1818 . . . it attests its composer as a gifted mind, full of force and invention – a major advantage, since everything else can be acquired; but it also shows at the same time that Herr Schubert's abilities lie in the direction of tragedy rather than comedy, for which reason we urgently advise him to choose the former category, at any rate for the present. The music for *The Twin Brothers* has much originality and many interesting passages, and the declamation is correct; but it is a blot on the work that the sentiments of simple country folk are interpreted much too seriously, not to say heavy-handedly, for a comic subject. . . . Comic music, it seems to us, does not take at all kindly to a very close adherence to the words, or to the composer's taking refuge in a modulation whenever pain, for instance, is mentioned; and both kinds, the higher and the lighter music, demand shapely pieces, each of which has its exposition, its development and its unravelling, like the scenes of a spoken play – for which see Mozart's operas. Herr Schubert is too much wedded to details of the text, and this chases him and his hearer restlessly through modulations and allows of no point of repose; he tries to express words in music instead of painting the nature of a whole speech by means of the character of a whole piece, which, as Mozart proves, is the only way of attaining to the highest aims of art and of conquering its greatest difficulties, by producing regular, rounded-off pieces and yet by making the whole call forth the required feeling. For this Herr Schubert has allowed himself to be led too far astray by his laudable endeavour to go his own way, and he has done away too drastically with the concluding formulas of musical numbers.

This is interesting criticism: the writer has described Schubert, the composer of Lieder, attempting to bring his Lieder technique into the opera house instead of adapting his technique to the wider canvas of the theatre. The writer goes on to describe, and to criticize quite constructively, the individual musical numbers of Schubert's score.

The remainder of the reviews were decidedly mixed. The *Conversationsblatt* thought that the general verdict on Schubert 'can only be favourable, although not to the point to which his numerous friends endeavour to force it', while the *Sammler* described the music as 'the neat minor product of a young composer' and added that some of the melodies were a little old-fashioned, 'and some even tuneless'. The foreign press was, on the whole, discouraging. The Dresden *Abendzeitung* castigated the first-night Viennese audience for acclaiming the operetta as a great masterpiece, 'which it is not', and observed that Vogl 'played the two twins in such a way that one knew only too well it was the same actor who interpreted them'. The Leipzig *Allgemeine Musikalische Zeitung* thought that 'in this first dramatic essay, [Schubert] seems to attempt to fly as high as Beethoven and not to heed the warning example of Icarus. Little true songfulness is to be found, whereas hardly any repose is to be met with in confused and supercharged instrumentation, anxious striving after originality, and continual modulation.'

Six performances of *Die Zwillingsbrüder* were given at the Kärntnertor theatre, the last being on 21 July when the second piece on the programme was *Aline, Königin von Golconda* (Aline, Queen of Golconda), a grand ballet in three acts with music by Karl Blum. Schubert's operetta was never revived during his lifetime (Vienna next saw it in 1882), but its moderate success was sufficient for him to be commissioned to compose the incidental music for a play which was to be staged during the summer at the Theater an der Wien. This was

Die Zauberharfe (The Magic Harp, D.644).

Die Zauberharfe was another adaptation by Georg von Hofmann of a French original, this time a magic play or pantomime, of the genre of Schikaneder and Mozart's *Magic Flute* but less pretentious, more nonsensical and, by all accounts, considerably boring. Schubert's commission to provide the incidental music was obtained through a friend, Hermann Neefe, who was to design the scenery for the production. Neefe had visited Schubert, bringing with him Friedrich Demmer, the stage-director of the Theater an der Wien, who staged the piece and also appeared in it, and had easily persuaded the composer to accept the commission. The play was in three acts, and Schubert's score consisted of two overtures (one an introduction to the third act), six choruses, and five pieces of melodrama, i.e. music in which a speaking voice declaims either simultaneously with the music, or in pauses between sections of music. (A well-known example is the gravedigging scene in Act II of Beethoven's *Fidelio*.)

The play was spectacularly staged at the Theater an der Wien on 19 August, Schubert having written his music quickly, in little more than two weeks; but, despite the many felicities of its score, the work itself was thought tedious by theatre-goers. Josef Karl Rosenbaum wrote in his diary after the first performance, 'Wretched trash, quite failed to please, the machinery jibbed and went badly, although nothing remarkable. Nobody knew his part: the prompter was always heard first.'

The several Viennese reviews made it clear that the failure of *Die Zauberharfe* was due to the paralysing tedium of its plot and dialogue. 'True, there is the music', wrote the critic of the *Theaterzeitung*, '– and real music! Many good ideas, forceful passages, cleverly managed harmonic pieces, insight and understanding.' And he praised the settings and the stage machinery, adding, however, that 'even these united forces are incapable of overcoming a flood of boredom'. 'What a pity', said the *Conversationsblatt*, 'that Schubert's wonderfully beautiful music has not found a worthier subject.'

(The overture was later published, and is today known as the overture to Schubert's *Rosamunde* music, although, as we shall see, it was not played as part of the *Rosamunde* music in December 1823. The *Conversationsblatt* had perspicaciously noted, after the *Zauberharfe* première: 'We think, too, that the overture has greater merit as a composition pure and simple than as a connection with this melodrama, and might as well be played before an opera as before a fairytale.')

Eight performances of *Die Zauberharfe* were given during the summer, but after October the work was heard no more. A happier occasion for Schubert that summer was the period of a few days which he spent at Atzenbrugg, about twenty miles north-west of Vienna, at the house of Franz Schober's uncle, who managed estates in the neighbourhood. It was Schober's custom to bring a band of friends to Atzenbrugg each summer for a country holiday, and 1820 was the first year in which Schubert was one of his guests. The band of friends made excursions into the surrounding country, played games in the fields and meadows, and held 'Schubertiad' evenings in the rooms of the small castle which were at their disposal.

In Vienna, Schubert evenings were often held at Ignaz Sonn-leithner's house. The Sonnleithner residence in the Gundelhof was one of the best-known musical salons in Vienna, where every Friday evening during the summer months, and at least once a fortnight during the winter, more than a hundred people would assemble to hear music performed by the finest Viennese musicians as well as by visiting foreign performers. Many of Schubert's most popular songs were first performed at the Sonnleithners' musical evenings.

It was through his friendship with the Sonnleithners and their son Leopold that Schubert, in the autumn of 1820, met the Fröhlich sisters, four young women who were all locally renowned for their artistic talents. Their father had been a merchant whose business failed, and the four sisters now lived by themselves in a house in the Singerstrasse. They later moved to a house nearby, in the Spiegel-gasse, near the Graben.

Anna Fröhlich, the eldest of the sisters, was three years Schubert's senior. Dark and vivacious, she had been a pupil of Hummel, sang soprano, and taught singing at the Conservatorium of the Society of Music Lovers. The second sister, Barbara, had also been musically trained but became a noted painter of flowers, and in 1825 married the flautist Ferdinand Bogner.

The two younger sisters were both musicians, and were probably the more talented. Katharina, or Kathi, three years younger than Schubert, was the most beautiful of the four. She sang soprano, as did the fourth sister, Josefine, who became a professional singer, appeared at the Kärntnertor theatre in 1821–2, and later toured abroad as a concert singer.

The Fröhlich sisters kept open house to anyone at all interested in music or with musical talent, and from the time of his first meeting with them in December 1820 until 1822 Schubert was frequently to be seen there. Some months after Schubert first visited the Fröhlich house, the poet Franz Grillparzer was introduced to the sisters. Schubert and Grillparzer became good friends, and Grillparzer developed an overwhelming passion for the third sister, Kathi. She returned his love, and was the inspiration for many of his poems, but their relationship was a stormy one, due to the instability of Grillparzer's temperament. The poet tortured himself with groundless jealousy, broke off his relations with Kathi, but later returned to the bosom of the Fröhlich family as a friend of all four women. Ultimately, he went to live in their house. 'I must love all four of them,' he said. 'I cannot love singly.'

The Fröhlich sisters were probably in the mind of the Styrian author Rudolf Hans Bartsch (1873–1952) when, in the early twentieth century, he wrote his Schubert novel, *Schwammerl* (Little Mushroom), which in turn inspired the musical play *Das Dreimäderlhaus*, or *Lilac Time*, for which Heinrich Berté (1857–1924) arranged familiar Schubert melodies. The fictitious trio of sisters in novel and play, with one of whom Schubert is supposed to be in love, would seem to have been suggested in outline by the Fröhlich sisters.

Anna Fröhlich in later years recounted to a friend her memories of Schubert:

When Schubert was introduced to us, he used to come to the musical evenings which I was then giving at our rooms. I can see Schubert now. He had folded his hands in deep emotion as if in prayer, and pressed them to his mouth, as he was accustomed to do when he listened to anything beautiful. . . . Within a few days he brought me his quartet, 'Gott ist mein Hirt' [The Lord is my shepherd, D.706], and soon afterwards the quartet 'Gott in der Natur' [God in Nature, D.757]. Poor Schubert, his was a magnificent soul. He was never jealous or grudging to others, as is the case with so many people. On the contrary, he was overjoyed when beautiful music was performed. He folded his hands, and placed them against his mouth, and sat there as if in ecstasy. The purity of his mind, the lack of all thought of guile, are beyond expression. Often he would sit down with us on the sofa, and rub his hands and say: 'Today I have composed something with which I believe I have been really successful.'

The quartet 'Gott ist mein Hirt', mentioned by Anna Fröhlich, is Schubert's superb setting for female voices of Psalm 23, 'The Lord is my shepherd', a work of great beauty and spiritual power. It was composed for Anna's female singing class at the Conservatorium.

Among other works written by Schubert in 1820, two stand out. One is incomplete, but masterly: a quartet movement (*Quartettsatz*) in C minor (D.703), intended to be the first movement of a full-scale string quartet. Schubert began to sketch the second movement, an andante, but, for some reason, abandoned it after forty-four bars. The existing movement, however, reveals Schubert writing at his peak. This is music worthy of the composer of that other incomplete masterpiece, the 'Unfinished' Symphony. Another outstanding composition of 1820 is the lyrical song 'Frühlingsglaube' (Faith in Spring, D.686), in which Schubert softly whispers his heart's secrets as the season of renewal comes round again.

More songs by Schubert were being printed in the musical journals, and more of his works were being performed in public. At the age of twenty-three, he was now a well-known figure in Viennese musical circles and beyond, and his name was no longer completely unknown outside Austria. But he had still not been taken up by any of the major publishers of music, and he now began to increase his efforts to achieve this kind of professional recognition of his genius.

Early in the new year, 1821, the Schubert-Mayrhofer household broke up, the cause, according to Mayrhofer, being 'circumstances, social engagements and changed views of life'. Schubert moved in with the artist Moritz von Schwind, who was living in a house in the same street, Wipplingerstrasse. Schwind was a youth of seventeen, seven years Schubert's junior. A self-portrait of the time shows him to have been slender, with large blue eyes and an earnest, romantic expression. 'His appearance', wrote Spaun in his reminiscences, 'bearing witness to the healthy soul in the healthy body, his beautiful intelligent eyes, his liveliness and good humour, prejudiced us strongly in the youth's favour, and we welcomed him as a new member of the circle which had been formed round Schubert by Schober and others.'

Schwind's was a highly romantic nature, given to hero-worship, and he offered Schubert a slavish devotion. The Schubertians called him 'Cherub' because of his youthful, almost effeminate good looks, and Schubert laughingly named him his 'Beloved', for Schwind's feelings were sometimes expressed in over-emotional language and behaviour. (In those innocent, pre-Freudian days, romantic friendships between males were accepted as such, quite distinct from homosexual relationships. There has never been a suggestion in the mass of Schubert literature that any of the composer's relationships with his male friends contained an overt sexual element, though a modern intelligence may perhaps be forgiven for occasionally suspecting something of the kind.)

In the early part of 1821, Schubert composed some of his Goethe songs, as well as a choral setting for tenor and bass voices and strings of Goethe's poem 'Gesang der Geister über den Wassern' (Song of the Spirits over the Waters, D.714), a magnificent piece which was performed, along with two other Schubert compositions, 'Das Dörfchen' and 'Erlkönig', at a concert in the Kärntnertor theatre on 7 March.

The concert at the Kärntnertor was an important event for Schubert. It was one of a series of annual concerts, held on Ash Wednesday, when the theatres were closed, which were organized by the 'Society of Ladies of the Nobility for the Protection of Good and Useful Charities'. (The concerts celebrated their 125th anniversary in 1936: unfortunately, though not surprisingly, the Society appears not to have survived the Second World War.) Works by other composers, among them Mozart and Rossini, were included in the programme of the 1821 concert, and Schubert's 'Gesang der Geister über den Wassern' was probably written specifically for the occasion. 'Erlkönig' was sung by Vogl, who was accompanied by Anselm Hüttenbrenner, Schubert himself being too shy to play the new Graf pianoforte which was being used. According to Hüttenbrenner, Schubert wrote a few more bars into the accompaniment here and there for this performance, at the request of Vogl, who needed more time to breathe.

The Vienna *Allgemeine Musikalische Zeitung* thought that 'the performance of the ballad "Erlkönig", music by Schubert, showed our master of declamatory song – Herr Vogl – in all his greatness. The music shows much imagination. Several successful passages were justly acclaimed by the public.' Surely the public did not applaud during the performance of the song? One wonders, however, how otherwise they could have directed their acclaim to 'several successful passages'.

Leopold Sonnleithner, Josef Hüttenbrenner and a few other friends were determined to have 'Erlkönig' published. They encountered no difficulty in enlisting subscribers, and indeed raised so much money that they were able to have 'Gretchen am Spinnrade' engraved as well. The music-publishing firm of Cappi & Diabelli acted as agents, and 'Erlkönig' was published as Schubert's opus 1, on 31 March, less than four weeks after Vogl's performance of it at the Kärntnertor theatre concert. Six hundred copies were sold immediately. 'Gretchen am Spinnrade' followed as opus 2, a month later, and sold almost as well. The critic of the Dresden *Abendzeitung*, writing of the concert after 'Erlkönig' had been published, said: 'What pleased above all was "Erlkönig", which Vogl performed with his accustomed mastery, and which had to be repeated. This splendid composition cannot fail to grip one: it has now appeared in print, at Cappi & Diabelli's, and I am convinced that I shall earn the gratitude of any reader who wishes to procure this masterpiece for having drawn his attention to it.'

During 1821 and 1822, twenty Schubert songs were published, with such success that the firm of Cappi & Diabelli accepted, on their own responsibility, the publication of further songs, piano music and part-songs. From then on, publication of works by Schubert proceeded regularly, until at the time of his death the list of his published works had reached to opus 100.

Another commission was offered to Schubert in the spring of 1821 to compose music for the theatre. At the invitation of the Kärntnertor management, he composed two pieces (D.723), a tenor aria and a comic duet, for insertion into the score of the French composer Ferdinand Hérold's operetta *La Clochette*, which was being given its Viennese première in German translation as *Das Zauberglöckchen* (The Magic Bell). Schubert wrote the two numbers quickly, and they were performed for the first time at the première on 20 June. The duet seems to have been preferred to the aria, which lay too high for the tenor who sang it.

In July, Schober's uncle again offered hospitality to the Schubertians at Atzenbrugg for a few days. One of the guests this time was the twenty-five-year-old painter Leopold Kupelwieser, who, while they were at Atzenbrugg, drew a portrait of Schubert (said to be an extremely good likeness), and also one of Schober, and painted two famous water-colours (now in the Schubert museum in Vienna), one of which is a delightful picture of an excursion by open carriage to nearby Aumühl, and the other an indoor scene showing the party acting out a charade. Schubert appears in both. During these days in the country, Schubert composed six 'Atzenbrugger Tänze' (Atzenbrugg Dances; D.145, nos. 1–3, and D.365, nos. 29–31) for piano. With a number of other Schubert waltzes, they were published in November.

The term 'Schubertiad' is nowadays used to describe the impromptu musical evenings which took place whenever and wherever the composer and his friends met together. The term was first used, however, to describe the private concerts which began as weekly affairs at the Sonnleithners' residence, but which, during the early 1820s, spread to many other houses. By popular choice, the whole of the music for the evening was by Schubert. The songs, often sung by Vogl, were a principal attraction, but Schubert also provided, and in many instances improvised at the piano, music for dancing. These were the first real Schubertiads.

In August, soon after his return from Atzenbrugg, Schubert began work on another symphony (in E major, D.729), which he left incomplete. All four movements of this Seventh Symphony exist in sketch form, but very little of the work was fully scored. Why the composer abandoned it is not known; perhaps he thought its level of musical inspiration insufficiently high for him to devote the time necessary for scoring it in detail. He put the manuscript aside, and forgot about it. Seventeen years after Franz Schubert's death, his brother Ferdinand gave the manuscript to Mendelssohn. In his letter of thanks Mendelssohn wrote:

Believe me that I know how to esteem the magnificent gift at its true value, that you could have given it to no one who would have greater joy in it, or who would be more sincerely grateful to you for it. In truth, it seems to me as if, through the very incompleteness of the work, the scattered, half-finished indications, I became at once personally acquainted with your brother more closely and more intimately than I should have done through a completed piece. It seems as if I saw him there, working in his room, and this joy I owe to your unexpectedly great kindness and generosity.

On Mendelssohn's death, the manuscript passed to his brother Paul, who, many years later, gave it to Sir George Grove, who was about to write long articles on both Schubert and Mendelssohn for his forthcoming *Dictionary of Music and Musicians*. At one time, Brahms considered completing the symphony, but found it too difficult a project. In England, Sir Arthur Sullivan expressed his intention of completing it. In the end, John Francis Barnett (1837–1916), a competent English composer and teacher, completed the work, which was performed, in his version, at the Crystal Palace in London in 1883. A new completion of the symphony, made in 1934 by the Austrian conductor and composer Felix Weingartner (1863–1942), is generally considered to be more satisfactory. In the 1970s, another version was made, by the English composer and academic Brian Newbould. An advance on Schubert's first six symphonies, this (No. 7) is his farewell to the old, Haydnesque symphony. His later essays in symphonic form, the 'Unfinished' (No. 8), the 'Great' C major (No. 9), and a recently discovered No. 10, were to be considerably greater in stature.

In September, Schubert left Vienna for a stay of some weeks at St Pölten, a country town twenty-eight miles west of Vienna, in the company of Schober. The bishop of St. Pölten was a relative of Schober's mother, and owned the neighbouring castle of Ochsenburg. Schubert and Schober stayed for a time in the castle, and were occasionally entertained by the bishop in his residence.

One of Schubert's friends, Josef Kenner, wrote of Schober, many years after Schubert's death, that he, Schober, was 'a seductively amiable young man of extraordinary talents, but lacking in moral character [who] gained over Schubert a lasting and injurious influence'. However, Schober's purpose in luring Schubert away from Vienna to St Pölten in September 1821 was not to entice him away from work but to encourage and supervise his composition. The two friends were at work together on an opera, *Alfonso und Estrella*, for which Schober was providing the libretto and Schubert the music.

Towards the end of October they returned to Vienna, and on 2 November jointly wrote to Spaun. Schubert told Spaun little more than that the opera had already progressed as far as the third act and that they had great hopes of it, but Schober wrote at greater length, giving a picture of their life in and around St Pölten:

Schubert and I have now returned from our half-country and half-town holiday, and we have brought back recollections of a lovely month. At Ochsenburg we were much taken up with the truly beautiful surroundings, and at St Pölten with balls and concerts; in spite of which we worked hard, especially Schubert, who has done nearly two acts, while I am on the last. I only wish you had been there to hear the glorious tunes as they arose: it is wonderful how once again he has poured forth music that is rich and teeming with ideas. Our room at St P. was particularly snug: twin beds, a sofa next to the warm stove, and a pianoforte made it all very domestic and cosy. In the evenings we always compared notes on what we had accomplished during the day, then sent for beer, smoked our pipes and read, or else Sophie and Nettel [Schober's sister Sophie, and her friend Anna ('Nettel')] came across and there was singing. There were a couple of Schubertiads at the bishop's, and one at the Baroness Münk's, of whom I am quite fond, where a princess, two countesses and three baronesses were present, all most generously ecstatic.

On their return to Vienna, Schubert did not return to his lodgings with Schwind, but stayed with the Schober family. The move may have been made in order to facilitate his work on the opera with Franz von Schober, but he continued to live with the Schobers for some months after the opera's completion at the end of February 1822.

Schubert spent Christmas Eve, 1821, with the actor Heinrich Anschütz and his wife Emilie. Anschütz, one of the leading German actors of his time, had been engaged at the Burgtheater since the summer. He was thus spending his first Christmas in Vienna, and determined to introduce to the Catholic city the Protestant custom of having a Christmas tree in one's house, and giving presents to one's family and friends. In his memoirs, he wrote:

This Christmas party was of especial interest to me, since it brought Schubert to my house for the first time. He was then one of the most active members of the late 'merry nonsense society'. It was through my brothers that he came to the house. His second visit happened on an evening that was spent in quite a different way. I had asked some friends, Schubert among them, including a number of young men and women. My wife was young, and my brother Gustav was passionately fond of dancing, and soon the conversation turned on this subject. Schubert, who had already played a few pieces, sat at the piano and broke into dances. They all joined in the circle round him, laughing and drinking. Suddenly I was called away; a stranger was announced. It was a Commissioner of Police, who forbade us to go on with the dancing because it was Lent! When I went back to the room and announced what had happened everybody was alarmed. But Schubert remarked: 'He has done that on purpose. The fellow knows that I like playing dance music!'

It was in 1821 that Schubert discovered the poems of Friedrich Rückert (1788–1866). No more than five songs were to come into being as a result, but they are all first-rate Schubert. The earliest, and the only one to be composed during 1821, was 'Sei mir gegrüsst' (My Greetings to You, D.741), a wonderfully sensuous serenade. The other four Rückert songs followed two years later, among them 'Dass sie hier gewesen' (That She Has Been Here, D.775), a remarkable love song in which Schubert's music is made to fit perfectly the syntax of the poem, and 'Du bist die Ruh' (You Are Repose, D.776), which is quite simply one of the most purely beautiful songs ever written.

CHAPTER FOUR

A Golden Age for the Arts

The second half of the eighteenth century had seen the rise of the great Viennese classical period in music: the operas of Gluck, the symphonies of Haydn, the wide-ranging genius of Mozart, and the emergence of the young Beethoven; a period which reached its culmination in Schubert's time, when Beethoven was at his peak and the younger composer packed a lifetime's work into a mere fifteen years of adult life.

Although Vienna appeared to the young poets of German Romanticism as a kind of Mecca, attracting to it such talents as those of Clemens Brentano, Friedrich Schlegel, Bettina von Arnim and Joseph von Eichendorff, German Romanticism did not itself ever take root in Vienna. The city pursued her own path; the Viennese writers of the day had little in common with their German contemporaries. The most popular novelist of the Biedermeier period was Caroline Pichler (1769–1843), whose romances of Viennese life were greatly to the taste of her readers, and whose collected works extended to no fewer than sixty volumes. She also wrote poems, one of which, 'Der Unglückliche' (The Unhappy Man), was set by Schubert in 1821 (D.713); but she was famous beyond Austria not so much for her writing as for her salon, which was frequented in the 1820s by Vienna's leading artists, actors and musicians, among them Franz Schubert.

The leading figure of Austrian Romantic literature was Nikolaus Lenau (1802–50), whose lyric poems combined striking imagery with a frightening intensity of temperament. In 1832 Lenau emigrated to the United States but returned, disillusioned, to Europe the following year, and later lost his reason. Much more characteristically Viennese was Adalbert Stifter (1805–68), a novelist and master of the short story whose emphasis on the importance of tradition marks him as very

75

much of his time and place. In the preface to his collection of narrative sketches, *Bunte Steine* (Coloured Stones), Stifter wrote that a boiling tea-kettle interested him as much as a volcano, and that in even the most trivial phenomena the universal harmony of nature could be discerned, provided that one knew how to observe it. Schubert, in many of his miniature pieces for the piano, as well as in his songs, said essentially the same thing.

Poetry played a role in Biedermeier Vienna but, perhaps because the Biedermeier way of life embraced poetry more naturally and spontaneously than did German society in the Romantic period, the actual poets of Austria were a lesser breed than their German contemporaries. Austria excelled in its profusion of minor poets. Prominent among them were Ernst von Feuchtersleben, Anastasius Grün and Johann Gabriel Seidl. Feuchtersleben was a respected physician who wrote his verses in a café between professional calls; Grün was the pseudonym chosen by a nobleman, Count Anton Alexander Auersperg, whose liberal views often brought him into conflict with the authorities; Seidl worked at various times as a lawyer, teacher and free-lance literary journalist, but was predominantly a lyrical poet, several of whose verses Schubert set to music.

The most distinguished literary figure of Biedermeier Vienna was Franz Grillparzer, poet, playwright and novelist. Six years Schubert's senior, Grillparzer lived on until 1872 but produced his finest work in his earlier years. (One of his poems was set by Schubert, whom he knew personally.) His love of Austria and of Vienna was so intense that he idealized both the country and its capital city in his journals and memoirs as well as in his short stories and poems. At the same time, however, he epitomized the Biedermeier delight in life as it is, and satisfaction with the status quo. His historical dramas, such as *Sappho, Das goldene Vliess* (The Golden Fleece) and *König Ottokars Glück und Ende* (King Ottakar's Success and Downfall), are of little interest to the present age, but his stories of Viennese life and his poems of young love read as freshly today as when they were written.

None of the other poets of Biedermeier Vienna approached the stature of Grillparzer; they were fortunate to have flourished at the same time as Franz Schubert, for he shared their attitudes and feelings and reached beyond their rather simple and often slipshod expression of those feelings to clothe their verses in the most beautiful melodies.

Above all, the Viennese of the time were theatre-goers. They had always viewed life as theatre and, in the first decades of the nineteenth century, theatre in Vienna flourished more brightly than it had ever done before. One of the most popular places of entertainment in Vienna was the new Theater an der Wien, a strong rival to the city's two classical theatres.

The Theater an der Wien was built by the impresario and playwright Emanuel Schikaneder. Schikaneder, best remembered today as the librettist of Mozart's *Die Zauberflöte* (and the first performer of the rôle of Papageno in that opera), had for some years been presenting popular plays and entertainments in his little sub-urban theatre, the Theater auf der Wieden, where *Die Zauberflöte* was first staged in 1791. In 1800, he petitioned the Emperor for a permit to build a new theatre, not far from the Theater auf der Wieden, but on the other side of the river Wien. Permission was granted, for Schikaneder's plays were by then attracting large audiences from among the working classes, and to have refused him his new theatre would have caused great public discontent.

In 1801, the Theater an der Wien opened its doors with the opera *Alexander*, by Franz Teyber. Schikaneder offered his audiences an extremely varied bill of fare which included not only his own hastily written farces, but also sentimental plays by modern German and Austrian playwrights, parodies, pastiches, operettas, Shakespeare and French plays. He also remained faithful to his association with Mozart by reviving *Die Zauberflöte* and staging other Mozart operas, and even commissioned Beethoven, to whom he gave a year's free lodging in the theatre building, to compose an opera. Beethoven's work was a failure at its first performance, but succeeded some years later when revived in the same theatre. The opera was, of course, *Fidelio*.

A more classical and traditional repertoire was presented at the Theater in der Leopoldstadt (though its impresario on one occasion staged *The Dog of Montargis*, a play whose leading rôle was played by a dog) and at the Burgtheater. The Burgtheater was, and is still, Austria's national theatre, founded in 1776 by Josef II as a German-language theatre to counteract such foreign cultural influences as French plays and Italian operas.

Despite their differing repertoires, these and other Viennese theatres were all engaged in rivalling one another, for they competed for the same audience. The aristocracy not only attended the operas but ventured out into the suburbs to see the latest shows, and the middle classes flocked to the operas and classical plays in the inner-city theatres as well as to Schikaneder's spectacular attractions at the Theater an der Wien.

Spectacle, in fact, was what all these productions had in common. 'As long as something is spectacular', it used to be said, 'the Viennese will enjoy it.' Thus, the Theater an der Wien would produce a pantomime with realistic effects of thunderstorms, cavalry charges and shipwrecks, while another theatre would respond with a play set in Egypt which filled the stage with camels. Battle scenes were so realistically staged, with cannon and rifles fired, that the police authorities had eventually to intervene. These battle scenes had become so great an attraction that it was customary to announce in the newspaper advertisements the number of shots that would be fired. After 1807 the use of gunpowder in theatres for fusillades or fireworks was forbidden by the authorities. The spectacles, however, continued in the open air.

The two great popular playwrights of nineteenth-century Vienna were Nestroy and Raimund; the plays of both, though rarely seen outside Austria, are still regularly performed in the theatres of Vienna. Johann Nestroy (1801–62) was a typical Viennese in that his racial background embraced several elements of the old Austria, among them Bohemian and Polish. He himself was born in Vienna into a prosperous middle-class family, was well educated, and discovered while still at school his great gifts as actor and singer. He made his professional début in 1822 singing the role of Sarastro in a revival of *Die Zauberflöte* at the Kärntnertor theatre, and went on to become a versatile actor-singer in plays, pantomimes, farces, tragedies, musical plays and operas. He was as much at home in the operas of Mozart and Rossini as in the plays of Goethe and Schiller or playing the clown in pantomime.

After some years of appearing in other men's plays, Nestroy began to write his own: satirical comedies of Viennese life with leading roles tailored to suit his own talents. The plays were interspersed with songs, and it is from these simply constructed musical plays that the great Viennese operettas of the later nineteenth century emerged. In his eighty-three comic plays, Nestroy affectionately yet sharply satirized all aspects of Viennese life. Perhaps the Nestroy play most frequently performed today in Austria is *Lumpacivagabundus*; certainly the one whose influence has spread most widely is *Einen Jux will er sich machen*. Itself based on *A Day Well Spent* by an English contemporary, John Oxenford (for Nestroy, like Shakespeare, was not averse to borrowing his plots from other writers), *Einen Jux will er sich machen* (He Wants to Have Some Fun) was adapted by the twentieth-century American playwright Thornton Wilder and staged in New York in 1938 as *The Merchant of Yonkers*. Sixteen years later, Wilder re-wrote *The Merchant of Yonkers* as *The Matchmaker*, and in 1965 it became the musical *Hello, Dolly!*

Eleven years Nestroy's senior, Ferdinand Raimund (1790–1836), although often thought of in conjunction with Nestroy, was a genius of a different kind. Satire was not absent from his plays, but sentiment played a larger part, and magical elements were also important. His *Zauberpossen*, or magic plays, involve their mortal characters in supernatural adventures, usually to point a serious moral about human behaviour. Unlike his younger contemporary, Raimund was born into a working-class Viennese family, and made his first theatrical appearance selling sweets during the intervals of plays. He, too, became an actor and wrote the leading rôles in his plays for himself to perform. Baroque and romantic elements mingle in his magic plays such as *Der Bauer als Millionär* (The Peasant Millionaire), *Der Alpenkönig und der Menschenfeind* (The King of the Alps and the Misanthrope) and *Der Verschwender* (The Spendthrift), and the gentle melodies which the characters pause to sing are as important a part of the plays as the dialogue. A chronic depressive, Raimund took his own life while in his mid-forties and still at the height of his fame.

An enduring creation of Viennese popular theatre, akin to Mr Punch or to the figures of the Italian *commedia dell'arte*, was Hanswurst (or Jack Sausage), a chameleon-like character who could transform himself, from play to play, into lover, fighter, brigand or philosopher. The rôle was handed down by Viennese actors from generation to generation. The original Hanswurst, Josef Stranitzky (1676–1726), was followed by Gottfried Prehauser (1699–1769). By the time of Schubert, the role of Hanswurst had several interpreters, and the character itself had spawned others, such as Bernadon, an impetuous youth who experiences a number of adventures in the world of magic; Hanskaspar; and Kaspar or Kasperle. The comic actor Johann Laroche (1745–1806) popularized the character of Kasperle at the Theater in der Leopoldstadt, incorporating into his creation many of the characteristics of the original Hanswurst.

Among the most charming comedies of the Vienna Congress period are those of Adolf Bäuerle, a journalist whose eighty plays include sentimental comedies as well as *Zauberpossen*. Bäuerle's most successful creation was the character of Staberl, a comic umbrella-maker who made his first appearance in *Die Bürger in Wien* (The Citizens of Vienna) (1813). As played by the popular comedian Ignaz Schuster, Staberl was such a success that Bäuerle was obliged to provide four sequels, while another famous actor-playwright, Karl Carl (1787–1854), wrote several more plays featuring the character of Staberl.

The sense of theatre of the citizens of Vienna extended well beyond the legitimate forms of opera, spoken drama or comedy and musical play. Anticipating modern theories of the happening as a work of art, the Viennese tended to invest almost any kind of event with the status of theatre, a theatre in which they were both spectators and performers. To them, the everyday life of their beloved city was in itself an entertainment or spectacle.

A fondness for rare and wild animals was another Viennese attribute. In 1828 a great sensation was caused in the city by the arrival of a giraffe which had been presented to the Emperor by the Viceroy of Egypt. The newspapers published daily bulletins on the animal's journey from Alexandria, and when it was finally installed in the Imperial and Royal Menagerie at Schönbrunn thousands hastened there to admire the giraffe. For several years thereafter, fashions in hair-styles were *à la giraffe*, and the animal was depicted on snuffboxes and trinkets of various kinds. Raimund wrote a comedy about it, and the owner of one of the dance-halls organized balls *à la giraffe*.

Puppet and marionette theatres, troupes of dancing dwarfs, displays by illusionists and magicians, waxwork museums and automata of various kinds, all were part of Vienna's world of theatre. Many of the automata were constructed by Johann Mälzel, the friend of Beethoven and inventor of the metronome. Mälzel's Panharmonicon, an automatic instrument of flutes, trumpets, clarinets, violins, cellos, drums, cymbals and triangle, which played music by Haydn and Mozart, and which was worked by weights acting on cylinders, was exhibited by its inventor in Vienna in 1804.

Many people suspected Mälzel of black magic, especially after they had witnessed his display on the day of Napoleon's wedding to Marie-Louise in 1810. Mälzel had installed on his balcony a robot-figure who sang in praise of the young couple. His masterpiece, however, which aroused the anxiety of both the police and the clergy, was the occasion when he arranged, in a window of his house in the Kohlmarkt, the appearance of the royal couple, who suddenly emerged from within, bowed to the crowd (who responded with wild cheering), and then solemnly retired within the house again. Many people were convinced that these were not mechanical figures but the real, flesh-and-blood couple.

In the early nineteenth century, as today, the great place for outdoor entertainment in Vienna was the Prater. A former imperial hunting ground, this stretch of acre upon acre of parkland by the Danube had in 1766 been dedicated to the public by Josef II. At the Prater were all the delights of a country fair, with stalls, games, entertainments, cafés, beer gardens, orchestras for dancing, and delightful country through which to wander. Here every Viennese could practise the art at which he excelled: the art of living. The Comte de Sainte-Aulaire, French Ambassador in Vienna in the first third of the nineteenth century, notes this characteristic in his *Mémoires*:

Country walks, music and dancing in the fresh air, always accompanied by good fare, are habitual among all classes of the population. At the end of the day, if time allows, the suburban artisan takes off his working clothes and puts on a neat suit; with his wife and children he goes to eat fried chicken in one of the innumerable small inns scattered over the rich countryside through which the Danube flows. The bastions and glacis of the city provide superior restaurants for the lower-middle-class and well-to-do artisans; in the public gardens which form a green belt round the town, the avenues are copiously supplied with refreshments and solid viands. In the centre of the gardens a huge space is always set aside for dancing, and numerous bands, which have been conducted by Strauss and Lanner themselves, play waltzes and operatic selections.

It is delightful to see this crowd of men and women of all ages enjoying life so calmly and appearing so well content with their lot; there is never the slightest disturbance, no sound is heard save the clink of knives on plates. Everyone talks quietly to his neighbour, the walkers process two by two round the space reserved for dancing; sometimes couples, abandoning their tranquil pace, break from the ranks of the spectators, dart into the whirling crowd and spin round in the waltz with an impetuosity for which the gravity of their demeanour and the seriousness of their expression had not prepared the foreigner.

During the Biedermeier period, the art of painting underwent a very distinctive development in Austria, and especially in Vienna. This was due as much to the political situation as to what one might call the lightly enforced political passivity of the populace, or the particular temperament of the Viennese. The themes most favoured by artists and their patrons were man himself and his environment. The portrait was popular, but the preference was for scenes of daily life not only in the city but also in the immediate rural surroundings.

The most important painter in Biedermeier Vienna, Ferdinand Georg Waldmüller (1793–1865), was renowned primarily for his family portraits. So happily does he convey the serene contentment of bourgeois life that he is generally held to be the embodiment of the era. The great portraitist of the period, remarkable for his depiction of character in his paintings of individuals, was Friedrich von Amerling (1803–87), whose art was inspired by the much admired English school of portrait painting.

Even more than in the portrait, the Biedermeier period found happy expression in genre painting, particularly in the work of such artists as Peter Fendi (1796–1842), Carl Schindler (1821–42), and Josef Danhauser (1805–45). Fendi concentrated upon scenes of lower-middle-class life, Schindler's most admired paintings were of military life, while Danhauser, the most versatile of the three, painted comical scenes, pictures of children, historical events, and even scenes of society containing elements of social criticism, something rare in the art of the time.

Different from all these painters with their classically based techniques was the primitive artist Michael Neder (1807–82), whose very direct and simple scenes of popular life radiate a charming lyricism.

Austrian landscape painting of the period is superb in its depiction of the moods of nature, from the romanticism of Carl Agricola (1779–1852) to the realism of Friedrich Gauermann (1807–62) and Friedrich Loos (1797–1890). But perhaps the artist who, more than any other, brings to life on canvas the essence of Biedermeier Vienna is Rudolf von Alt (1812–1905), whose work spans nearly seven decades from Biedermeier to the *Jugendstil* of the turn of the century. Alt's numerous city views are both topographical documents and works of art, and his Biedermeier characteristics are still discernible in the paintings he executed towards the end of his life.

Not easily fitted into any of these categories is Schubert's friend

The house in which Schubert was born, Nussdorferstrasse 54

On the right, the Imperial and Royal City Seminary, where Schubert was a pupil from 1808 to 1813. On the left is the University church.

A lithograph of 1821 showing the Karlskirche and the Polytechnic School, with the river Wien in the foreground

'The grand Congress of Vienna for peace and the restoration of freedom and order in Europe', from a watercolour by L. Zutz (1815), showing some of the monarchs and ministers of state assembled in Vienna

The Kärntnertor theatre, where *Die Zwillingsbrüder* was staged in 1820, stood close to the present site of the Vienna State Opera. It was demolished in the 1860s during the construction of the Ring, the circular road now surrounding the inner city.

The Theater an der Wien, where *Die Zauberharfe* was staged in 1820, and *Rosamunde* in 1823. The theatre is still used for opera and operetta.

The music room in the castle of Zseliz in Hungary, where Schubert spent two summers as music tutor to the family of Count Johann Karl Esterházy, in 1818 and 1824

The young Countess Caroline Esterházy, for whom Schubert felt a tender affection

The talented Fröhlich sisters: (LEFT TO RIGHT) Barbara, Katharina and Anna

The castle at Atzenbrugg, scene of convivial summer gatherings of Schubert and his friends

'The ball game at Atzenbrugg, or the Atzenbrugg feast' (etching by Ludwig Mohn, 1820, after a drawing by Franz von Schober [landscape and buildings] and Moritz von Schwind [figures]). Of the three seated figures in the centre foreground, the one on the left is Schober, and the one on the right smoking a long pipe is Schubert.

'The outing' (lithograph after a drawing by Moritz von Schwind)

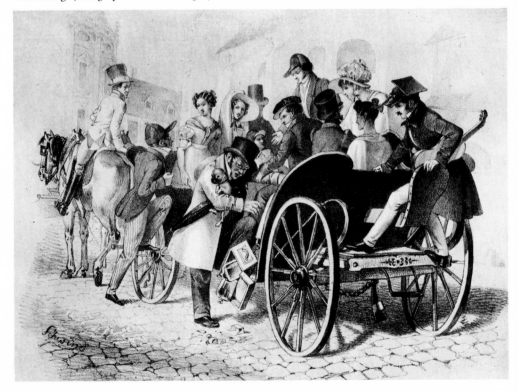

LEFT TO RIGHT Johann Baptist Jenger, Anselm Hüttenbrenner and Schubert (drawing by Josef Teltscher, *c.* 1827)

'Excursion of the Schubertians', from Atzenbrugg to Aumühl (watercolour by Leopold Kupelwieser, 1820). The two figures on the extreme left are Kupelwieser and Schubert (on the right).

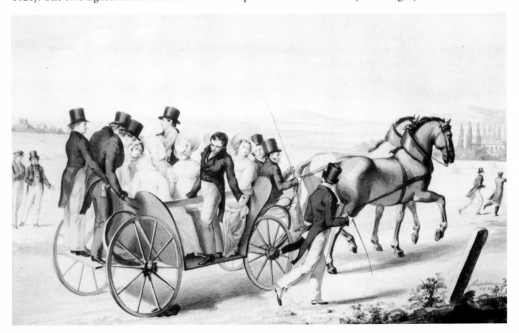

Schubert (watercolour by Wilhelm August Rieder, 1825). Many later likenesses of Schubert are based on this, the best-known of the contemporary portraits. More than fifty years later, Rieder himself painted several oil portraits from this original.

Schubert's close friends
TOP LEFT Bauernfeld (lithograph after Moritz
Michael Daffinger, by Franz Stöber, c. 1837)
TOP RIGHT Vogl (etching after a drawing by
Kupelwieser, c. 1821)
CENTRE LEFT Schober (oil painting by
Kupelwieser, 1823). In the background is
Schober's birthplace, Torup Castle near
Malmö, in Sweden, after one of his own
drawings.
ABOVE Spaun (oil painting by Kupelwieser,
1835)
LEFT Schwind (portrait by Josef Kriehuber,
1827)

The house in which Schubert died, Kettenbrückengasse 6

OPPOSITE PAGE Some of Schubert's favourite inns as they appear today. TOP The former *Café Bogner* is now 'Styl', an antique furniture showroom. BELOW LEFT The inn *Zum grünen Anker* still exists under the same name as a restaurant. BELOW RIGHT The *Café Rebhuhn* is still in business.

'Michael Vogl and Franz Schubert setting out for combat and victory' (caricature in pencil, *c.* 1825, probably by Schober)

Moritz von Schwind (1804–71), whose relationship with the composer is discussed elsewhere. Schwind was a painter who allowed his fantastic imagination a free rein. So in love with his native Vienna that he could be persuaded only with difficulty to visit Rome or Munich, Schwind found his reality in the fantastic world of fairytale and painted the scenes of fantasy and enchanted landscape which filled his mind. He took his inspiration from historical romanticism, in tales of knights and bewitched princesses in a world of fable and courtly chivalry.

The applied arts of the time have almost as much to convey about life in Biedermeier Vienna as the fine arts. The production of exceptionally elegant, delicate writing-tables and desks is widely regarded as a predominant achievement of the Viennese craftsmen of the period. All kinds of furniture, especially chairs, possess a lightness which becomes lost as the century progresses. The crafts of the goldsmith and silversmith flourished. The products of the Vienna Porcelain Factory, which had its greatest period from the time of the Congress of Vienna to the middle of the century, are today most highly sought after, as is Viennese glassware of the Biedermeier time. The textiles of the period, thousands of samples of which are today preserved in Vienna in the Austrian Museum of Applied Art, are exquisite in design.

However, the art form in which the Viennese excelled, during the Biedermeier years as in most other periods of their history, was music. In music, Vienna did not produce representative artists, but great artists. Schubert's Biedermeier characteristics were more strongly defined than were Beethoven's, but no one could call either man a Biedermeier composer. They transcend their time and their own society, though Schubert, while transcending his local society, contrived to represent it as well. Schubert's light music (mostly for piano) lies closer to the central core of his being than Beethoven's light music does to his.

Beethoven was Schubert's only great contemporary in the realm of music: it was extraordinary enough that two composers of genius should exist in the same city at the same time. Haydn, whom they both revered, had died in Vienna at the age of seventy-seven, when Schubert was twelve years of age, and Beethoven thirty-nine. Haydn had experienced the crowning moment of his long career a year before his death when, on 27 March 1808, a performance of his oratorio *Die Schöpfung* (The Creation) was given at the university of Vienna. The

83

military had to be called out to control the crowds, and a distinguished audience of the aristocracy and the middle classes included Beethoven, Hummel, and several other Viennese composers. By now too weak to walk, Haydn was carried into the Great Hall of the university in an armchair to the sound of trumpet flourishes and cries of 'Long live Haydn!' Salieri conducted Haydn's oratorio, and at the passage 'And there was light', the audience burst into spontaneous applause. With tears in his eyes, the aged composer of *Die Schöpfung* raised his hands towards heaven. 'Not from me,' he exclaimed, 'but from Him everything comes.' Beethoven knelt before the musician he acknowledged as his master, and kissed his hands.

The following year, 1809, when the French army occupied Vienna, Napoleon personally ordered a guard of honour to be posted outside Haydn's house. On 31 May, after sitting at his piano and playing the Austrian national anthem, his own composition, the great composer quietly breathed his last.

It was during Schubert's lifetime that the Viennese waltz entered upon its period of greatest popularity. Together with his friend and colleague Johann Strauss (1804–49, father of the 'waltz king'), Josef Lanner (1801–43) was largely responsible for introducing the waltz to the city of Vienna. At the age of seventeen, Lanner formed a group of five musicians, with himself as first violin and Strauss playing the viola, to play for dancing in the taverns and coffee-houses, and in the Prater. Schubert and his companions heard them play, and danced to their music, in taverns such as *Der rote Hahn* (The Red Rooster) or *Zum grünen Jäger* (The Green Hunter), or the favourite coffee-house of artists and musicians, *Das Rebhuhn* (The Partridge).

Soon the band was so popular that Lanner was able to split it into two, directing one ensemble himself, and entrusting the other to Strauss. In 1825, the colleagues separated, Strauss formed his own orchestra, and Lanner marked the occasion by composing 'Trennungswaltzer', or 'Parting Waltz'. Vienna delighted in paying homage to them both, playing them off against each other. When Chopin came to Vienna to give concerts in 1830, two years after the death of Schubert, he wrote that he found it difficult to interest the Viennese in his music, for 'Lanner, Strauss and their waltzes dominate everything'.

CHAPTER FIVE

1822–1825
Holy Fears and Purer Spheres

By the end of February 1822, Schubert and Schober had completed work on their opera, *Alfonso und Estrella* (D.732). This is Schubert's most successful attempt at a full-scale romantic opera, a work which is musically composed throughout, and not simply a succession of numbers separated by spoken dialogue. It could be enjoyed by modern audiences, despite its shortcomings as drama. Schober's libretto is no literary masterpiece, but then the same could be said of the libretti of many famous and much-loved operas. A more serious fault is the metrical dullness of Schober's verses and his complete lack of feeling for dramatic form or construction. When one clothes those verses in music by a composer who writes the most beautiful melodies but whose genius is not, by its nature, dramatic, and who therefore requires in his librettist a strong theatrical instinct, one has *Alfonso und Estrella*, a work full of musical invention which is superb but of predominantly a lyrical and essentially non-dramatic kind. Some of the opera's arias and ensembles are, in fact, dramatic, but the overall pacing of the entire work lacks momentum. Schubert had not learned, and indeed was never to learn, how to shape his music to the needs of the drama. (Incidentally, it is interesting to note that when, more than five years later, Schubert was composing his *Winterreise* cycle of songs, he took as the melody of 'Täuschung' [Illusion] a section of a ballad sung by Alfonso's father, Troila, near the beginning of Act II of *Alfonso und Estrella*.) Schubert submitted *Alfonso und Estrella* to the opera management, but heard nothing from them for several months.

A new friend had entered Schubert's circle. This was Eduard von Bauernfeld, a twenty-year-old student of philosophy who was later to become a successful writer of comedies for the Burgtheater, and a translator of Shakespeare and Dickens. Bauernfeld met Schubert when Schwind brought the composer to a musical evening on 21 January at the house of Professor Weintridt, an ex-professor of theology who had become a free-thinker. Schubert sang several of his most recent songs, Bauernfeld was charmed by the composer and by his music, and a close friendship soon developed between the two young men. Indeed, for a time Schubert, Bauernfeld and Schwind became an almost inseparable trio.

In February, the German composer Carl Maria von Weber visited Vienna, where, the following month, he was to conduct perform-ances of his opera *Der Freischütz* at the Kärntnertor theatre, which had now come under the management of the Italian impresario Domenico Barbaia. Schubert met Weber, and showed him the manuscript of *Alfonso und Estrella*, which Weber declared he would recommend for production in Germany. After one of the *Freischütz* performances, leaflets were scattered from the gallery of the theatre. On them was printed an adulatory poem by Schober, whose title read: 'To Carl Maria von Weber, after a performance of *Der Freischütz*, with a wreath.'

An interesting commission, early in 1822, came from the director of the Theresianum, a school for sons of the nobility. The school wished to honour the Emperor's birthday with a new hymn, in the style of Haydn's famous 'Gott erhalte Franz den Kaiser', on a poem which had been written by Johann Deinhardstein, a member of the Theresi-anum's teaching staff. Schubert accepted an invitation to compose the work. His hymn, or cantata, 'Am Geburtstag des Kaisers' (On the Emperor's Birthday, D.748) was sung by the school choir on the eve of the birthday.

On 24 February Schubert induced Weber to attend a performance of an oratorio by Friedrich Schneider, a composer eleven years Schubert's senior, whose work he admired. What Weber thought of the music is not known, though he was delighted by the bass soloist, Karl Gottlieb Reissiger. That Schubert was spending time in the company of the celebrated Weber seems to have upset some of the Schubertians. On 22 February, a former school friend of Schubert, Anton Holzapfel, wrote to Albert Stadler in Linz: 'I rarely see [Schubert] nor do we hit it off very well, his world being a very different one, as it should be. His somewhat gruff manner stands him in very good stead and will make a strong man and a ripe artist of him; he will be worthy of art.'

Holzapfel's reference to a 'somewhat gruff manner' suggests that Schubert's success in having had a number of works published, and one operetta performed on the stage, may have gone to his head. Or perhaps Schubert was already suffering from the disease which was to strike him down in the autumn. Meanwhile, more success, or at least more recognition, was coming his way. An article entitled 'A Glance at Schubert's Songs' by Friedrich von Hentl appeared on 23 March in the *Wiener Zeitschrift*, in which Schubert's songs were said to

raise themselves by ever undeniable excellences to the rank of masterpieces of genius, calculated to restore the present debased taste; for never has the true force of genius failed in its effect on heart and mind. Let the divine spark be buried deeply under the ashes smouldering upon the altar on which we sacrifice to the idol of sensuality, it will blaze up into the brightest flame of enthusiasm on being fanned by the breath of genius, which we can never describe, but only profoundly feel.

In the greatest work by our composer, 'Erlkönig', it is neither the melodic expression nor the succession of notes in the voice-part which gives organic unity to the whole, but rather the harmonic expression, the tone, imparted to the work by the accompaniment. This is the foundation here, on which the tone-picture is laid, and indeed quite in accordance with the text, where night and tempest and the father on horseback with his child compose the background. With profoundly moving truth the melodic expression characterizes the inner meaning of the action, the changing emotions of the father, the child and the Erl King, while its outward aspects, such as the galloping horse and the intermittent howling of the gale, are outlined by the most appropriate figures of accompaniment. Such a treatment was the only possible one in this case, since the uniform romance-like tone of the poem demanded a similarly uniform tone in the musical representation. In order to weave this tone into the whole, without sacrificing anything of the necessarily different characteristics in the words of the acting exponents, the separate melodies, the disparate parts of the significant vocal expression, had to be unified by the accompaniment. The latter did not only serve as a foil to the voice-part, but also as musical painting outlining the atmosphere.

The writer went on to describe and criticize in similar detail several other of Schubert's published songs, among them 'Der Wanderer', 'Schäfers Klagelied' and 'Memnon', before summing up:

I believe that I have said enough and need therefore not proceed from particulars to the general characteristics of Schubert's muse. His works will reveal to everyone at a first glance the marks of genius and of a thinking artist, and if the cultivated mind, deeply touched, declares that here music expresses

87

in perfect truth and beauty what has been said in the same way in poetry, it will be better to silence such questions of the cavilling mind as whether this is the proper manner of doing it, whether there might not be another, and whether this or that master had proceeded in the same way or not. Each genius bears his own measure within himself and is inspired by feelings which pour the deepest inner consciousness, the highest wisdom and the only true sources of perception into works of great and noble art.

In April, Schubert's Eight Variations on a French Song, for piano, four hands (D.624), composed four years earlier, was published as his opus 10, 'dedicated to Herr Ludwig von Beethoven by his worshipper and admirer Franz Schubert'. Having always cherished a desire to meet Beethoven, whom he had occasionally seen sitting in an inn surrounded by friends, or in a music shop, but whom he had been too shy to approach, Schubert is said to have delivered a copy of the Variations to Beethoven's house in person, but to have left without seeing the great composer, who was not at home. Whether or not Schubert went to Beethoven's house, it is known that Beethoven approved of the Eight Variations on a French Song and that he and his nephew Karl played the work together frequently during the months following its publication.

A curious prose manuscript by Schubert exists, which is dated 3 July 1822. Written in pencil, it bears a title and signature added in ink by the composer's brother Ferdinand, 'Mein Traum [My Dream]. Franz Schubert':

I was one of many brothers and sisters. Our father and mother were good people. I felt a deep love for them all. – One day my father took us to a feast. My brothers became very merry there. I, however, was sad. Then my father came up to me and bade me enjoy the delicious foods. But I could not, whereupon my father in his anger banished me from his sight. I turned on my heel and, with a heart full of infinite love for those who disdained it, I wandered off into a far country. For years I felt torn between the greatest love and the greatest sorrow. Then the news of my mother's death reached me. I hastened back to see her, and my father, softened by grief, did not hinder my entrance. I saw her lying dead. Tears flowed from my eyes. I saw her lying there, looking just as she used to in the old happy past in which, according to her wishes, we ought still to live and move and have our being.

We followed her in mourning to the grave, and the coffin slowly sank to earth. – From that time on, I again remained at home. Then one day my father took me once again into his favourite garden. He asked me whether I liked it. But the garden wholly repelled me, and I did not dare to reply. Then he asked me a second time, and more impatiently, if I liked the garden. – Trembling, I told him no. At that my father struck me, and I fled. For the second time I turned away, and, my heart filled with infinite love for those who had disdained it, I wandered once more into distant lands. For many long years, I sang my songs. But whenever I wished to sing of love, it turned to sorrow, and when I wanted to sing of sorrow, it was transformed into love.

Thus were love and sorrow divided in me.

And one day I had news of a gentle maiden who had just died. And a circle formed around her grave, in which many youths and old men walked as though in everlasting bliss. They spoke softly so as not to awaken the maiden.

Heavenly thoughts like bright sparks seemed to be showered unceasingly on the youths from the maiden's gravestone, falling on them with a sound of gentle rustling. I longed to walk there, too. But only by a miracle, they told me, could one enter the circle. However, I went forward to the gravestone, slowly and devoutly, and before I knew it I found myself in the circle, from which there sounded the most wondrous of melodies. And I felt as though eternal bliss were gathered together into a single moment. My father I saw, too, reconciled and loving. He took me in his arms and wept. And I wept even more.

This odd piece of allegory has been treated by some Schubert biographers as pure autobiography, which it most decidedly is not. It has an emotional factual basis, in the death of Schubert's mother ten years earlier when he was still at school, and in Schubert's quarrel with his father, who did not want him to leave home and live alone. But no 'gentle maiden' of Schubert's acquaintance had died, and a summer spent as a tutor in Hungary can hardly be described as wandering off into a far country. Why Schubert should have written these paragraphs of prose is not clear. He did occasionally dabble in poetry, but as far as is known he made no other attempt to write imaginative prose. Did he, at some time, tell his brother Ferdinand that it was the description of a dream? Or was it, perhaps, written as an exercise, or as part of one of the word-games or competitions in which the Schubertians were wont to indulge? There is now no way of knowing.

Among the compositions of the summer of 1822 are the popular *Marches militaires* (D.733) for pianoforte duet, and the impressively dramatic chorus 'Gott in der Natur' (God in Nature, D.757) for female voices. Performances of Schubert's choruses and part-songs, as well as his solo songs, were becoming increasingly frequent, not only in

Vienna but also in provincial towns. Three part-songs in particular, the sentimental, Biedermeierish 'Das Dörfchen' (The Little Village, D.598), the charming 'Die Nachtigall' (The Nightingale, D.724) and the solemn 'Geist der Liebe' (Spirit of Love, D.747), were especially popular in Schubert's lifetime.

During the summer, Schubert's manner seemed to some of his old friends to have altered. There was an estrangement from Vogl, the exact reason for which is not known, which is mentioned in a letter of 20 July from Spaun's brother Anton to his wife. Anton was staying at Steyr during the summer, and had encountered Vogl there on the famous singer's annual pilgrimage to his birthplace:

To me Vogl is extremely pleasing. He told me all about his relationship to Schubert with the utmost frankness, and unfortunately I am quite unable to excuse the latter. Vogl is very much embittered against Schober, for whose sake Schubert behaved most ungratefully towards Vogl and who makes the fullest use of Schubert in order to extricate himself from financial embarrassments and to defray the expenditure which has already exhausted the greater part of his mother's fortune. I wish very much that somebody were here who would defend Schubert at least in the matter of the most glaring reproaches. Vogl also says Schober's opera is bad and a total failure, and that altogether Schubert is quite on the wrong road.

It is clear that, by this time, many of the Schubertians were distrustful of Schober's influence over their friend. In particular, they were distressed that Schubert had begun to ape the loose-living ways of Schober, who seemed to delight in initiating others into his own style of life, in which wine and women certainly played as large a part as song. But, whatever lay behind the references in Anton von Spaun's letter, Schubert and Vogl appear to have been reconciled by the autumn, even though Vogl's opinion of *Alfonso und Estrella* ('Schober's opera') may have been the deciding factor in the Kärntnertor management's rejection of that work.

Among Schubert's songs of 1822 are two of his finest settings of Goethe. The entrancing 'Der Musensohn' (The Son of the Muses, D.764) is so similar to the German folk-song 'Im Wald und auf der Heide' (In the Forest and on the Moors) that clearly one must derive from the other. Since so many German folk-songs turn out on close inspection to be the work of minor but known nineteenth-century composers, it is quite probable that Schubert's song came first.

The other superb Goethe setting is the last song that Schubert wrote

in 1822, one which is known today as 'Wanderers Nachtlied II'
(Wayfarer's Night Song II, D.768), a companion piece to an earlier
Schubert-Goethe song, 'Wanderers Nachtlied I' (D.224). The poem of
'Wanderers Nachtlied II' is Goethe's 'Ein Gleiches' (A Resemblance),
perhaps the most famous short lyric in the German language, a calm
acceptance of approaching death. The lines were written by the
thirty-year-old Goethe on the walls of his bedroom in a lonely hunting
lodge in the Thuringian hills. In Schubert's wonderful setting, which
is as simple, direct and poetic as the words, all the stillness and peace of
the world seem to reside. Music and words are fused into one
statement.

Baron Karl Schönstein, who, after he had got to know the
composer at Zseliz in the summer of 1818, devoted himself to
performing Schubert's songs, recalled in later years a story which he
had from Vogl:

One morning Schubert brought some new songs for Vogl to look through,
in other words for his criticism. But the latter was very busy that day and
could not, at that moment, undertake the usual perusal of the songs at the
piano, so he kept the songs and bade Schubert call back another time.
Meanwhile, Vogl looked over the songs for himself, one of which appealed
to him very particularly. Some time after this, it might have been a fortnight,
after Vogl had sung it, without saying a word beforehand about the song and
without having made the slightest change in it – at times he liked to take
liberties with Schubert's songs – Schubert cried out in his simple way, 'You
know, that song isn't bad! Who's it by?' After a fortnight he no longer
recognized his own creation.

It is much more likely that Vogl *had* taken liberties in his
performance of the song, and that Schubert's comment and question
were intended ironically.

Three important compositions, two of them among Schubert's
most popular works today, were written during the latter part of 1822:
the Mass in A flat major (D.678), the 'Unfinished' Symphony (D.757)
and the 'Wanderer' Fantasy (D.760). The Mass had been begun as
early as November 1819, and Schubert had probably worked on it
intermittently before finishing it in a burst of energy in the autumn of
1822. His six settings of the Catholic Mass can be divided into four
early works, composed before the end of 1816, and two mature
masterpieces, of which this in A flat is the first. (The second, in E flat,
was composed in the last months of his life.) The A flat Mass is a lyrical

rather than a dramatic setting of the Latin text, and possesses a sweetness perhaps verging on the sentimental. An engaging work, its finest sections are the 'Et incarnatus est' and the 'Crucifixus'. It was first performed, not long after its composition, in the parish church of Alt Lerchenfeld, a suburb of Vienna.

In October Schubert sketched, in piano score, three movements of a new symphony, his eighth. At the end of the month, he began to score the work, and completed the first two movements but broke off after the first few bars of the third movement, a scherzo. Why he did not sketch a fourth and final movement before embarking upon the full scoring of a work only partially sketched out is a mystery. If sketches for a fourth movement ever existed, they have not been discovered. Sometime in November he set the work aside and never returned to it. This is the composition known to the world today as Schubert's 'Unfinished' Symphony (No. 8) in B minor.

The 'Unfinished' Symphony was never performed during its composer's lifetime, and the story of how it came to light after his death is a strange one. At some time in 1823 Schubert gave the incomplete manuscript of the orchestral score to Josef Hüttenbrenner, intending him to pass it on as a gift to his brother Anselm, in Graz. This Josef did. In view of the beauty of these two movements, it is astonishing that Anselm did not bother to have them performed in Graz or at least to urge Schubert to complete the symphony. It was not until twenty-five years after Schubert's death that Anselm made a piano duet arrangement of the two completed movements, which he played with his brother. That they were both well aware of the symphony's stature is proven by Josef's letter of 8 March 1860 to the conductor of the Vienna Musikverein:

[Anselm] possesses a treasure in Schubert's B minor Symphony, which we rank with his great C major Symphony, his instrumental swan song, and with all the symphonies of Beethoven – only it is unfinished. Schubert gave it to me for Anselm to thank him for having sent the diploma of the Graz Musical Society through me. [See pp. 100–101.]

It was not until five years after this that Anselm Hüttenbrenner actually yielded up the score. The conductor of the Vienna Musik-verein, Johann Herbeck, visited him in Graz, ingratiated himself with Anselm by offering to perform one of his compositions in Vienna, and then innocently brought up the name of Schubert. Anselm produced the score of the 'Unfinished' Symphony, and, as he turned over the pages, Herbeck realized he was handling a masterpiece. He asked if he might have the score copied, whereupon Anselm exclaimed, 'Oh, take the manuscript back with you.' The result was that the symphony's two completed movements were played for the first time in Vienna on 17 December 1865.

Listening today to the 'Unfinished' Symphony one is struck immediately by its flowing lyricism and its wealth of melody. One feels it to be inconceivable that Schubert could not have realized he was creating a masterpiece. How could he, one wonders, simply have set it aside and failed to return to it? None of the explanations offered by critics and biographers is completely satisfactory: that, having written two such superb movements, he knew he could not sustain that level of genius; that he had intended to write only a two-movement work; that, at this stage of his life, music was flowing from him at such a rate that the composer himself could hardly keep up with it, and simply forgot to complete this particular work. If a work is going well, a composer completes it; he does not agonize over whether or not he will be able to. The nature of the two movements of the 'Unfinished' Symphony indicates that they were intended as part of a conventional, four-movement symphony; in any case, the first nine bars of the third movement exist in full score, and the piano sketch of all three movements can be seen today in the library of the Gesellschaft der Musikfreunde in Vienna. (The third movement is a boisterous scherzo, with a gentler trio.) One is forced to consider more seriously the third possibility: that, having for whatever reason put the work aside, Schubert simply lost interest in completing it. He may, so to speak, have lost the thread of that particular musical argument, and he was certainly not at a loss for other musical ideas.

It has also been suggested that Anselm Hüttenbrenner may have been given a complete score, and have mislaid the last two movements at some time between 1822 and 1860. This is an attractive theory, but untenable in the light of recent documentation. The adventures of the piano sketches, however, are interesting. The three movements (still incomplete, for the scherzo-like nature of the third adumbrates a fourth, concluding movement) passed into the possession of Ferdinand Schubert when his brother died. Ferdinand's son, Karl, sold the sketches in 1885 to someone who, in turn, bequeathed them to the Vienna Gesellschaft der Musikfreunde.

These sketches have been used by more than one composer or musicologist as a basis on which to construct a completion of the Symphony. There have been performances of the work (the first was in London in 1881) in which the two movements have been followed by the 'Entr'acte' in B minor which Schubert composed for the play *Rosamunde* in the autumn of 1823. This is a practical solution, for the 'Entr'acte' is itself a masterpiece. However, the theory that the 'Entr'acte' is really a missing movement, which Schubert simply tore from the Symphony to use as an entr'acte since he was fighting against time to complete the *Rosamunde* score, cannot be maintained against the facts. Whatever existed of the symphony was already with Anselm Hüttenbrenner in Graz at the time when Schubert was composing his *Rosamunde* music.

It is just possible that Schubert turned aside from working on his Symphony in B minor because an idea for a large-scale piano work had come into his mind and taken precedence. It is certainly the case that in November 1822 he composed his Pianoforte Fantasy in C Major (D.760), now popularly known as the 'Wanderer' Fantasy (though Schubert never called it that) because it incorporates a theme from his famous song of 1816, 'Der Wanderer'.

The 'Wanderer' Fantasy is, in effect, a piano sonata in one huge movement containing four sections which correspond to the usual four movements of a sonata. It is in the second section, an adagio theme and variations, that the composer uses as his theme the tune which, in the song, is sung to the words 'Die Sonne dünkt mich hier so kalt,/Die Blüte welk, das Leben alt,/Und was sie reden, leerer Schall;/Ich bin ein Fremdling überall' (The sun here seems so cold to me, the bloom faded, life old, and what people say is merely empty sound; I am a stranger everywhere). If the use of this tune suggests a sentimental romanticism, the suggestion is not borne out by the evidence of the work itself, which has the toughness of intellectual fibre of a late Beethoven sonata. Listening to the 'Wanderer' Fantasy ignorant of the words of the song, one would never be in danger of interpreting it as a despairing cry against the emptiness of life from a romantic wandering exile. It is a vigorous, dramatic work with episodes of lyrical contrast and, incidentally, it makes the heaviest demands on a player's technique of any composition for piano by Schubert.

Schubert's writing for the piano in the 'Wanderer' Fantasy seems continually to be striving for something more than pianistic expression. As the composer Robert Schumann wrote of it, 'Schubert would like, in this work, to condense the whole orchestra into two hands, and the enthusiastic beginning is a seraphic hymn to the Godhead; you see the angels pray; the Adagio is a gentle meditation on life and takes the veil off it; then fugues thunder forth a song of endless humanity and music.' In 1851, Liszt made an arrangement of the Fantasy for piano and orchestra. It is a valid piece of music in its own right, but it in no way supplants Schubert's original.

Schubert, then, may have been diverted from his 'Unfinished' Symphony by the urge to compose the 'Wanderer' Fantasy. He may, however, have been diverted from it as the result of a different kind of urge. Sometime towards the end of 1822 he contracted a venereal disease, which was probably syphilis. (It was not until ten years after Schubert's death that it became possible to make a clear distinction between syphilis and gonorrhoea.) It may be that the sexual act which caused the disease occurred when Schubert was working on the symphony, and that he subsequently associated the unfinished work with events he preferred to forget, and thus chose not to return to it. This seems less unlikely than the other suggestions that have been put forward to explain the unfinished state of the B minor Symphony.

The onset of Schubert's disease led to his leaving the Schober residence and returning, in December, to his father's school-house in the Rossau district. Although the nature of his illness was known to his family and his immediate circle of friends, it did not find its way into any of their written reminiscences or memoirs, nor have any documents or letters referring to it survived. There can be no doubt, however, that his syphilis must have had a profound effect upon the composer's psyche and upon his personality. In this first stage of the disease he was ill for several months, but from this time until his death six years later periods of good health and creative energy alternated with those of depression, illness and inability to compose.

Most of Schubert's other friends were convinced that his disease was the direct result of his having been led by Schober into casual sexual liaisons, possibly with prostitutes. Josef Kenner, who was on the fringes of the Schubert circle of friends and acquaintances, referred obliquely to the matter in material he provided in 1858 for a projected biography of Schubert. Kenner, whose personal contacts with Schubert were for the most part limited to their student days before

1816, wrote:

With the year 1816, these close contacts between us came to an end.

Schubert's genius subsequently attracted, among other friends, the heart of a seductively amiable and brilliant young man, endowed with the noblest talents, whose extraordinary gifts would have been so worthy of a moral foundation and would have richly repaid a stricter schooling than the one he unfortunately had. But shunning so much effort as unworthy of genius and summarily rejecting such fetters as a form of prejudice and restriction, while at the same time arguing with brilliant and ingratiatingly persuasive power, this scintillating individuality, as I was told later, won a lasting and pernicious influence over Schubert's honest susceptibility. If this was not apparent in his work it was all the more so in his life. Anyone who knew Schubert knows how he was made of two natures, foreign to each other, how powerfully the craving for pleasure dragged his soul down to the slough of moral degradation, and how highly he valued the utterances of friends he respected, and so will find his surrender to the false prophet, who embellished sensuality in such a flattering manner, all the more understandable. But more hardened characters than he were seduced, for longer or shorter periods, by the devilish attraction of associating with that apparently warm but inwardly merely vain being into worshipping him as an idol.

This intimation seemed to me indispensable for the biographer's grasp of the subject, for it concerns an episode in Schubert's life which only too probably caused his premature death and certainly hastened it.

But it must, of course, remain a mere intimation and no name may be mentioned, for Schubert's fame should not be misused as a pillory for the purpose of perpetuating the memory of wicked people.

The 'episode in Schubert's life which only too probably caused his premature death' was, of course, the sexual encounter which led to his syphilis. A few days after writing those words to Ferdinand Luib, whose intention it was to publish a biography of Schubert, Kenner wrote again to make it clear that

by Schubert's seducer I meant Franz von Schober, whom I had known, and known intimately, since 1808 at the Kremsmünster Seminary . . . under the guise of the most amiable sociability, and even of engaging affection, there reigned in this whole [Schober] family a deep moral depravity, so that it was not to be wondered at that Franz von Schober went the same way. Only he devised a philosophical system for his own reassurance and to justify himself in the eyes of the world as well as to provide a basis for his aesthetic oracle, about which he was probably as hazy as any of his disciples; nevertheless he found the mysticism of sensuality sufficiently elastic for his own freedom of movement; and so did his pupils. The need for love and friendship emerged with such egotism and jealousy that to his adherents he alone was all, not only prophet, but God himself, and apart from his oracles he was willing to tolerate no other religion, no morals, no restraint.

Schober seems to have been a *fin de siècle* character in advance of his time, someone who could have stepped from the pages of Wilde's *The Picture of Dorian Gray*. It is not always easy to extract an exact meaning from the flowery circumlocutions of nineteenth-century language on the subject of sexual morality, which inhibited Kenner from using such terms as 'sexual intercourse' and 'venereal disease', but unless he is accusing Schober of a physical, homosexual seduction of Schubert (which is possible, though somewhat improbable), he seems to be blaming Schober for having led Schubert into the company of prostitutes and other women of loose morals.

A letter from Schubert to Spaun survives from the end of 1822, when the composer's illness first declared itself. The letter, sent from Vienna to Spaun in Linz, is dated December 7th:

I hope that the dedication of these three songs will give you a little pleasure. You deserve so much more for all that you have done for me that I really ought to give you, *ex officio*, something infinitely greater, and I would too if only I were in a position to do so. You will be satisfied with the selection, for I have chosen those songs which you yourself specified. Apart from this volume, two others are appearing at the same time: one is already printed, and I have enclosed a copy for you, and the other is actually in the printer's hands. The first volume contains, as you will see, the three songs of the Harper, the second of which, 'Wer nie sein Brot mit Tränen ass' [He Who Never Ate His Bread With Tears, D.480], is new, and is dedicated to the Bishop of St Pölten. The other contains, as you will not see, 'Suleika' [D.720] and 'Geheimes' [Secrets, D.719], and is dedicated to Schober. In addition to these, I have composed a Fantasy for pianoforte, two hands, which is also being printed, and is dedicated to a certain wealthy person. I have also set to music some more Goethe poems, such as 'Der Musensohn' [The Son of the Muses, D. 764], 'An die Entfernte' [To the Distant One, D.765], 'Am Flusse' [By the River, D. 766], and 'Willkommen und Abschied' [Hail and Farewell, D.767]. As to my opera, there is nothing to be looked for in Vienna. I asked for it back again, and have received it. Vogl too has definitely left the theatre. I shall shortly send it either to Dresden, whence I had a most encouraging letter from Weber, or to Berlin. My Mass is finished and is to be performed before long. I still cling to my old idea of dedicating it either to the Emperor or the Empress, for I think it is a successful piece of work. Now I have told you all the news I have about myself and my music. Let me add some news about someone else. *Libussa*, a grand opera by C [onradin] Kreutzer, has just been performed here for the first time, and was a success. The second act is said to be especially fine, but I heard only the first, which left me cold.

And now, how are you? I certainly hope you are well and that thus I may be forgiven this tardy enquiry. How is your family? What is Streinsberg up to? Do write to me soon about everything. If I were not so vexed over this miserable business with the opera, I should be fairly content. Now that Vogl has left the theatre and my troubles in that direction are consequently over, I have taken up with him again. I even think I may accompany, or follow, him into the country again this summer, and am looking forward to this very much, for I shall see you and your friends again. Our companionship in Vienna is very pleasant nowadays. We meet at Schober's three times a week for readings, as well as a Schubertiad at which Bruchmann also makes an appearance. And now, dear Spaun, farewell. Write to me very soon, and fully, so as to mitigate somewhat the gaping void your absence will always cause for me. Remember me to your brothers, also to your sister and Ottenwalt, as well as to Streinsberg and all the others, etc.

Your faithful friend,
Franz Schubert

Address your letter to the school-house, Grünthorgasse, in the Rossau, for that is where I am living now.

(The three songs dedicated to Spaun are the set published as opus 13, which consists of 'Der Schäfer und der Reiter' [The Shepherd and the Horseman, D.517], 'Lob der Tränen' [In Praise of Tears, D.711], and 'Der Alpenjäger' [The Alpine Hunter, D.524], all three minor but delightful pieces. The 'wealthy person' to whom the 'Wanderer' Fantasy was dedicated was Emanuel Karl, Edler Liebenberg de Zsittin, a Jewish landowner who had been ennobled by the Emperor in 1821, and who had been a piano pupil of Hummel. The opera referred to in the letter is *Alfonso und Estrella*, and it would seem that the temporary estrangement of Schubert from Vogl may have been due to Vogl's unwillingness to recommend the work to the management of the Kärntnertor theatre. Vogl had retired from the theatre the previous month at the age of fifty-four, but continued to sing in public until after Schubert's death. 'Readings' had become a favourite occupation of the Schubertians, and Schubert apparently found them useful to him as a composer of vocal music.)

At the beginning of 1823, Schubert was too ill to move outside his father's house. Uncharacteristically, at this time he rejected several commissions or requests for works from the Philharmonic Society and other organizations, and seemed disinclined to compose. He was still, however, keen to arrange a production of *Alfonso und Estrella*, and on 28 February wrote to Ignaz Franz Mosel, who was an official of the imperial court:

Please forgive me for troubling you again with a letter, but the state of my health does not yet allow me to venture out of doors.

I have the honour to send you now, sir, the third and last act of my opera and also the overture to the first act, with the request that you will be so good as to let me know your valued opinion of them. Should I still be unable to visit you in person, would you very kindly let me know when I may send for the whole opera, together with your highly esteemed criticism? May I remind you, sir, of your very kind promise of a letter of recommendation to Weber? I would even venture to ask, if you could see your way to do so, to return my opera with a similar covering letter to Baron von Könneritz, who according to Weber is in charge of the theatre in Dresden.

And now, since I have importuned you with so many requests already, may I very humbly add this last one, namely, that you would be so kind as to let me have in the meantime the libretto which you intended for my unworthy self, which I assure you most solemnly I shall take great care of and shall not allow anyone else to see.

This letter must have been preceded by one from Schubert to Mosel, accompanying the first two acts of *Alfonso und Estrella*. Mosel was himself a composer and also a librettist, and Schubert was either interested in, or pretending an interest in, one of his libretti.

In February the 'Wanderer' Fantasy was published, within three months of its composition, and Schubert, still confined to the house, began to work again, this time at another piece for piano, the A minor Sonata, the first of his mature sonatas. A more restrained, inward-looking composition than the 'Wanderer' Fantasy, the A minor Sonata (D.784, published posthumously in 1839) is a deeply personal work, whose slow movement is one of Schubert's most original. Oddly, during these weeks of illness and depression, he also composed for the piano a set of thirty-four of his most delightful, and, in some instances, sweetly sentimental, dances, the *Valses sentimentales* (D.779). Though most of his dance music was written to be danced to, these waltzes were surely intended for concert performance.

Foolishly, or perhaps desperately, in order to raise funds, Schubert sold outright to the publishers Cappi & Diabelli the works which they had published. Then, in a somewhat tart letter of 10 April, he severed his relations with the firm when he suspected them of not having dealt honestly with him in their most recent statements of account:

Your letter has indeed surprised me, for I understood from Herr von Cappi's own statement that the account was completely settled. During the earlier negotiations over the publication of the waltzes I became aware of the not over-scrupulous intentions of my publishers; and their conduct, therefore, on this second occasion is easy to explain: and you gentlemen yourselves will have no difficulty in the circumstances in finding a natural explanation for the long-term contract which I have now entered into with another publisher. Neither am I able to understand your suggestion of a debt of 150 Viennese florins, for the estimate you gave me for copying the opera amounted only to 100 florins. Be that as it may, I feel that the extremely small purchase price which you paid for my earlier things, including the Fantasy at 50 florins, long ago wiped out this debt which you so unjustly put upon me. However, since I very much doubt whether you will take so human and reasonable a view, I am compelled to call your attention to my legal right to 20 copies of the latest and 12 copies of the earlier sets of songs, and my even more justifiable claim to repayment of the 50 florins which you know how to get out of me in so ingenious a way. Kindly reckon all this together and you will find that my claim is not only greater than yours but fairer too, though I should never have made it if you had not reminded me of it in so unpleasant a fashion. As you will be good enough to see for yourselves, my debt was wiped out in this way long ago, nor can there be any question whatever of your publishing any more of my songs, whose worth you could never estimate cheaply enough, though I now receive 200 Viennese florins a volume for them. Herr von Steiner too has made me several offers of publication for my works. In conclusion I must ask you please to send me back all my manuscripts, the engraved as well as the unengraved works.

Yours faithfully,
Frz. Schubert
Composer

N.B. Please let me have an exact account of the number of copies delivered to me since our first agreement of sale, for I find that my calculation greatly differs from yours.

Schubert had already come to terms with another firm, Sauer & Leidesdorf, who in fact published three of his songs on the day on which he wrote his letter to Cappi & Diabelli. Also on the same day, though Schubert would have heard of it only some days later, the Styrian Musical Society in Graz elected him as a non-resident honorary member. The Society's diploma, delivered to Schubert through the Hüttenbrenner brothers, states that this honour was accorded to the composer 'in full recognition of your already generally acknowledged merits as a musical artist and composer'. The Society had, the previous year, similarly honoured Beethoven, although in his case the wording read 'to do honour to the high merits of the greatest composer of this present century'.

During April, although he was still ailing and depressed, Schubert made yet another attempt to compose for the theatre. The libretto of the one-act Singspiel, *Die Verschworenen* (The Conspirators, D.787) by Ignaz Franz Castelli, a prolific writer of comedies for the Viennese theatres, is a variation on the theme of Aristophanes' *Lysistrata*: several Viennese wives, at the time of the Crusades, deny conjugal rights to their husbands until they promise to remain at home instead of going off to war. Castelli's *Die Verschworenen* had been published in February with a preface which stated: 'Most German-speaking composers make the same complaint, that they would love to write operas if only someone would furnish them with decent texts. Gentlemen, here is one!'

Schubert accepted the challenge, and composed eleven numbers, but no overture. His score is quite delightful, from the opening soprano-tenor duet, through the lively ensembles, to the exuberant finale of reconciliation, but, although *Die Verschworenen* is, along with *Alfonso und Estrella*, probably the most stageworthy of all of Schubert's operas or operettas, it failed to achieve performance during his lifetime. Before it was submitted for production, its title was changed from *Die Verschworenen* to *Der häusliche Krieg* (Domestic Warfare) in deference to a nervous Austrian political censorship. The change was unavailing, and the first performance of the work did not take place until March 1861 in Vienna, when the aged librettist, who was hearing the music for the first time, exclaimed in amazement at its gaiety and charm, remarking that he had been told at the time of its composition that Schubert had provided a rather gloomy score. (The March 1861 Viennese performance was a concert version. The first staging of *Die Verschworenen* was at Frankfurt, later in 1861. In October of that year, the work reached the Viennese stage at last, and was subsequently produced in several German towns as well as in London, New York, Budapest, Prague, Paris, St Petersburg and a number of other places. It has been kept alive during the twentieth century, and makes an excellent half of an operatic double-bill.)

Schubert's illness increased to such an extent that, for a few days in May, he was committed to the Vienna General Hospital. It was at this time that he wrote the poem 'Mein Gebet' (My Prayer):

Deepest longing, holy fears
Striving up to purer spheres,
Would lift this darkling space above
To the almighty realm of love.

Give thy son, O mighty father,
As reward thy sorrows rather,
And at last, him to redeem,
Send thy love's eternal beam.

See, destroyed in dust and mire,
Scorched by agonizing fire,
Lies my life, its mortal woe
Nears eternal overthrow.

Slay it, and slay me at last,
In the stream of Lethe cast,
And, O great one, let me then
Stronger and purer rise again.

The poem, as well as being rather poor, is clearly the product of a mind debilitated by illness. How astonishing, therefore, that the first songs of the *Schöne Müllerin* (Fair Maid of the Mill, D.795) cycle should have been composed during the same month. In addition, Schubert embarked upon yet another opera, which he began in May, worked on in Upper Austria during the summer, and completed in September.

The opera was *Fierrabras* (D.796), a three-act piece with a libretto by Josef Kupelwieser, Leopold's brother. (There are also sketches, dating from May, for the first two numbers of an opera called *Rüdiger*.) Schubert's score for *Fierrabras* is even more attractive than that of *Alfonso und Estrella*, more concerned with the needs of the stage, and makes interesting use of what in Wagner is called *Leitmotif*; but the libretto is a lamentably poor and unnecessarily complicated piece of romantic nonsense, set in the time of Charlemagne. The impresario Barbaia, to whom the work was submitted, kept it for several months and then rejected it, giving the poor quality of the libretto as his reason.

Towards the end of July, Schubert was well enough to travel to Upper Austria, where he met up with Vogl in Linz. There, he and Vogl were introduced by Josef von Spaun and Albert Stadler to the Hartmann family, at whose house on 28 July they performed several of Schubert's songs. From Linz, they made their way to Vogl's home town of Steyr, whence on 14 August Schubert wrote to Schober:

Although I am rather late in writing, I hope that this letter will still find you in Vienna. I am in constant correspondence with Schäffer and am fairly well, though whether I shall ever completely recover I am inclined to doubt. Here I lead a very simple life in every way, go for walks regularly, work hard at my opera, and read Walter Scott.

I get on very well with Vogl. We were at Linz together, where he sang a good deal, and splendidly. Bruchmann, Sturm and Streinsberg visited us in Steyr a few days ago, and they too were sent off with a fresh load of songs. I shall hardly see you before your journey home, so I must once again wish you the best of good fortune in your undertaking, and assure you of my everlasting love, which will make me miss you grievously. Let me hear something of you from time to time, wherever you may be.

(The Schäffer with whom Schubert was 'in constant correspondence' was his physician, who, it seems, was worried about the composer's condition and wanted regular reports from him while he was absent from Vienna. In general, Schubert appears to have avoided a number of his friends at this time, even after his return to Vienna in mid-September. Beethoven was told by his nephew Karl, in August, 'They greatly praise Schubert, but it is said that he hides himself.')

More of the *Schöne Müllerin* songs were composed during the summer. Schubert did not work constantly upon these settings of Wilhelm Müller's poems, but interspersed them with other songs, and instrumental works. It was not until the following March that he finally completed the cycle. In October 1823 Weber came to Vienna for the first performance of his opera *Euryanthe*, at the Kärntnertor theatre. Schubert was present at the first performance on the 25th and, the following day, when Weber asked him how he had liked the opera, he was tactless enough to reply that he had quite enjoyed it, but preferred *Der Freischütz* as it had more melody. It is likely that, after this exchange, Weber's efforts to have Schubert's *Alfonso und Estrella* staged in Germany slackened somewhat.

On 30 November, Schubert wrote to Schober, who was now in Breslau attempting to pursue a career as an actor:

I have been longing to write to you for some time now, but I could never find a moment. You know how it happens.

First of all, I must pour out a lament over the sad state of our circle, as well as all other circumstances here, for, with the exception of my health, which seems at last (thank God) to have definitely improved, everything goes miserably. Just as I saw, our circle has lost its central focus without you. Bruchmann, back from his travels, is not the same as he used to be. He seems to cling now to social conventions, and in consequence is losing that halo of his which, in my opinion, was due entirely to his consistent abstention from all contact with the world. Kupelwieser, as you probably already know, has gone to Rome (but is not particularly pleased with his Russian). As for the others, you know better than I. It's true that four individuals have come to fill the places left vacant by you and Kupelwieser; namely, the Hungarian Mayr, Hönig, Smetana and Steiger, but the majority of such people weaken our society instead of strengthening it. What do we want with a succession of quite ordinary students and clerks? If Bruchmann is ill or absent, one hears by the hour – with Mohn presiding over everything – nothing but endless talk of riding and fencing, horses and dogs. If it goes on like this, I shall probably not be able to stand their company much longer.

Things are going very badly also with my two operas. Kupelwieser has suddenly left the theatre. Weber's *Euryanthe* was a failure, and in my opinion its poor reception was deserved. These circumstances, and a new split between Pálffy and Barbaia, leave me with scarcely any hope for my opera. As a matter of fact, it would not be a great stroke of fortune, for everything nowadays is indescribably badly produced.

Vogl is here, and sang once at Bruchmann's, and once at Witteczek's. He interests himself almost exclusively in my songs. He writes out the voice-parts himself, and makes, so to speak, a living out of it. For this reason, he is very polite and docile with me. And now, let's hear something of you. How are you? Have you already appeared before the public eye?

Please let me have news of you really soon. Tell me of your life and doings in order to still my longing for you to some extent. Since the opera I have composed nothing except a few more *Schöne Müllerin* songs. These will be published in four sets, with vignettes by Schwind.

For the rest, I hope to regain my health, and this recovered treasure will help me forget many a sorrow: but you, dear Schober, I can never forget, for no one else can ever be to me, alas, what you once were.

And now, keep well, and do not forget
　　your eternally affectionate friend.

Schubert's letter is addressed from the Stubentor Bastei, near the present Stadtpark, where he shared lodgings with one of the circle of friends, Josef Huber, from the time of his return to Vienna in the autumn of 1823 to the spring of the following year.

An important commission came Schubert's way at the end of 1823. This was to compose the incidental music for a new play, *Rosamunde, Fürstin von Zypern* (Rosamunde, Princess of Cyprus), by Helmina von Chézy (the librettist of Weber's *Euryanthe*), which was performed for the first time at the Theater an der Wien on 20 December. The text of the play has not survived, but Schubert's music (D.797) has remained popular to this day in concert performances. He wrote ten pieces: choruses, ballet music, orchestral entr'actes and one song. For an overture, he used the one he had written for *Alfonso und Estrella*.

When the *Rosamunde* music is performed now at concerts, the overture used is that which Schubert wrote three years earlier for *Die Zauberharfe*. The entr'actes are in turn tragic, lyrical and poetic, and all of symphonic stature; the song 'Der Vollmond strahlt' (The Full Moon Shines) is exquisite and the chorus of spirits romantically mysterious. The third entr'acte (in B flat) is surely one of Schubert's most delicate yet deeply felt pieces for orchestra: a slow movement in search of a symphony. The opening theme of the final ballet is one of the best-known of Schubert melodies.

The programme of the Theater an der Wien described *Rosamunde* as a 'Grand Romantic Drama in Four Acts, with Choruses, Musical Accompaniment and Dances'. The play proved to be a disaster, and after a second performance on 21 December it disappeared for ever. Schwind described the première in a letter to Schober, dated 22 December:

The day before yesterday the Theater an der Wien produced a piece by the wretched Frau von Chézy, *Rosamunde of Cyprus*, with music by Schubert. You may imagine that we all went to it. As I did not go out all day on account of my cough, I could make no arrangements, and sat alone in the third tier while the others were in the pit. Schubert has taken over the overture he wrote for *Estrella* as he thinks it too 'homespun' for *Estrella*, for which he wants to write a new one. It pleased so much that, to my great joy, it had to be repeated. You may imagine how I followed the basses and the scoring. You were worried about them, I know. I noticed that the flute, to which half the score is given, comes in a bit too soon, but that may have been due to the player. Otherwise, it is easy to understand and well-balanced. After the first act, there was a piece which proved not sufficiently brilliant for the place it occupies, and too repetitive. A ballet made no impression, nor did the second and third entr'actes. Well, people are accustomed to talking immediately the curtain has dropped, and I do not see how they can be expected to notice such serious and lovely things. In the last act was a chorus of shepherds and huntsmen, so beautiful and so natural that I cannot remember ever hearing the like before. It was applauded and repeated, and I believe it will deal the chorus in Weber's *Euryanthe* the sort of blow it deserves. An aria too, though most atrociously sung by Mme Vogel, and a little bucolic piece were applauded. A subterranean chorus could not be heard, and even the gestures of Herr Rott, who was brewing poison the while, could not make it materialize.

Two days later, on Christmas Eve, Schwind wrote again to Schober, with news of Schubert's health:

Schubert is better, and it will not be long before he goes about with his own hair again, which had to be shorn owing to the rash. He wears a very nice wig. He is much with Vogl and Leidesdorf. The wretched doctor is often with him, too. He is now thinking (the doctor) of a concert or a public Schubertiad. If it comes off, I'll write to you.

(Schubert's rash was caused by the secondary stage of his syphilis. The idea of a public concert of Schubert's work took more than four years to come to fruition.)

Schubert's second doctor at this time was Dr Bernhardt, who, like Dr Schäffer, was an amateur poet and a member of the Schubert circle. On New Year's Eve, Schubert and Dr Bernhardt turned up at the circle's party, announcing themselves by throwing stones at the window and shattering a window-pane. Schubert was well enough, then, to participate in the season's festivities, but prudent enough to keep one of his doctors in tow.

The most important of Schubert's compositions in 1823 is the song-cycle *Die schöne Müllerin* (D.795). It is said that Schubert came across the poems in a volume which he found in a friend's house, and that he simply walked off with the volume and began immediately to set some of the poems to music. The volume, however it came into his possession, was *Seventy-seven Poems from the Posthumous Papers of a Travelling Horn-Player* by Wilhelm Müller (1794–1827), which had been published in 1821. The first twenty-three poems formed a cycle, 'Die schöne Müllerin, im Winter zu lesen' (The Fair Maid of the Mill; to be Read in Winter), and these were the poems which first attracted Schubert's attention. Müller was a German Romantic poet whose verses were mostly in the folkish style affected by several of the nature poets of the period, and his 'Schöne Müllerin' sequence tells the story of the unhappy love of a young apprentice for a country miller's daughter who rejects him for a huntsman.

Schubert discarded three of Müller's poems, and composed his cycle on the remaining twenty, tracing the apprentice's story from the time he sets out on his wanderings ('Das Wandern': Wandering), through his coming to work at the rustic mill ('Am Feierabend': The Hour of Rest), his growing love for the miller's daughter ('Ungeduld': Impatience), his conviction that his love is returned ('Mein!': Mine), and the arrival on the scene of a hunter ('Der Jäger': The Huntsman) whom the girl clearly prefers ('Die liebe Farbe': The Beloved Colour), to the apprentice's despair ('Trockne Blumen': Withered Flowers), and his suicide in the brook to which he had been wont to confide his hopes and fears ('Der Müller und der Bach': The Miller and the Brook).

Critical opinion generally, and no doubt rightly, rates the tragedy of Schubert's second cycle, *Winterreise* (Winter Journey), more highly than the sweet sentimentality of *Die schöne Müllerin*. Yet this first cycle is no less remarkable in its way. Schubert's apprentice is a genuinely touching creation. He appears in *Winterreise*, older, sadder, embittered and on the way to despair and madness, having died in *Die schöne Müllerin* only a physical death, not the spiritual death of the later cycle. These songs of young love and romantic desperation reveal that charm and delicacy which are at the heart of one aspect of their composer's genius.

Among the single songs of 1823 are 'Auf dem Wasser zu singen' (To be Sung on the Waters, D.774), one of Schubert's most delightful water songs, its accompaniment suggesting a rippling brook, and the serene setting of Rückert's 'Du bist die Ruh' (D.776), mentioned earlier.

After the failure of *Rosamunde*, Schubert never again made any serious attempt to write for the theatre, other than one or two sketches for an abortive opera project with Bauernfeld, *Der Graf von Gleichen* (Count von Gleichen, D.918), in the summer of 1827. At the beginning of 1824, he renewed his interest in chamber music, which he had neglected for some two or three years, and produced a number of superb chamber works. These were preceded by one which is somewhat less than superb, though it is a pleasant enough piece: a set of variations for flute and piano (D.802), composed for the flautist

Ferdinand Bogner (who the following year married Barbara Fröhlich). The variations were based on the melody of the song 'Trockne Blumen' from the *Schöne Müllerin* cycle.

The three really fine chamber works, each a mature masterpiece, are the String Quartets in A minor (D.804) and D minor (D.810) and the Octet (D.803), all three written in the first two months of the year. Schwind kept Schober informed of Schubert's activities at this time. They included a party for his birthday (31 January) at which Schubert slept, surrounded by tipsy friends. Ten days later, 'Schubert now keeps a fortnight's fast and confinement. He looks much better, and is very bright, very comically hungry, and writes quartets and German dances and variations without number.'

The A minor Quartet of 1824 is a work dear to all who love the music of Schubert, for it is one of those quintessentially Schubertian compositions, like the 'Unfinished' Symphony, *Die schöne Müllerin*, or indeed the companion chamber music works of 1824. A work of lyrical beauty and emotional power, it reveals itself at first hearing: it is not intellectually demanding in the manner of a late Beethoven quartet. Its poetic slow movement is based on the entr'acte in B flat from the *Rosamunde* music which Schubert had written only some months earlier; the failure of *Rosamunde* on the stage had probably suggested to him that he would be wise to salvage some of that score for use elsewhere.

The second quartet which Schubert worked on early in 1824 (though he did not complete it until the beginning of 1826) is the famous D minor Quartet (D.810), whose slow movement is a set of variations on the melody associated with the character of Death in the 1817 song 'Der Tod und das Mädchen' (Death and the Maiden). The title of the song not surprisingly became associated throughout the nineteenth century with the entire quartet, and commentators tended to read fanciful and sentimental death-related meanings into every movement. There is, however, no reason to connect the D minor Quartet with thoughts of death. It was not unusual for Schubert to use the melodies of his songs in instrumental compositions, but he chose those melodies for musical reasons divorced from their texts.

The fact that all four movements of the quartet are in a minor key ought to make for monotony, but curiously does not. To listen to this work is to enter its world and to surrender completely to it. The D minor Quartet is not only one of Schubert's greatest compositions in the realm of chamber music but indeed one of the finest achievements of the Romantic spirit in music.

The Octet was commissioned by Ferdinand, Count Troyer, an excellent clarinettist who was chief steward to the Archduke Rudolf. Troyer was in search of a work that could be performed by the Archduke's musicians, and stipulated to Schubert that it should be modelled on Beethoven's Septet of 1799–1800, a work which was still very popular in Vienna. Schubert obliged: there are a number of similarities between Beethoven's Septet and Schubert's Octet, which was given its first performance in the spring at Count Troyer's residence with Troyer himself playing the clarinet part, and Ignaz Schuppanzigh the first violin. (Schuppanzigh, a famous Viennese violinist, was Beethoven's friend and an important interpreter of his music.)

The Octet, a lengthy piece taking nearly an hour to perform, is scored for string quartet, double-bass, clarinet, horn and bassoon. A genial, indeed lovable, work in six movements, in character some-what like a divertimento, the Octet is today very popular. However, it received only two performances during Schubert's lifetime: its first, private performance at Count Troyer's residence, and then a public concert at the Musikverein in April 1827, organized by Schuppanzigh. The amiable theme of its fourth movement is adapted from a duet in Schubert's 1815 operetta, *Die Freunde von Salamanka*, which the composer was by now fairly certain was not likely to be heard in its original context. Only at the beginning of its final movement does the Octet admit moments of despondency. For most of its length it reveals Schubert in his most *gemütlich* vein.

'Schubert is quite well,' wrote Schwind to Schober on 22 February. 'He has given up his wig, and reveals a charming cygnet's down. . . . Of the *Schöne Müllerin* songs the first book has been published.' It was the carnival season, and Schubert, his hair beginning to grow again, was to be seen at several balls and parties, for many of which he wrote waltzes and other dances for the piano. Schwind wrote to Schober again on 6 March:

Schubert is pretty well already. He says that after a few days of the new treatment he felt how his complaint broke up and everything was different. He still lives one day on panada [bread boiled to a pulp and flavoured with sugar or nutmeg], and the next on cutlets, and lavishly drinks tea, goes bathing a good deal besides, and is superhumanly industrious. A new quartet is to be performed at Schuppanzigh's, who is quite enthusiastic and is said to have rehearsed particularly well. He has now long been at work on the octet, with the greatest zeal. If you go to see him during the day, he says 'Hello, how are you? – Good!' and goes on writing, whereupon you depart.

Schubert had, in fact, finished the Octet five days before the date of Schwind's letter. The 'new quartet' was the A minor (D.804), which Schubert dedicated to Schuppanzigh, whose quartet gave the first performance at one of the violinist's subscription concerts on 14 March. 'Schubert's quartet has been performed,' wrote Schwind, 'rather slowly in his opinion, but very purely and tenderly. It is on the whole very smooth, but written in such a way that the tune remains in one's mind, as with the songs, all feeling and thoroughly expressive. It got much applause, especially the minuet, which is extraordinarily tender and natural. A mandarin next to me thought it affected and devoid of style. I should just like to see Schubert affected! A single hearing, what can that mean to the likes of us, let alone to such a gobbler-up of notes? Afterwards we had Beethoven's famous septet.'

Although he had not kept a diary since the summer of 1816, Schubert seems to have done so again for a few days in March 1824. The pages, which were published some months after his death, read as follows:

25 March
Sorrow sharpens the understanding and strengthens the character, whereas happiness seldom troubles about the former and only makes for weakness or frivolity in the latter.

With all my heart I hate that narrow-mindedness which makes so many wretched people believe that only what they happen to be doing is best, and that everything else is worthless. One kind of beauty should inspire a man throughout his life, it is true; but the glow of that single inspiration should illuminate everything else.

27 March
No one to feel the other's grief, no one to understand the other's joy! People imagine that they can reach one another, but in reality they only pass one another by. Oh what torture for those who realize this!

What I have created is born of my understanding of music and of my own sorrow: that which sorrow alone has produced seems to please the world least of all.

28 March
One step alone divides the sublime from the ridiculous, and the greatest

wisdom from the grossest stupidity.

Man comes into the world armed with faith, which is far superior to knowledge and understanding: for in order to understand something, one must first of all believe in it. Faith is that higher basis on which weaker intellect erects the first pillars of conviction.

Reason is nothing more than analysed faith.

29 March

O imagination! Man's greatest treasure, inexhaustible source at which both art and learning come to drink! O remain with us still, though recognized and venerated only by the few, so that we may be safeguarded from so-called enlightenment, that hideous skeleton without flesh or blood!

[Undated] 2 o'clock at night

Enviable Nero! You were strong enough to destroy a corrupt people with the sound of stringed instruments and with song!

Eduard von Bauernfeld, in his recollections of Schubert written in 1869, suggested that the occasion for this last note was a violent altercation between the composer and some members of the Vienna Opera House orchestra:

It was on a summer's afternoon and, with Franz Lachner and others, we had strolled over to Grinzing for the *Heuriger* [new wine] to which Schubert was especially partial, though I was quite unable to acquire a taste for its acute tartness. We sat over our wine, indulging in lively conversation, and it was not until the dusk of the evening that we walked back; I wanted to go straight home, as I was living in an outlying suburb at that time, but Schubert dragged me forcibly to an inn, and I was not even spared the coffee-house afterwards, at which he was in the habit of winding up the evening, or rather the late hours of the night.

It was already 1 o'clock, and an extremely lively musical discussion had arisen over the hot punch. Schubert emptied glass after glass and had reached a sort of elated state in which, more eloquent than usual, he was expounding to Lachner and me all his plans for the future. At this point a singular misfortune had to bring a couple of professional artists, celebrated members of the Opera House orchestra, into the coffee-house. As these people came in, Schubert stopped short in the middle of his impassioned discourse; his brow puckered, his small grey eyes gleamed out fiercely from behind his spectacles, which he pushed restlessly to and fro. But scarcely had the musicians caught sight of the master when they rushed up to him, grasped him by the hands, paid him a thousand compliments and almost smothered him with flattery. Finally it transpired that they were extremely anxious to have a new composition for their concert, with solo passages for their particular instruments, and they were sure that Maestro Schubert would prove accommodating, etc.

But the master turned out to be anything but accommodating; he remained silent. After repeated entreaties he said suddenly: 'No! For you I will write nothing.'

'Nothing for us?' asked the men, taken aback.

'No! Not on any account.'

'And why not, Herr Schubert?' came the rejoinder, in rather a nettled tone. 'I think we are just as much artists as you are! No better ones are to be found in the whole of Vienna.'

'Artists!' cried Schubert, hurriedly draining his last glass of punch and getting up from the table. Then the little man pulled his hat down over his ears and faced the virtuosi, one of whom was tall of stature and the other more inclined to stoutness, as though threatening them. 'Artists?' he repeated. 'Musical hacks are what you are! Nothing else! One of you bites at the brass mouthpiece of his wooden stick and the other blows out his cheeks on the horn! Do you call that art? It's a trade, a knack that earns money, and nothing more! You, artists! Don't you know what the great Lessing says? How can anyone spend his whole life doing nothing but bite on a piece of wood with holes in it! That's what he said – (turning to me) or something of the kind! Didn't he? (Once more to the virtuosi:) You call yourselves artists? Blowers and fiddlers are what you are, the whole lot of you! I am an artist. I! I am Schubert, Franz Schubert, whom everybody knows and recognizes! Who has written great things and beautiful things that you don't begin to understand! And who is going to write still more beautiful things – (to Lachner:) that is so, my friend, isn't it? – the most beautiful things. Cantatas and quartets, operas and symphonies! Because I am not just a composer of *Ländler*, as the stupid newspapers say and as the stupid people repeat – I am Schubert! Franz Schubert! And don't you forget it! And if the word "art" is mentioned, it is *I* they are talking about, not you worms and insects, who demand solos for yourselves that I shall never write for you – and I know very well why! You crawling, gnawing worms that ought to be crushed under my foot – the foot of the man who is reaching to the stars – *sublimi feriam sidera vertice* – (to me:) translate that for them! To the stars, I say, while you poor puffing worms wriggle in the dust and with the dust are scattered like dust and rot!!'

A tirade like this, probably much worse, but substantially just as I have given it, was flung at the heads of the dumbfounded virtuosi, who stood there gaping, unable to find a word in reply, while Lachner and I endeavoured to get the overwrought composer away from the scene of the incident, which, to say the least, was unpleasant. With soothing words we brought him home.

The next morning I hurried round to my friend's to see how things were, as his condition had seemed to me serious. I found Schubert still in bed, fast asleep, with his spectacles on his head as usual.

In the room his clothes of the previous day lay strewn about in wild disorder. On the writing-table lay a half-written sheet of paper, with a sea of ink spilled over it from the overturned inkwell. On the paper was written, '2 o'clock at night' – there followed a few half-confused aphorisms, violent outbursts of feeling. There was no doubt he had written them down yesterday, after the violent scene.

Although one can hardly fail to sympathize with the innocent musicians who had done nothing to bring such a torrent of abuse down upon their heads, there is a certain magnificence in Schubert's uncharacteristic outburst, compounded of drink, despair and disease. There was somewhere, waiting to be released, an aspect of Schubert quite different from the gentle, unassuming, genial fellow which was that part of his personality he generally revealed to his friends and the world. Schubert had earned the right to his tirade.

That his state of mind and of health was at best variable at this time can be deduced from Schubert's despondent letter to Leopold Kupelwieser, addressed to him in Rome (whither he had gone to study painting) care of the *Café Greco*. The letter is dated 31 March 1824:

Dear Kupelwieser,
For a long time now I have felt the urge to write to you, but could never hit upon the when and where. Now comes an opportunity through Smirsch, and at last I am able to pour out my whole heart to someone again. You are so good and faithful, you are sure to forgive me things which others might take in very bad part. To be brief, I feel myself to be the most unhappy and wretched creature in the world. Picture to yourself someone whose health will never be right again, and who in sheer despair over this does everything to make it worse instead of better; picture to yourself, I say, someone whose most brilliant hopes have come to nothing, someone to whom love and friendship have nothing to offer but bitterness, someone whose inspiration (whose creative inspiration at least) for all that is beautiful threatens to fail, and then ask yourself if that is not a miserable and unhappy being.

'Meine Ruh ist hin, mein Herz ist schwer, ich finde sie nimmer und nimmermehr' [My peace is gone, my heart is sore, I shall find it never and nevermore]. That could be my daily song now, for every night, when I go to bed, I hope never to awaken again, and each morning I am only recalled to yesterday's grief. So I pass my days, joyless and friendless, except when Schwind comes now and again to see me and brings with him a ray of light from those sweet days of the past. Our circle [reading circle], as you probably know already, has dealt itself its own death-blow by swelling its ranks with a rowdy chorus of beer-drinkers and sausage-eaters, and it is being dissolved in two days' time – though I myself have hardly ever attended it since you went away. Leidesdorf, whom I have got to know very well, is a really thoughtful and good-hearted man, but of such a melancholy disposition that I am afraid in this respect his company may have influenced me rather too much. Things are going badly with him as with me, and therefore we never have any money. They declared that your brother's opera was unplayable – he made a mistake in leaving the theatre – and, together with my music, it was not accepted. Castelli's opera *Die Verschworenen* [The Conspirators] has been set to music in Berlin by a local composer, and enthusiastically received, so it seems that once again I have composed two operas for nothing! I have written very few new songs, but I have tried my hand at several kinds of instrumental music and have composed two quartets for violins, viola and violoncello, and an octet, and so prepare the way for grand symphonic works. The latest news in Vienna is that Beethoven is giving a concert at which his new symphony, three movements from the new Mass, and a new overture will be performed. I too should like to give a similar concert next year, God willing. I must end now so as not to use up too much paper, and kiss you 1,000 times. If you were to write to me about your present mood of inspiration, and about your life in general, nothing could more greatly please

My address would then be
c/o Sauer and Leidesdorf's
music shop, for I am
going to Hungary with
Esterházy at the beginning of May.

your
faithful friend,
Frz. Schubert.
Fare well!
Very well!!

(The quotation in the letter is, of course, from the poem in Goethe's *Faust* which Schubert had set as 'Gretchen am Spinnrade'. 'Your brother's opera' is *Fierrabras*. Castelli's libretto, which Schubert had himself set, had now been used by the Berlin horn player, oboist and composer Georg Abraham Schneider [1770–1839]. Despite what Schubert says about its reception, Schneider's opera was performed only twice in Berlin.)

The tone of Schubert's letter to Kupelwieser is despairing, but it appears that his depression came and went quite frequently at this stage of his illness. Often he was for weeks on end his old cheerful self. However, it is clear that, to Schubert, his periods of comparative happiness must have seemed like small oases in a desert of misery. According to Schwind, on 10 April, Schubert was 'almost wholly well', but in Schwind's letter to Schober four days later one reads:

'Schubert is not very well. He has pains in his left arm so that he cannot play the pianoforte at all. Apart from that he is in good spirits.'

On 25 May Schubert departed on the mail-coach for Hungary, where he again joined the Esterházy family in their summer castle, as music tutor to the family. He took with him a libretto by his friend Dr Bernhardt, based on the epic poem *Die bezauberte Rose* (The Enchanted Rose), but appears not to have worked on it at Zseliz. (Later, Bauernfeld was to produce a libretto on the same subject for Schubert.) He had also been asked by the management of the Theater an der Wien to provide the music for a play, *Der kurze Mantel* (The Short Cloak), by Johann Gabriel Seidl, and in July the libretto was forwarded to him in Hungary. However, Schubert seems not to have written this music, and when the play was produced in November it was with music by Philipp Jakob Riotte (Act I), Josef von Blumenthal (Act II) and Ignaz von Seyfried (Act III).

Schubert's brother Ferdinand wrote most affectionately to him from Vienna on 3 July, and mentioned his surprise at hearing the mechanical clock at the inn, *Zur ungarischen Krone* (The Hungarian Crown), playing tunes by brother Franz: 'I felt so strange at that moment, I hardly knew where I was: it did not cheer me up by any means at all; rather did it strike my heart and soul with such an anxious pain and longing that, at last, melancholy threw its veil over me and I involuntarily shed – .'

The mechanical clock at the Hungarian Crown had, in fact, been playing Schubert since 1822. Apparently in the meantime it had acquired a few more cylinders with Schubert melodies, mainly dance tunes. In his letter, Ferdinand also mentioned that a Herr Hugelmann had called at the Schubert house to collect some scores of Mozart quartets which he had earlier loaned to Franz:

However, as I did not find them after searching three times, I could not satisfy his request. After that, he came to me twice more, once in the training-college corridor, and once at my home, where he gave me not a little annoyance by inveighing so violently against your thoughtlessness, blustering, screaming and using such coarse expressions that I very much cursed the honour of his acquaintance. Be good enough, therefore, to let me know where the music in question might possibly be, so that I can pacify this raging monster.

Schubert replied to Ferdinand from Zseliz in a long letter begun on 16 July and finished on the 18th:

Beloved Brother,

You can take my word for it that I was really rather hurt at not receiving news either from home or from you for such a long time. Neither do I hear anything from Leidesdorf, although I wrote to him. Do go and look him up in his music shop, and get him to send me what I asked for. (You will have to be really forceful with him, though, for he is rather negligent by nature.) You might also enquire about the publication of Volume III of the *Schöne Müllerin* songs. I see nothing in the paper about it. The formation of your quartet astonishes me, and all the more since you have induced Ignaz to join!!! But it will be better for you to stick to quartets by other composers, for there is nothing in mine to commend them, except that perhaps they please you, who are pleased with anything of mine. Your thinking about me is what I like best about it, especially as my quartets do not seem to affect you as much as the waltzes at the *Ungarische Krone*. Was it only grief at my absence that drew tears from you, and could you not trust yourself to write the word? Or did you feel, on thinking of my person, oppressed by an ever incomprehensible longing, that its dark veil was closing about you too? Or did all the tears which you have seen me shed come into your mind again? Whatever it was, I feel in this moment more strongly than ever before that you are my closest friend, bound to me by every fibre of my being! Lest these lines should perhaps lead you wrongly to suppose that I am not well, or in poor spirits, let me hasten to assure you of the contrary. True, that blessed time is over when everything appeared to us in a nimbus of youthful glory, and we have to face instead the bitter facts of existence, which however I endeavour to beautify as far as possible with my own imagination (for which God be thanked!). We turn instinctively to places where we found happiness before, but in vain, for happiness is to be found only within ourselves. I have had an unpleasant disappointment in renewing here an experience I had already undergone at Steyr, although I am now better able to find inner peace and happiness than I was then. A grand sonata and some variations on a theme of my own, both for four hands, which I have already composed, will prove this to you. The variations have met with particular success. As regards the songs you handed to Mohn, I comfort myself with the thought that only a few of them seem good to me, for instance those in the set which includes 'Das Geheimnis' [The Secret, D.250], the 'Wanderers Nachtlied' [Wayfarer's Night Song, D.224] and 'Der entsühnte Orest' [Orestes Absolved, D.699], not 'entführte' [abducted], a mistake that made me laugh very much. Try at least to get these back as soon as possible.

Has Kupelwieser not said what he thinks of doing with the opera? Or where he is sending it?

Through an oversight I have brought here with me the quintets (not quartets) belonging to that jackass Hugeltier [i.e. 'Hugel-animal' instead of 'Hugel-man'], and, by heaven! he shall not have them back until he atones for his disgusting rudeness by a written or oral apology. If, moreover, I get an opportunity to administer a good dressing-down to this dirty swine, I shall not hesitate to take the fullest advantage of it. But enough of that miserable creature!

That you are so well makes me all the happier, in that I hope to enjoy to the utmost the same good health through the coming winter.

Remember me most lovingly to our parents, brothers and sisters, and friends. A thousand kisses both to you and your good wife and children. Write as soon as possible, and keep very, very well!!!
P.S. How are Karl and Ignaz? If only they would write to me.

With eternal affection,
Your brother Franz

P.S. Has Resi perhaps already presented the world with another inhabitant?

Helmina von Chézy, the ill-fated authoress of the texts of Weber's *Euryanthe* and of *Rosamunde, Princess of Cyprus*, wrote to Schubert, sending him a copy of her revised *Rosamunde*, which she hoped still might be staged again elsewhere, and asking him what fee he would accept as a lump sum for his music. (He would have been paid by the Theater an der Wien only for the two performances at that theatre.) Schubert replied from Zseliz on 5 August:

Madam,
Convinced as I was of the value of *Rosamunde* from the moment I read it, I am very glad that you have undertaken to remove, and I am sure to the best advantage, certain minor defects which only a prejudiced audience could have censured so severely, and I feel especially honoured at receiving a revised copy of the same. As to the fee for the music, I do not feel I can fix it at less than 100 florins (Assimilated Currency) without being derogatory to the music itself. Should this price, however, be too high, I would ask you, madam, to name one yourself, without diverging too greatly from the amount I have suggested, and to have it sent in my absence to the enclosed address.

With the greatest respect,
Yours,
Frz. Schubert

Address: Franz Schubert, teacher at the school-house in the Rossau, in Vienna.

On receipt of this tactful epistle, Madame von Chézy must have agreed to Schubert's fee and paid it, for after his death she offered both play and music to theatre managements in Stuttgart and Karlsruhe.

(Both theatres rejected the offer.)

In August, Schubert wrote to Schwind in Vienna:

Dear Swind,

At last, after three months, a letter from Schubert, you will say. True, it is a pretty long time, but as my life here is as uneventful as possible, I have very little news for you or the others. Indeed, were it not for my longing to know how you and my other close friends are faring – and above all to hear how things are with Schober and Kupelwieser – then, forgive me for saying it, but I might perhaps not have written even now. How is Schober's enterprise succeeding? Is Kupelwieser in Vienna or still in Rome? Is the reading circle still holding together or, as I suspect, has it completely gone to pieces? What are you working at??? I am still in good health, thank God, and I should be very content here if only I had you and Kupelwieser with me, but as it is, in spite of the attractive star, I feel at times a desperate longing for Vienna. I hope to see you again by the end of September. I have composed a grand sonata, and variations for four hands, which latter have met with a particularly good reception here, but as I do not entirely trust Hungarian taste I shall leave it to you and the Viennese to decide their true merit. How is Leidesdorf? Is he making good, or is he barking up the wrong tree? Please answer all these questions as exactly and as quickly as possible. You have no idea how much I long for a letter from you. And since there is so much for you to tell me, about our friends, about Vienna, and a thousand other matters, whereas I have nothing to relate, it really would not have hurt you to have told me some of the news. But perhaps you did not know my address. Above all, I lay it on your conscience to scold Leidesdorf *scandaleusement* for neither answering my letter nor sending me what I asked him for. What the devil does he mean by it? The *Schöne Müllerin* songs are making very slow progress, too: a volume comes out every three months. And now goodbye, remember me to anyone you will, and (I repeat) write very soon, or else . . .

Your

faithful friend,

Frz. Schubert

(Schubert addresses his friend Schwind jokingly as 'Swind'. The 'attractive star' he refers to is probably his pupil, the young Countess Caroline Esterházy, who by now was nearly twenty. Schubert felt affectionately towards her, but he can hardly have seriously entertained the possibility of a love affair with someone who was not only the daughter of his employer but also socially far above him. He may, of course, have romanticized to his friends his feelings for the young lady. On the other hand, it is just possible that he is referring to Pepi, the chambermaid with whom he was undoubtedly on affectionate terms on his previous visit to Zseliz. Though whether he would have called Pepi an 'attractive star' is doubtful. The vocal quartet for mixed voices, 'Gebet' [Prayer, D.815], not one of Schubert's finest part-songs, was certainly written for Caroline Esterházy one day in September, Schubert being given the words by the countess at the family breakfast table and presenting his finished composition for rehearsal that evening in the drawing-room. Baron Schönstein, who sang the tenor part, had come from Vienna in August to join the family. He subsequently became a great Schubert enthusiast and a fine interpreter of his songs.)

The 'grand sonata' mentioned by Schubert in his letters from Zseliz is the work which was composed in June, and published post-humously under the title 'Grand Duo' (D.812). It is the supreme example of Schubert's epic style, a spacious work so broadly planned that its proportions suggest a symphony rather than a sonata. The nature of Schubert's writing for the piano is such as to suggest to some commentators that he may have been composing with an orchestra in mind. Much more likely is that the composer was seeking to discover what kind of orchestral effect he could achieve with a piano played by four hands. The andante is almost an act of homage to Beethoven, and the trio of the scherzo is a curious anticipation of the romantic style of Schumann.

Some time after Schubert's death, writers began to speculate as to whether the 'Grand Duo' might not be a piano reduction of the symphony which Schubert is known to have sketched in the summer of the following year, 1825, at Gmunden and Gastein. There is really no evidence to connect the so-called 'Gastein' Symphony with the 'Grand Duo' for piano which Schubert composed at the Esterházy estate at Zseliz in 1824, though this has not prevented several musicians from orchestrating the 'Grand Duo', among them the Austro-Hungarian violinist and composer Joseph Joachim in 1855, the English conductor Anthony Collins in 1939, and the Israeli pianist and conductor Karl Salomon in 1946.

The variations which Schubert says he composed at Zseliz are the Eight Variations on an Original Theme (D.813), a work for piano, four hands, which was published soon after he returned to Vienna. Schubert's masterpiece in variation form, it is music of great warmth and poetic feeling. A third piece for piano, four hands, was written at

Zseliz in September: the long and uneven *Divertissement à l'hongroise* (D.818). This Hungarian divertissement was published in Vienna in April 1826, and became fairly well known in the nineteenth century. It does not represent Schubert at his best: Wagner's ˙criticism of its triviality and Mendelssohn's of its rhythmic monotony are not entirely unjustified, though perhaps overstated. This divertissement is a charming and relaxed piece, written for the purposes of domestic music-making.

One further letter by Schubert survives from the summer of 1824. It is addressed to Schober in Breslau, and is dated 21 September:

Dear Schober,

I hear that you are not happy and that you have to get over a bad attack of despair. So Schwind writes to me. Although I am exceedingly grieved to hear this, I am not at all surprised, this being the lot of most intelligent people in this miserable world. And, after all, of what use is happiness, misery being the only stimulant left to us? If only we were together, you, Schwind, Kuppel [Kupelwieser] and I, any misfortune would be easy enough to bear, but instead we are all separated, each in a different corner, and that is what makes me really unhappy. I want to exclaim with Goethe: 'Ach, wer bringt die schönen Tage,/Jene holde Zeit zurück!' [Ah, who will bring those fair days, that sweet time back!]. That time when, in our intimate circle, each showed the other, with motherly shyness, the children of his art, and waited, not without apprehension, for the verdict to be pronounced by affection and truth; that time when each inspired the other with a common striving towards the ideal that animated one and all. Now I sit here alone in the depths of Hungary, whither I unfortunately let myself be enticed for a second time, without a single person near me to whom I can really talk. Since you went away I have written scarcely any songs, but have tried my hand at several instrumental things. Heaven knows what will happen to my opera! Although I have been in good health for the past five months, my spirits suffer from your absence and Kuppel's, and I have very wretched days sometimes. In one of these fits of depression, when the sterility and insignificance that characterize the life of today were painfully brought home to me, there came into my head the following verses, which I am showing to you only because I know that you treat even my weaknesses with love and indulgence:

COMPLAINT TO THE PEOPLE

Undone art thou, O youth of this our day!
Wasted and spent the countless people's starkness,
Not one stands out from all that mass of darkness
Which, without meaning, floods along the way.

It is too great a pain that gnaws at me,
Of all my one-time strength the last poor fraction;
It is the age that dooms me to inaction,
Preventing all the greatness that might be.

Decrepit, old, the people crawl around,
The deeds of youth seem to them but a vision,
On their own golden rhymes they cast derision,
Nor heed the mighty scene behind the sound.

O powerful art, the sacred task is thine!
Hold up thy mirror to the noble past.
Thy strength alone can sorrow's strength outlast,
And mock its triumph over our decline.

Up to the time of writing, things are going very badly with Leidesdorf. He cannot pay, and no one buys either my things or anybody else's, but only wretched fashionable stuff.

I have now acquainted you pretty well with how matters stand with me, and I anxiously await the earliest possible news of your own affairs. What I should like best is for you to come back to Vienna again. That you are in good health I do not doubt.

And now fare you very well, and write to me as soon as you can.

Your
Schubert
Adieu!!!

Schubert left Zseliz on 16 October, and travelled to Vienna with Baron Schönstein, who took his own carriage but borrowed Count Esterházy's horses. They made an overnight stop at Diószeg; in a letter to Esterházy from Vienna a few days later, Schönstein states that 'the lackadaisical Schubert managed to smash the window at the back of the coach as soon as we were out of Diószeg, whereby the ghastliest of cold winds was given free play about our ears'. Schubert's spirits rose as soon as he was back in his beloved Vienna. 'Schubert is here,' Schwind wrote to Schober on 8 November, 'well and divinely frivolous, rejuvenated by delight and pain and a pleasant life.' The composer returned to his father's school-house to live, and remained there until early the following year.

In November, at the request of Vincenz Schuster, who had invented a new instrument, the arpeggione, Schubert composed the Sonata for Piano and Arpeggione (D.821), which Schuster first performed some weeks later. The arpeggione, also known as bowed guitar, violoncello guitar or *guitare d'amour*, was a six-stringed instrument played with a bow, which was in use for no more than ten years or so. Schubert's sonata, though a minor work and hastily written, is not unattractive in its *gemütlich* Biedermeier style. It is occasionally played by cellists, and has also been arranged for violin or viola.

The Austrian soprano Anna Milder-Hauptmann (for whom Beethoven had written the rôle of Leonore in *Fidelio*) was now a member of the Berlin Court Opera. In December 1824 she wrote to Schubert, enclosing a poem which she hoped he would set to music for her to sing, and offering to use her influence to secure a production of one of his operas in Berlin. Schubert did not set the poem, but instead sent her a song he had already composed, as well as a copy of the full score of his opera *Alfonso und Estrella*, which, however, was not accepted for production in Berlin.

Schubert and Schwind had now resumed their former intimacy, and were said by their friends to be almost inseparable. Schubert led a more active social life than he had for some time, and also, before the end of the year, began to extend his business relationships. A new publisher, Thaddäus Weigl, included in a collection of forty waltzes which he published on 22 December an arrangement for solo piano of a delightful *Ländler* in E flat (D.366, No. 17) which Schubert had composed for four hands (D.814, No. 1) the previous July at Zseliz, as the last of a set of seventeen *Ländler*. (Schubert made little distinction between the *Ländler* and the waltz, both dances in 3/4 time.) This was the beginning of an agreeable business arrangement by which Weigl published several important works by Schubert, whose music was now appearing in the lists of several publishers. In February 1825 Diabelli & Co. published not only songs by Schubert but also arrangements by other hands of his *Deutsche Tänze* and *Écossaises*. Schubert had written these for solo piano: the arrangements were for piano duet, and also for violin and piano. The publisher's advertisement for the songs in the *Wiener Zeitung* of 11 February claims that 'the excellence of Schubert's songs is already so generally acknowledged that they no longer require any recommendation'.

In February Schubert moved once again from his father's school-house to take rooms in a house next to the Karlskirche, so that he could be close to his 'beloved', Schwind, who lived next door. He remained there until the summer of the following year, except for the time he spent travelling with Vogl in the summer of 1825. It was in February, too, that the period of Schubert's close relationship with Eduard von Bauernfeld (1802–1890) began. Bauernfeld was twenty-three (five years younger than Schubert), a light-hearted youth who had yet to make his name as playwright and translator. He was, at this time, still a student of philosophy. He had met Schubert previously on several occasions, but it was after Schwind and Schubert paid him a visit one evening in February that their friendship blossomed. On that evening Bauernfeld read his unperformed and unpublished drama, *Madera*, to the others, and he and Schubert played piano duets. 'Then to the inn and coffee-house', Bauernfeld wrote in his diary.

Schubert's reputation grew steadily during 1825. His songs and quartets were performed at concerts in the Musikverein, more works were published, and the Schubertiads became popular once again, with Vogl taking an active part. The Schubertiads were held at all the usual houses, and also now at the house of Sophie Müller (1803–30), a popular Viennese actress and singer who, according to Anselm Hüttenbrenner, sang Schubert's songs 'most touchingly'. Sophie Müller lived at Hietzing, near the palace of Schönbrunn; Schubert became a frequent visitor there, bringing with him his most recent songs, which he and Sophie would play and sing for hours on end. On 3 March, the actress noted in her diary: 'After lunch Schubert came and brought a new song, "Die junge Nonne" [The Young Nun, D.828]; later, Vogl came, and I sang it to him; it is splendidly composed.'

'Die junge Nonne' is indeed splendidly composed: a superb dramatic landscape of the soul, it is one of Schubert's finest songs, contrasting a fierce tempest with the storm raging within the heart of a young nun. At the end, the nun's repeated 'Alleluja' asserts that her conflict has been resolved, though the bass octaves in the piano part suggest otherwise.

Two piano sonatas date from the early months of 1825: the Sonata in A minor (D.845), a restrained yet poetic work, and the Sonata in C major (D.840), known as the 'Reliquie'. This latter is planned on a larger scale than its predecessors, but was left unfinished. Its third and fourth movements have been completed by Badura-Skoda. A magnificent work, it deserves to be far better known than it is. Its first two movements can bear comparison with that other marvellous torso, the 'Unfinished' Symphony, and Badura-Skoda's sensitive completion of the work has helped it to become more accessible.

At the end of March Vogl went off on his annual visit to his country seat at Steyr, and Schubert joined him there two months later. Three settings of Goethe poems, dedicated to the poet, were published by Diabelli & Co. at the beginning of June. These were 'An Schwager Kronos' (To Coachdriver Chronos, D.369); 'An Mignon' (To Mignon, D.161); and 'Ganymed' (D.544). Copies were sent by the publisher to Goethe in Weimar, together with a letter which Schubert must have left with Diabelli before he went off to Upper Austria. The letter to Goethe reads:

Your Excellency,
Should I succeed with the dedication of these settings of your poems in expressing my boundless admiration of Your Excellency, and at the same time in earning perhaps something of respect for my unworthy self, the gratification of this wish would be for me the happiest event of my life.

With the greatest respect,
Your most humble servant,
Franz Schubert

Like Josef von Spaun's letter to Goethe on Schubert's behalf nine years earlier, this remained unanswered.

There appears to have been a temporary rift between Schubert and Schwind at this time, perhaps due to young Schwind's jealousy of Schubert's other friends. In March, Bauernfeld noted in his diary an occasion on which, for no apparent reason, 'Moritz [von Schwind] behaved with studied rudeness towards [Vogl]'; and in May he wrote, somewhat obscurely: 'Schubert to Steyr. Moritz complains about him: "If anything is done expressly to spite me, I can only feel disgusted." (The cap fitted me too.)' The affair is hardly clarified by Schwind's references to it in a letter he wrote Schubert on 2 July:

Let me be frank and confess to you what it is that still rankles. You will no doubt remember that you did not come to Hönig's last time. I should be quite idiotic if I took offence, nay if I even allowed it to annoy me, if you do as you please and take no notice of what I happen to want. Still, had you thought of how much affection was awaiting you, you would have come. Little as I shall allow myself to be deterred from meaning to you and doing for you what had so far always been acceptable to you, I am almost afraid of getting as much pleasure from you, seeing how ill I have succeeded all these years in overcoming your mistrust and your fear lest you should not be loved and understood. That may be the reason for some malicious pranks which I was unable to refrain from, much as they hurt me myself. It is no doubt altogether this sort of thing which is responsible for that accursed spirit of mockery. Why should I not say it? Ever since I knew you and Schober, I have been accustomed to find myself understood in all things. Then others come, mocking and spying out associations and thoughts of which they have caught some glimpse or other; we let them carry on at first, then take part in it ourselves, and, man not being made of diamond, we lose irreplaceable things for the despicable price of merely tolerable intercourse. If that is too bitter, I was unhappily often too complaisant. I beg you to give me your answer to this, as rude and candid as I am myself, for anything is better than these torturing thoughts, of which I cannot rid myself.

Schubert appears not to have replied to this sad outpouring of a heart which loves and fears it is not loved in return, and Schwind's embarrassed references to it in a further letter are incomprehensible. Their friendship was not for long impaired: by the autumn the quarrel, if there had been one, was forgotten.

Vogl and Schubert spent four months in Upper Austria, travelling, for the most part, together. From 30 May to 4 June, Schubert is known to have been at Steyr, during which time he paid a short visit to Linz. From 4 June to 15 July he was in Gmunden, after which he returned to Linz for ten days, and was in Steyr again from 25 July to 13 August. He was in the beautiful mountain spa of Bad Gastein from 14 August to 4 September and, after return visits of several days each to Gmunden and Steyr, he and Vogl were back in Vienna on 3 October. Throughout the tour, Schubert encountered many old friends and admirers of his music, and made several new acquaintances.

Among the works composed during the summer were five songs (D.837, 838, 839, 843, 846) and two part-songs (D.835, 836) from Sir Walter Scott's novel *The Lady of the Lake*. Schubert used an Upper Austrian lake, Traunsee, as inspiration, in place of Scott's Loch Katrine. One of the songs was the beautiful and now universally known 'Ave Maria' (D.839). From Linz, on 21 July, Schubert wrote to Spaun, who had paid a brief visit to his family in Linz, but had left to return to his post in Lemberg (Lvov) the day Schubert arrived:

Dear Spaun,
You can imagine how annoyed I am at having to write a letter in Linz to you in Lemberg!!! The devil take this infamous duty that tears friends so cruelly apart when they have scarcely sipped the cup of friendship. Here I am sitting in Linz, sweating my heart out in this preposterous heat, a whole volume of

new songs with me, and you are not here! Aren't you ashamed of yourself? Linz without you is like a body without a soul, or a horseman without a head, or soup without salt. If Jägermayr did not keep such good beer, and there were not so passable a wine on the Schlossberg, I should really have to hang myself on the promenade, with this superscription: 'Died of grief for the departed soul of Linz.' As you see, I am treating the rest of Linz very unfairly, for in the company of your sister, Ottenwalt and Max, I am having a very pleasant time at your mother's house, and I seem to see your spirit flash from out of the body of many another Linzer. My only fear is that this spirit of yours may gradually flicker out, and then one would burst out of sheer dejection. It is really distressing how bone-dry and prosaic everything in the world is becoming nowadays, how the majority of people, too, look on unperturbed at this state of affairs, and even thrive on it, and how comfortably they slide down through the mire into the abyss. To go upwards is naturally harder, but the guiding hand of someone superior could easily make something even out of this crowd. Well, do not go grey with worry at being so far away from us. Defy the foolish fate that has taken you there, and show your scorn by letting your fertile fancies blossom like a flower garden: reveal your divine descent, and diffuse life-giving warmth throughout the frozen North. Sorrow is not worthy to creep into a noble heart! Away with it, and trample under foot the vulture that would gnaw at your vitals.

Of Schober, we have had some odd, almost comical news. To begin with, I read in the Vienna *Theaterzeitung* of 'a female with the pseudonymous name of Torupsohn'??? What can that mean? Surely he has not married? That would be a bit of a joke. Secondly, his best role is said to be that of the clown in the travesty of *Aline*. Rather a mighty fall from all his expectations and plans! And thirdly, he is said to be returning to Vienna. I wonder what he will do there. However, I am looking forward very much to seeing him again, and hope that he will enrich once more our sadly depleted society with a livelier and wiser being. I have been in Upper Austria since 20 May, and was very vexed to hear that you had left Linz a few days earlier. I should have liked so much to see you once more before the devil took you to Poland. I stayed only fourteen days in Steyr, and then we (Vogl and I) went on to Gmunden where we spent a full six weeks very pleasantly. We lodged with Traweger, who has a magnificent pianoforte and is, as you know, a great admirer of my humble self. My life there was delightfully free and easy. At Councillor von Schiller's there was frequent music, among other things some of my new songs from Walter Scott's *Lady of the Lake*, the Hymn to the Virgin Mary in particular being approved by all and sundry. I am very glad that you are seeing something of young Mozart. Remember me to him. And now goodbye! My dear good Spaun! Think often of

your sincere friend,
Franz Schubert.

('Torupsohn' [Torupson] was the pseudonym adopted by Schober for his brief and inglorious stage career, Torop being the name of his birthplace in Sweden. The *Theaterzeitung* had referred to a 'pseudonymous Torupsohn who here makes her first appearance on the stage': 'her' must have been simply a mistake or misprint. 'Young Mozart' is Wolfgang Amadeus Mozart Jr, son of the composer.)

From Steyr on 25 July, Schubert wrote a long and informative letter to his father and his stepmother:

Dear Parents,

I justly deserve your reproach for my long silence but, as the present time offers very little of interest and I dislike writing empty words, you must forgive me for not offering an account of myself until I received your affectionate letter. I am very glad to hear that you are all in good health and, God be praised, I can now say the same. I am back again in Steyr, but have been in Gmunden for six weeks, where the surrounding country, which is heavenly, touched me very deeply, as did also the inhabitants, particularly the good Traweger. They all did me a world of good. I lived freely and easily at Traweger's, just as though I were at home. Later, after the appearance of Councillor von Schiller, who is monarch of the whole Salzkammergut, we (Vogl and I) had our meals every day at his house, and had music there, and also very frequently at Traweger's. My new songs from Walter Scott's *Lady of the Lake* especially had a great success. There was a good deal of surprise too at my piety, which I had expressed in a Hymn to the Blessed Virgin, which seems to have moved all hearts and created quite a devotional atmosphere. I fancy this is because my religious feeling is never forced, and I never compose hymns or prayers of this sort unless I am involuntarily overcome by a sense of devotion, and then the feeling is, as a rule, genuine and heartfelt. From Gmunden we went by way of Puchberg, where we met some acquaintances and stayed a few days, to Linz, where we spent eight days, partly in Linz itself and partly in Steyregg. In Linz I lodged at the Spauns' house, where they are still very sad·at Spaun (the one you know) being transferred to Lemberg. I wrote to him and pulled him up sharply for his weakness, though, if I were in his place, I suspect I should be even more miserable than he. In Steyregg we called on Countess Weissenwolf, who is a great admirer of my humble self, possesses everything I have written, and sings many of the songs very prettily too. The Walter Scott songs made such an extremely good impression on her that she made it clear that she would be by no means displeased if I were to dedicate them to her. But with the publication of these songs I intend to use a very different procedure from the usual one, which brings in so little profit. I feel that these songs, bearing as they do the celebrated name of Scott, are likely to arouse more curiosity and, if I add the English words, might also make me better known in England. If only honest dealing were possible with these d——d music publishers. But the wise and beneficent regulations of our Government have taken good care that the artist shall remain for ever the slave of these wretched money-grabbers.

As regards the letter from Mme Milder, the favourable reception of 'Suleika' gave me great pleasure, though I wish I could have had a look at the reviews myself to see if there was anything to be learned from them. A review, however favourable, can be at the same time ridiculous if the critic lacks the required understanding, which is not altogether rarely the case.

I have come across my compositions all over Upper Austria, but especially in the monasteries of St Florian and at Kremsmünster, where, assisted by an excellent pianist, I gave a very successful recital of my variations and marches for four hands. The variations from my new sonata for two hands met with special enthusiasm. These I played alone, and not unsuccessfully, for several people assured me that under my fingers the keys were transformed into singing voices, which, if it is true, pleases me very much, as I cannot abide the accursed thumping of the instrument to which even first-class pianists are addicted: it pleases neither the ear nor the heart. I am back in Steyr now, and should you wish to cheer me with a quick letter it would still reach me here, for we shall stay another 10 to 14 days, and then set out for Gastein, one of the most famous watering-places, about 3 days' journey from Steyr. I am looking forward very much to this journey, for in this way I shall get to know the most beautiful country, and on the way back we shall visit Salzburg too, which is renowned for its splendid position and surrounding country. We shall not get back from this expedition before the middle of September, and have then promised to re-visit Gmunden, Linz, Steyregg and Florian, so I shall hardly get to Vienna before the end of October. Will you therefore engage me my old rooms near the Karlskirche, and also please pay 28 florins, Viennese Currency, for them, which sum I shall gratefully refund you on arrival, for I have promised it already, and it is quite possible that I may get back earlier than I thought. Throughout the whole of June and half of July the weather here was very unsettled, then for 14 days it was so hot that I got quite thin merely from perspiring so much, and now it has rained for 4 days practically without ceasing. My best greetings to Ferdinand and his wife and children. I suppose he still crawls to the 'Cross' and cannot get rid of Dornbach. I am certain he has been ill 77 times again, and fancied himself 9 times at least on the point of death, as though dying were the worst that can happen to a man! If only he could see these marvellous mountains and lakes, whose aspects threaten to crush us or swallow us up, he would become less enamoured of the tiny span of human life, and would be ready joyfully to give his body to the earth, to be quickened by its incomprehensible forces into new life. What is Karl doing? Will he leave home or not? He must have plenty to do nowadays, for a married artist is obliged to produce both works of art and works of nature, and when both kinds are successful he is to be doubly congratulated, for that is no trifling performance! It is not for me! Ignaz is, I expect, at Hollpein's just now, for as he is there morning, noon and night, he will hardly be at home. I cannot refrain from admiring his perseverance, though I am not at all sure if it be a merit or otherwise, nor whether he is the more deserving thereby of heaven or hell. I wish he would enlighten me about that. Schneider and his Schneideress must take great care of the little Schneider or Schneideress now on the way. May the race of Schneiders become as innumerable as the sands of the sea! Only they must see to it that they produce no liars [Aufschneider], cutters [Zuschneider], slanderers [Ehrenabschneider] or cut-throats [Gurgelabschneider]. And now I must put an end at last to all this prattle, though I felt that I must make up for my long silence with an equally long letter. . . . A thousand kisses to Marie and Pepi and André, the little provost. Indeed, please remember me most kindly to everyone possible. Hoping for an answer soon, I remain, with all my love,

your
faithful son,
Franz.

(The 'Cross' to which Ferdinand 'still crawls' is the *Rotes Kreuz* [Red Cross] Inn, a haunt of the Schubert family, though Franz himself did not like it, for he suspected the wine there to be watered down. Schneider is Schubert's brother-in-law, whose name, meaning 'tailor', Schubert uses for his series of puns. Marie, Pepi and André are his stepsisters and stepbrother. The two-year-old André is 'the little provost' because he was fat, and reminded Schubert of a well-fed cleric.)

The idea, often encountered in books on the composer, that Schubert was an untutored simpleton through whom music unaccountably chose to flow must have been current even during his lifetime, for there is an interesting, indeed moving, passage in a letter from Anton Ottenwalt in Linz to Josef von Spaun, in which he refutes this false picture of the composer:

On Sunday, after Vogl had left at 9.30, [Schubert] remained with us: there were Max and I, Marie and Mama, who retired between 10 and 11 o'clock. We sat together until not far from midnight, and I have never seen him like this, nor heard: serious, profound, and as though inspired. How he talked of art, of poetry, of his youth, of friends and other people who matter, of the relationship of ideals to life, etc. I was more and more amazed at such a mind, of which it has been said that its artistic achievement is so unconscious, hardly

revealed to or understood by himself, and so on. Yet how simple was all this!
I cannot tell you of the extent and the unity of his convictions, but there were
glimpses of a world-view that is not merely acquired, and the share which
worthy friends may have in it by no means detracts from the individuality
shown by all this.

Schubert's favourite brother, Ferdinand, reproached the composer
for having travelled to the most beautiful parts of Austria without
him: 'That you have already visited the Salzkammergut is more than I
had supposed,' Ferdinand wrote on 4 August, 'since I hoped you
would travel through that wondrously beautiful region with me only
at the beginning of September. . . . Oh, you fortunate brother! Even
beautiful Salzburg with its glorious environs, and the famous, wild
watering-place of Gastein, discovered as long as 1,000 years ago, will
be visited by you. Well, I shall ask you for a nice, detailed description
of the latter.'

Ferdinand in due course received his detailed description, though he
had to wait until his brother returned to Vienna, for Schubert began a
letter to him from Gmunden on 12 September, continued it at Steyr on
the 21st, but failed to finish it, and handed what he had written to
Ferdinand in Vienna in October. (The text of this lengthy travel diary
will be found on pp. 188–92.)

Bauernfeld wrote to Schubert from Vienna in mid-September to
say that he and Schwind thought that, when Schubert returned to
Vienna, the three of them should find lodgings together. 'How are
you, fattest of friends?' he added. 'I suppose your belly will have
increased; may God preserve it and let it prosper.'

Schubert replied from Steyr, in a letter dated '18 or 19 September':

Dear Friend,
Your scribble had slipped indeed right out of my mind! All-destroying Time
and your own unconscionably hasty handwriting have brought things to this
pass! As regards the latter, I propose to pay you back in your own coin. As to
my quarters in Frühwirth's house, I mean to keep them on, and have already
tried through my family to let him know this, but it seems that they have
forgotten to do so, or else he is being over-anxious and fussy. In any case,
would you be so good, one or all of you, to pay him 25 Viennese florins on
my behalf, and to assure him that I shall be back without fail at the end of
October? As to setting up house together, I should be pleased enough to do
so, but I know these bachelor and student plans only too well, and do not
want in the end to fall between two stools. Should anything suitable turn up,

however, I could always find some good excuse for parting on friendly terms from my present landlord. The 25 florins mentioned above should be handed over to him for October, and on my arrival I will pay them back without delay. I am very eager to see Schober and Kupelwieser and see how a man looks, in the case of the former when all his plans have gone up in smoke, and in the case of the latter when he has just come back from Rome and Naples. Schwind is a dithering wool-gatherer, for I do not know which of the two letters he wrote me is the more muddle-headed. Such a grotesque mixture of sense and nonsense has never come my way before. Unless he has done some really fine work during this time, such brainless chatter is not to be forgiven him. My greetings to all three, and also to Rieder and Dietrich if you see them. My congratulations to Rieder on his professorship. Steiger and Louis Hönig came to see me in Gmunden, which pleased me very much. If only your otherwise excellent brains had reached a little farther, the idea of honouring me with your presence would have occurred to you too. But that is asking too much of lads as head-over-ears in love as you all are. How often, I wonder, have you been reduced to fresh despair, and had to drown your sighs and lamentations in beer and punch! Ha! ha! ha! ha! I nearly forgot to tell you that I have been in Salzburg and Gastein, where the country surpasses the wildest flights of fancy.

Farewell!
Your
Schubert
Greetings to all friends.

Write to me, but
write sense,
perhaps a musical
poem(?)!

P.S. Vogl has just told me that he may possibly be going to Italy with Haugwitz at the end of this month or the beginning of October. In that case, I should be back earlier, at the beginning of October.

Among the works which Schubert composed during his summer travels are the highly romantic and individual Piano Sonata in D major (D.850) with its cheerfully quirky final movement, and two songs which are settings of poems by Ladislaus Pyrker, Patriarch (or Archbishop) of Venice. Pyrker, born in 1773 in Hungary, was not only a prince of the Church but also a poet. A cousin of Spaun, he had met Schubert in Vienna more than once, some years earlier, and Schubert had dedicated the publication of a group of three songs to Pyrker. When Schubert and Vogl arrived at Bad Gastein, they found

Pyrker taking the waters, and also supervising a hospital which he had founded at Gastein for invalid soldiers.

The two songs which Schubert composed at Gastein on poems by Pyrker are 'Das Heimweh' (Homesickness, D.851) and 'Die All-macht' (The Almighty, D.852). 'Die Allmacht' is despised by some writers on Schubert as a piece of overwrought romanticism, but it is a magnificent song in which Schubert's response to the grandeur of the country around Gastein finds full and exalted expression. Both Pyrker's poem and Schubert's music are born of a love for the Austrian mountain landscape: the theme of God in nature always brought a rapturous response from Schubert, and 'Die Allmacht' is noble, harmonically rich, and exhilarating in its effect. 'Das Heimweh', an over-long piece of nostalgia, suffers by comparison with the superb 'Die Allmacht'.

It was at Gastein that Schubert completed a symphony that he had begun to sketch at Gmunden. But the suggestion made by several writers that the Grand Duo for piano of 1824 (D.812) and the 'Gastein' Symphony are one and the same work was never really feasible. It is now generally accepted that the symphony composed by Schubert in the summer of 1825 is the work popularly known as the 'Great' C major Symphony (D.944).

Schubert was back in Vienna in early October, and for the first few days spent a great deal of time with his friends Schober, Schwind and Bauernfeld, drinking and carousing at taverns and coffee-houses, 'often,' according to Bauernfeld's diary, 'until two or three in the morning'. An indication of his growing reputation is the fact that an 'Extremely Good Likeness of the Composer Franz Schubert' was advertised in the *Wiener Zeitung* on 9 December as being on sale at the firm of Diabelli & Co. This was an engraving by Johann Nepomuk Passini after a water-colour portrait painted in May by Wilhelm August Rieder. Rieder's portrait was thought by many who knew Schubert to be a fine speaking likeness of the composer, and it became the basis for most of the posthumous portraits.

CHAPTER SIX

'Alt Wien'

The first years of the nineteenth century in Vienna were years of deprivation and war. The city's occupation by Napoleon did little to improve matters, and by the time of the Vienna Congress it was clear that what the citizens wanted was to be able to turn their backs on tragedy, and to live in a safe and secure present. For this safety and security they were willing to trade a certain liberty of the spirit. Cosy domesticity now seemed to them to be preferable to adventurousness, and good humour more important than deep thought. It is this age of cosiness, of *Gemütlichkeit*, that, when we contemplate it now, we characterize as the age of Biedermeier.

The word 'Biedermeier' is a combination of the German adjective *bieder*, meaning 'plain', in the sense of unpretentious and inoffensive, with 'Meier', one of the most frequently encountered German-Jewish surnames. The term itself came into use only after the age which it described had begun to fade into the past. Biedermeier was the name of an imaginary poet, the invention of Adolph Kussmaul and Ludwig Eichrodt, who published poems ostensibly by Gottlieb Biedermeier in the humorous journal *Fliegende Blätter*, from 1855 onwards. By the 1890s, 'Biedermeier' had become a standard derogatory term for the style of the 1820s and 1830s. Its derogatory overtones now largely gone, the term survives to describe the art and the life-style of Germany and Austria from the time of the 1815 Congress of Vienna to the revolutionary year of 1848. In Austria, especially, it survives as the enduring image of *Alt Wien*, Old Vienna. The city has known other great periods, under Maria Theresia in the eighteenth century, and under the elder Franz Josef in the *Jugendstil* years at the birth of the twentieth century: but it is still the Vienna of Schubert, of Raimund, of the Congress, of Lanner and Strauss, which is conjured up by the term *Alt Wien*. Old Vienna is Biedermeier Vienna.

Nostalgia, of course, distorts reality. But then memory itself distorts reality. All views of the world (except God's, the religious would say) are partial. Schubert and most of his friends chose a partial view of their world which tended to evoke an instant nostalgia, for they preferred to accept the agreeable surface of Biedermeier life and to ignore its murkier depths. That those depths existed is not in question: even Schubert had his one or two brushes with the police. But Schubert was no revolutionary, not even in his music. He is the Biedermeier composer *par excellence*, and he is something far greater. But the far greater gift he carried within him and which produced some of his most distinctly un-Biedermeier music – the String Quintet, the last piano sonatas, the *Winterreise* songs – has little to do with revolution, whether revolution against political authority or against musical traditions. It is music which comes from personal depths, which speaks of personal loneliness, and which offers personal solace. Metternich, the reactionary Chancellor of Austria, would have understood the language of Beethoven more easily that that of Schubert.

Metternich, not a Viennese but a German from the Rhineland, was obsessed with the idea of student revolt. 'I feel certain that a whole generation of revolutionaries is bred at the universities,' he wrote in 1819 to his secretary Friedrich von Gentz. Under the Emperor Franz, the state remained, in Gentz's words, 'calm and happy in the paternal care of a virtuous sovereign'. An anonymous German traveller in Austria wrote of the Viennese under Franz:

The ordinary people of Vienna, of Austria and Styria, possess an indestructible fund of harmless sincerity, cheerfulness and good humour. The man in the street is charming. Franz, by nature a suspicious, crafty, cold-hearted and narrow-minded prince, without magnanimity, yet with a sharp eye for the weaknesses of the broad masses of the people; so cultured that he could express himself with diplomatic care and precision in both French and Italian, disguised his most carefully calculated thoughts in the simple Viennese dialect, and aped the homely simplicity of the people in gesture, expression and movement, so regularly and for so long that the mask eventually became his regular face.

Even this unprepossessing monarch was sufficiently Viennese to play second violin in a string quartet, though that appears to have been the extent of his musicianship. An excellent description of the society over which he presided is provided by the Viennese writer Karl Kobold:

The *Gemütlichkeit*, but at the same time the essentially intellectual intercourse of the time, influenced its artistic life. The Congress of Vienna had been the impetus to noble festivities on the grand scale. The Viennese had seen much beauty and exalted elegance, and had modelled themselves thereon. A new standard and style of living were evolved for the citizen class out of this richly endowed atmosphere, a romantic continuation of a heroic empire. A certain specific Viennese style bound in close relationship the music of Schubert and Lanner, the art of Schwind, the writings of Raimund. The Biedermeier Viennese created a home and mode of life for himself, full of grace and comfort. The furniture was of walnut or cherry-wood and brightly polished. The cupboards had at their corners little sculptured pillars of wood. Through the panes of the glass doors glittered the finest porcelain from the Vienna factory, and over them was carved delicately a tiny lute in gold; the backs of the chairs had slender pilasters. The round table, often with inlaid ornamentation, rested on pillared castor legs. Near the door hung a peal of bells decked with pearls. Fancy work of tatting and crochet and the finest native embroidery covered everything – armchairs, cushions, footstools. Of course, in accordance with the musical spirit of the time, the piano of cherry-wood was not missing, or the black alabaster timepiece, whose solemn tick reminded you of the impermanence of all earthly things. There was the dainty work-table, with work-basket of finest china, and there, too, was the big easy chair to rest in and spin dreams. From the walls laughed the portraits of handsome young men, with a *soupçon* of romance, and pretty girls' heads and beautiful women by Daffinger, Kriehuber, Rieder, Teltscher. Black silhouettes looked out dreamily from cherry-wood frames, half-length portraits in oils breathed parental dignity, and above the canopy reigned also in oils the likeness of the worthy patriarch of the kingdom, Emperor Franz.

'The whole aspect of the town with its surroundings', wrote Varnhagen von Ense, another surveyor of the scene, 'has something about it suggestive of riches, well-being and personal contentment. The people here seem healthier and happier than elsewhere, the evil spirits which are generally supposed to accompany, torment and stick to human beings in this air would find it difficult to breathe, and would be obliged to take up their abode somewhere else.' Trade and commerce prospered, politics could be safely left to the professionals, and life could be lived in an atmosphere of 'Wein, Weib und Gesang'.

To a certain extent, the average Viennese citizen's lack of interest in politics was due to his religion. That the Viennese, by and large, were not politically minded was surely a consequence of their Catholicism, as opposed to the Protestantism of most Germans. Political and religious passivity, acceptance of temporal and spiritual authority, these traits went hand in hand. Their spiritual welfare was in the hands of the Pope and his cardinals, and their temporal welfare could safely be entrusted to the Emperor and to the bureaucracy of the civil service. Freed of these anxieties, the Viennese could devote their attention to gastronomic delight, to enjoyment of the natural world and its produce, and to contemplation of the passing parade. A Protestant bookseller from Berlin who visited Vienna was shocked at what he called Viennese gluttony, for which he blamed both the Austrian monarchy and its Catholicism, which seemed to him a religion 'all in show, lacking high culture and preoccupied with sordid material matters, with results that are worse than the paganism of old'.

Today, Vienna is architecturally a mixture of *Jugendstil*, nine-teenth-century stateliness, Biedermeier cosiness and baroque-rococo splendour. In Schubert's time, the contemporary Biedermeier mingled only with the baroque and with considerably more Gothic and mediaeval buildings than exist in the city today. Our picture of the period of Schubert and Beethoven is one in which the fashions of the day are seen against the background of the baroque palaces and churches of Fischer von Erlach: the elegant lightness of the Karlskirche, the imposing magnificence of the royal palace at Schönbrunn, and much else. Also part of the background are the Belvedere, that masterpiece by Fischer's rival, Hildebrandt; the Schwarzenberg palace with its superb gardens; the Hofburg, which unites all styles from Gothic to mid-nineteenth-century; the domestic palaces or town houses of such noble families as Lobkowitz, Harrach, Kinsky, Pálffy or Lichnowsky, almost all of which are still standing today, for Vienna is conservative and prefers to conserve what it cherishes rather than to demolish in the hope that something better may arise.

The pleasures of the Viennese were, and are, equally conservative. Chief among these is to repair to one's favourite café: to drink coffee, of course, but also to read the newspapers, and to talk. Schubert and his circle favoured the taverns such as *Zum grünen Anker* (The Green Anchor) in the Grünangergasse or the hotel *Zur ungarischen Krone*; but they also met at the *Café Bogner* in the Singerstrasse. The cafés were more sedate places than the taverns, and those that remain in Vienna have changed hardly at all since the time of Schubert. After the waiter has brought the customer his desired brew (*Mocha, Mélange, Einspänner*, or any one of twenty or more different kinds of coffee), accompanied always by a glass of cold water, and a selection of newspapers, the customer may stay all day and until closing time, savouring the sweetness of life and watching the passing show. The waiter will approach only to renew the water or the newspapers.

In Schubert's day, the *Café Hugelmann* was popular, not only because it was an open-air restaurant on the banks of the Danube where one could watch the traffic of the river, but also because of its Billiards Academy. 'People go to see the best billiards players at Hugelmann's,' wrote Franz Fräffer, a contemporary observer, 'as they go to see the actors at the theatre.' In other cafés, the great attraction was the music, played on zithers, guitars and violins, and sung by tenors with high, sweet voices. In the wine suburbs such as Grinzing, as well as in the inner city, the sound of music was to be heard at all hours.

The beginning of the Biedermeier period coincided with the rise of the middle classes to a position of power and influence which had formerly and traditionally been that of the aristocracy. The Napoleonic wars followed by the Congress of Vienna had placed monarchs and rulers increasingly in the hands of financiers, who were the leaders of the new, influential bourgeoisie. This bourgeoisie gradually came to impose its way of life and its view of the world upon society, as the influence of the old nobility waned and as monarchies began slowly to disappear. In Austria, this change was accomplished without the violence of revolution which, in France, had exchanged one rule of terror for another. The success of the Austrian middle classes was largely due to the fact that the whole economic future of the country lay in its hands. In the eighteenth century the leading figures in science and philosophy came from the aristocracy: by the time of the Biedermeier period, the leading figures were predominantly middle-class. For more than a generation, the members of the bourgeoisie retained their influence. They did not, of course, entirely lose it in the revolutionary year of 1848: they were merely forced to acknowledge the rise of a new power, that of the proletariat.

Austria's revolution was not only sixty years later than France's; it was also completely different in kind. It did not lead to a change in régime, but merely to reforms extracted from the ruling régime, i.e. from the Habsburg monarchy, primarily because the majority of the Viennese remained attached to their monarchy – it took a twentieth-century world war to wrest it from them – and because the easy-going Austrian temperament precluded any serious thoughts of violent revolutionary change. In the Biedermeier Vienna of the 1820s, not even the events of 1848 could have been imagined. To the increasingly prosperous bourgeoisie, it must have seemed that the finest of all ages had arrived. Even to the working class, life was by no means intolerable. One has to imagine real liberty before one is able to yearn for it. Schubert and his friends were neither unimaginative nor insensitive, and several of them were prone to that uneasy melancholy which is the reverse side of the coin of Viennese gaiety. But their unrest was personal, was never socially orientated. If, after all, life was not absolutely perfect, then, they must have reasoned, surely the fault lay within themselves.

An Austrian chronicler of events, Walter Pollak, summed up the Biedermeier age in these words:

Under the cloud of the Metternich system, there blossomed with the Biedermeier one of the most charming and sensitive epochs. It is hardly an exaggeration to describe this rich intellectual and artistic development as the consequence and result of a kind of 'inward immigration'. People, given no say in matters political, barred from all participation in public affairs and the shaping of social conditions, withdrew from outward concerns into the intimate circle of the family and friendly relations with their fellow creatures. The harmless, gay parlour game, the sentimental literary salon, the cultivation of music at home: these formed the basis of a widely ramified, deeply rooted cultural life.

CHAPTER SEVEN

1826–1828
Winter Journey

The Schubertians welcomed in the new year of 1826 with a New Year's Eve party at Schober's, though without the leading member of their circle. Bauernfeld's diary entry for 2 January reads:

New Year's Eve at Schober's, without Schubert, who was ill. A dramatic parody on all the male and female friends read after midnight, with great success. Moritz appears in it as Harlequin, Netti as Columbine. Schober is Pantaloon, Schubert, Pierrot. Moritz and I slept at Schober's, and I remained with him until midday.

What was wrong with Schubert is not known, but his illness seems not to have been serious, for none of the friends felt an urge to visit him on New Year's Day to enquire after his condition.

By 14 January Schubert was out and about again, for two days later Bauernfeld wrote in his diary: 'The day before yesterday a sausage ball [*Würstelball*] at Schober's. Schubert had to play waltzes.' (A *Würstelball* was an evening of dancing at which sausages were served to the men by the women. The sausages, strung in pairs and eaten hot, were called frankfurters in Vienna, while at Frankfurt-on-Main they were known as Vienna sausages.)

It was during January that Schubert composed what were to prove the last of his Goethe songs: four 'Gesänge aus "Wilhelm Meister"' (Songs from *Wilhelm Meister*, D.877), all of which he had set before. No. 1, 'Mignon und der Harfner', is the familiar 'Nur wer die Sehnsucht kennt' (Only he who knows yearning) set as a duet for Mignon and the Harper. The famous poem of loneliness and longing for love seems unsuitable material for a duet, although in Goethe's novel it is sung by these two characters. Schubert's No. 4 is the same poem, this time set as a solo for Mignon, and much more appealing than the duet. Nos 2 and 3 are also songs for Mignon: 'Heiss mich nicht reden' (Bid me not speak) and 'So lasst mich scheinen' (So let me appear), both deeply felt responses to the poems.

Schubert also finally completed his D minor Quartet ('Death and the Maiden', D.810), which was given its first rehearsal on 29 January at the apartment of the Hacker brothers in the Schönlaterngasse, with Karl (violin) and Franz (viola) Hacker, Joseph Hauer (violin), and the Court Opera cellist Bauer, under Schubert's direction. A second rehearsal was held the following day, when Schubert was still making corrections and alterations to his score. The first performance of the quartet was given by these musicians at the residence of Josef Barth on 1 February.

The publication early in the year of the 1825 A minor Piano Sonata, (D.845) helped to enhance Schubert's status as a composer for the piano. The Leipzig *Allgemeine Musikalische Zeitung* on 1 March wrote that 'it can probably be compared only with the greatest and most free-ranging of Beethoven's sonatas', adding:

We are indebted for this uncommonly attractive and also truly significant work to Herr Schubert, who is, we hear, a still quite young artist of and in Vienna. To us, as doubtless to northern Germany in general, he is known only by his extremely diversified songs for one or more voices, with or without pianoforte accompaniment.

Schubert may have been known, until then, by the north Germans primarily as a composer for the voice, but that his fame had more generally spread abroad is attested to by the fact that the Zürich composer and publisher Hans Georg Nägeli mentioned him in a series of lectures given two years earlier in six German towns. Schubert and nine other composers, among them 'the boy Mendelssohn', were singled out by Nägeli as 'among the pianoforte composers now living' who were 'apt to increase the artistic blessings of our time'.

A number of works by Schubert were published during 1826, some by firms with whom he had not previously dealt. These include the Grand Funeral March for piano duet (D.859) on the occasion of the death of Tsar Alexander, who had visited Vienna twice since the days of the Congress; several songs; the *Divertissement à l'hongroise* (D.818) and the three *Marches militaires* (D.733) of 1822, the first of which has become universally popular in countless arrangements.

'Schubert and I hold faithfully together against many a Schoberish folly. Moritz wavers.' Thus wrote Bauernfeld in his diary at the end of March. Among Schober's follies at this time would appear to have been an attempt to raise idleness to a high art: this is certainly what had been suggested in the New Year's Eve satire. Schubert, on the other hand, was not being idle: on 7 April, he wrote a petition to the Emperor Franz, asking to be appointed as Vice-Director of the Imperial and Royal Court Chapel. The Music Director, Antonio Salieri, had retired in 1824, and the Vice-Director, Josef Eybler, had been promoted to replace him. The position of Vice-Director had since then been vacant. Schubert's petition reads as follows:

Your Majesty, Most Gracious Emperor,
With the deepest submission, the undersigned humbly begs Your Majesty graciously to bestow upon him the vacant position of Vice Music-Director to the Court Chapel, and supports his application with the following quali-fications:

(1) The undersigned was born in Vienna, is the son of a school teacher, and is 29 years of age.

(2) He enjoyed the privilege of being for five years a pupil of the Imperial and Royal City Seminary as a boy-chorister of the Court.

(3) He received a complete course of instruction in composition from the former chief Music Director of the Court Chapel, the late Herr Anton Salieri, and is fully qualified, therefore, to fill any post as Music Director. (See Enclosure A.)

(4) His name is well known, not only in Vienna but also throughout Germany, as a composer of songs and instrumental music.

(5) He has also written and arranged five Masses for both smaller and larger orchestras, and these have already been performed in various churches in Vienna.

(6) Finally, he is at the present time without employment, and hopes in the security of a permanent position to be able to realize at last those high musical aspirations which he has ever kept before him.

Should Your Majesty be graciously pleased to grant this request, the undersigned would strive to the utmost to give full satisfaction.

Your Majesty's most obedient humble servant,
Franz Schubert

'Enclosure A' was the testimonial which Salieri, who had died in 1825, had supplied in September 1819 at Schubert's request. It reads:

That Herr Franz Schubert has completely learnt the art of composition and already furnished very good compositions both for the church and for the stage; and that he is therefore entirely suited to any chapel master's post, in regard to his thorough knowledge as well as his moral character, is herewith confirmed in praise of him.

Ant. Salieri,
Imperial and Royal Music Director of
the Court Chapel

The appointment was not made immediately. By the end of the year, a short list of suitable applicants had been presented to the Lord High Chamberlain: Schubert was one of those short-listed, and his friend Anselm Hüttenbrenner was another. In the following January it was announced that Josef Weigl, the Court Theatre conductor, who had not applied, had been appointed. Schubert's petition was returned to him on 27 January 1827, with a note on the reverse side: 'His Majesty having condescended to fill the post herein applied for, no further steps can be taken concerning it.' Josef von Spaun reports that, on receiving his petition back, Schubert said to him, 'Much as I should have liked to receive this appointment, I shall have to make the best of the matter, since it was given to so worthy a man as Weigl.'

Bauernfeld went to the country, to the province of Carinthia, for most of the summer of 1826. 'Greetings to thee, boredom, mother of the Muses!' he wrote in his diary, and continued: 'Thus I thought of the libretto for Schubert and set to work on *Der Graf von Gleichen* [The Count of Gleichen]. Dramatic and musical contrasts: Orient and Occident, janissaries and knighthood, romantic wooing and wedded love, etc. In short, a Turkish-Christian outline. The verses flow pretty easily for me.' (He completed his libretto for Schubert, who, the following year, began to sketch music for it, despite the fact that what Bauernfeld had written was hardly better than the nonsense he had turned out for the Schubertians' New Year's Eve party. However, Schubert did not persevere with his sketches.)

At the end of May 1826, Schubert wrote to Bauernfeld:

That you have written the opera text is an excellent move, and I only wish that I had it before me now. They have asked for my operas to see if anything could be done with them, and if only your libretto were ready I could submit this to them instead, and as soon as its worth was recognized – about which I have no doubts – why then, God willing, I could get to work on it, or else send it to Mme Milder in Berlin. Mlle Schechner has made her appearance here in *Die Schweizerfamilie*, and was very enthusiastically received. In some ways she is very like Milder and on that account should be popular with us here.

Do not stay away too long. Everything here is very miserable and depressing. The general tediousness of life has already gained too strong a hold upon us. Schober and Schwind give vent only to lamentations that are far more heartrending than those we listened to during Holy Week. Since you left, I have scarcely been to Grinzing once, and never with Schwind. . . . From all this you can deduce a fine sum-total of gaiety! *Die Zauberflöte* was very well produced at the Theater an der Wien, and *Der Freischütz* very badly at the Imperial and Royal Kärntnertor theatre. 'Herr Jacob and Frau Babel' are incomparable at the Leopoldstadt theatre. Your poem which appeared in the *Modezeitung* is very good, but the one in your last letter is finer still. Its sublime humour and comic loftiness of sentiment, and especially the gentle cry of anguish at the end, where you take advantage in a masterly fashion of the good city of Villach – 'woe, woe!' – place it among the finest examples of its kind.

I am not working at all. The weather here is really terrible, and the Almighty seems to have forsaken us entirely. The sun refuses to shine. It is already May, and one cannot even sit in the garden. Fearful! Dreadful!! Appalling!!! For me, the greatest cruelty one can imagine. In June, Schwind and I want to go to Linz with Spaun. We might all arrange to meet there, or in Gmunden, only you must let us know definitely and as soon as possible if you could manage it. Not in two months' time!

Goodbye!

(*Die Schweizerfamilie* [The Swiss Family], an opera by Josef Weigl, the newly appointed Vice-Director of the Imperial and Royal Court Chapel, was immensely popular throughout Europe in the nineteenth century. 'Herr Jacob and Frau Babel' is actually *Herr Josef und Frau Baberl*, a comedy with songs.)

Schubert's plan to travel to Gmunden in June was not realized. On 10 July he wrote again to Bauernfeld:

It is impossible for me to get either to Gmunden or anywhere else, for I have absolutely no money, and everything else is going very badly with me too. However, I am bearing up, and am in good spirits.

Do come back to Vienna as soon as you can. Duport wants me to write an opera for him, but he does not like any of the texts which I have already used, so it would be really splendid if your libretto were accepted.

Schwind has quite lost his head as regards Nettel. Schober is now a business man. Vogl is married!!!

Please come as soon as you possibly can! On account of the opera.

Your
Schubert

You have only to mention my name in Linz, and you will be well looked after.

(Nettel was Annette Hönig, to whom Schwind was for a time engaged; Schober was managing a lithographic institute; and the fifty-eight-year-old Vogl had, the previous month, somewhat unexpectedly married. Louis Antoine Duport was connected with the management of the Court Opera. Nothing came of his desire that Schubert should write a new opera.)

Towards the end of April, Spaun returned to take up an appointment in Vienna; he and Schubert resumed their former relations, and were to be seen frequently in the inns and coffee-houses. During July, while he was staying in the outer suburb of Währing at the Schober house, Schubert composed his three Shakespeare songs: 'Trinklied' from *Antony and Cleopatra* (D.888) is 'Come, thou monarch of the vine', a jolly but unremarkable drinking song; far better, in fact purely delightful, though perhaps more Viennese than Shakespearian, are 'Ständchen' (Serenade) from *Cymbeline* (D.889), a joyous *Ländler* to the words of 'Hark! hark! the lark at heaven's gate sings', and 'Gesang (an Sylvia)' (Song to Sylvia) from *The Two Gentlemen of Verona* (D.891), which is, of course, 'Who is Sylvia?', the most graceful and endearing of pastoral love songs.

The story persists that Schubert composed 'Hark! hark! the lark' on the back of a menu in a beer-garden. He certainly did not use the back of a menu, as all three Shakespeare songs and one other were written in a little note-book, with the music staves drawn in pencil. But it is possible that they, or one of them, were written in the garden of the inn which was next door to Schober's residence.

Another of the many Schubert legends is that, in 1826, he obtained a job as assistant conductor at the Kärntnertor theatre, but was unable to hold it down, due either to (according to one version) his insobriety and unpunctuality, or to his rudeness to or dissatisfaction with a prima donna. None of this can be substantiated. Bauernfeld, in an obituary article published only some months after the death of Schubert, refers to 'the function of conductor at the Kärntnertor theatre, which, if memory serves, was offered him in 1827 by the manager of that time [but] which he did not accept'. However, it seems more likely that Schubert informally applied for the position but without success.

Hans Georg Nägeli, the Zürich composer and publisher who had mentioned Schubert in his lectures in Germany, wrote to the Viennese pianist and composer Karl Czerny in June, asking him to pass on to Schubert an invitation to compose a piano sonata for a collection of miscellaneous compositions for the piano which Nägeli intended to publish. Schubert replied to Nägeli on 4 July:

Sir,
My Sonata in A minor made you no doubt better acquainted with me, since you have now done me the honour of commissioning, through Herr Karl Czerny, a pianoforte sonata which you propose to include in a selection of similar compositions (under the title 'Ehrenpforte' [Portal of Honour]). The good reception which you have been kind enough to accord to my sonata and, above all, your extremely flattering request make me very willing to comply with your desire without delay.

In that case, I must request you to make the fee of 120 florins [Assimilated Currency] payable in advance to me in Vienna.

Let me add how gratifying it is to be in correspondence with such an old-established and famous publishing house.

With the greatest respect, I remain,
yours faithfully,
Franz Schubert.

My address is: Auf der Wieden, No. 100, in Frühwirth's house, 5th staircase, 2nd floor.

No further correspondence between Schubert and Nägeli has survived, and neither of the two published volumes of Nägeli's 'Portal of Honour' contains anything by Schubert. Either the publisher did not accept Schubert's terms or Schubert failed to complete the composition. The next piano sonata he wrote was the G major (D.894), but this was not until October.

In the last ten days of June, Schubert had composed what was to prove his final string quartet, the G major (D.887), a work which, though it lacks the popular appeal of its predecessors in A minor and D minor ('Death and the Maiden'), is nevertheless a superb work whose violence and nervous energy are almost Beethovenian.

In August, ill again and having run out of money, Schubert wrote two desperate letters to publishing houses in Leipzig. His letters to

Breitkopf & Härtel and to H. A. Probst were written on the same day, 12 August, and their texts are virtually identical. To Breitkopf & Härtel, the oldest music publishing house in Germany, he wrote:

In the hope that my name is not wholly unknown to you, I am venturing to ask whether you would be disposed to take over at a moderate price some of my compositions, for I very much want to become as well-known as possible in Germany. Your selection could be made from the following: songs with pianoforte accompaniment, string quartets, pianoforte sonatas, pieces for four hands, etc., etc. I have also written an octet. Should you avail yourselves of this suggestion, I should feel it a special honour to be associated with such an old-established and well-known publishing house.

Breitkopf & Härtel replied, very much *de haut en bas*, offering to try out one or two piano pieces but to remunerate the composer only with free copies. (This was the firm which, nine years earlier, when Schubert submitted 'Erlkönig' to them, had confused him with one Franz Schubert of Dresden!) Schubert did not pursue the matter. Probst's reply was more promising, so Schubert then sent three of his piano compositions. However, these were rejected by Probst several months later.

In September, Leopold Kupelwieser married. Schubert played for the dancing at the wedding celebrations, refusing to let anyone else near the piano. One of the waltzes he improvised was remembered by the bride, Johanna Lutz, and handed down from generation to generation of her family. It was never put on paper, until Richard Strauss heard it from a member of the family in 1943 and wrote it down, a pleasant little waltz tune in G major.

The powerful Rondo in B minor for violin and piano (D.895) was composed in October, and in the same month Schubert sent to the Gesellschaft der Musikfreunde the manuscript of a symphony, accompanied by the following note:

Convinced as I am of the noble aim of the Society of Music Lovers to give whole-hearted support to every effort made in the cause of art, I venture now, as an Austrian musician, to dedicate to, and to commend to the good care of, the Society this symphony of mine.

One cannot be certain which symphony is referred to, for the Society of Music Lovers, far from taking good care of the work, managed to lose it. Nevertheless, as a token of their thanks, the Society on 12 October awarded a grant of 100 florins (Assimilated Currency) to the

146

composer.

Schubert's activities in November and December are well documented in the diaries of Franz von Hartmann, who had studied law in Vienna in 1824–5 and who returned to live in the capital again in November 1826 with his brother Fritz, who had been at the university since 1823. 'With Fritz to the *Anker*,' Franz von Hartmann wrote on 19 November, 'where there was a large gathering, including Schwind, who presented me with a small nosegay, Schubert and Bauernfeld. Spaun joined us later, too. At 11.30 we parted.'

The *Anker* was *Zum grünen Anker*, the inn in a little cobbled street near the Stephansdom. (It is still there, and looking rather as it must have done in Schubert's day, though now it is an Italian restaurant.) Schubert and his companions had been frequenting the *Anker* for at least two years: the beer was good and the atmosphere convivial, and it was on the way to Bogner's, which remained Schubert's favourite coffee-house.

The overture which Schubert had composed for his opera *Alfonso und Estrella* in 1822, and which he subsequently used for *Rosamunde* in 1823, was to be performed at a concert at the Kärntnertor theatre on 2 December. Nine days before the concert, the score and parts had not been found, and on 23 November Schubert wrote to Ignaz von Seyfried, Music Director of the Theater an der Wien:

Please be so good as to let me know by the bearer of this whether my overture to *Rosamunde* has been found. Otherwise I should find myself in terrible embarrassment, for it is supposed to be given on 2 December.

So, once again, I beg you to let me have word as soon as possible.

Seyfried must have found and returned the manuscript, for the concert on 2 December began with an item called 'Overture by Schubert', which was favourably reviewed and in the following June was mentioned in the London *Harmonicon*: 'In another concert, given by the brothers Lewy, the novelties [included] a revived Overture by Schubert, full of striking effects, and worthy of being better known.'

From Franz von Hartmann, who seems to have been at the *Anker* almost every evening in December, we learn that Schubert was present on the 5th, 7th, 12th, 15th, 17th, 19th, 20th, 21st, 27th, and 30th. On the 8th, at Spaun's, Schubert 'played a magnificent but melancholy piece of his own composition' (perhaps the first movement of his recently composed piano sonata, the G major, D.894), and

'Schubert and Schwind then sang the most lovely Schubert songs'.

A 'big, big Schubertiad' was held at Spaun's on 15 December. 'On entering,' writes Franz von Hartmann,

I was received rudely by Fritz and very saucily by Haas. There was a huge gathering. The Arneth, Wittczek, Kurzrock and Pompe couples, the mother-in-law of the Court and State Chancellery Probationer Wittczek; Dr Watteroth's widow, Betty Wanderer, and the painter Kupelwieser, with his wife, Grillparzer, Schober, Schwind, Mayrhofer and his landlord Huber, tall Huber, Derffel, Bauernfeld, Gahy (who played gloriously *à quatre mains* with Schubert) and Vogl, who sang almost 30 splendid songs. Baron Schlechta and other court probationers and secretaries were also there. I was moved almost to tears, being in a particularly excited state of mind today, by the trio of the fifth march, which always reminds me of my dear, good mother. When the music was done, there was grand feeding and then dancing. But I was not at all in a courting mood. I danced twice with Betty and once with each of the Wittczek, Kurzrock and Pompe ladies. At 12.30, after a cordial parting with the Spauns and Enderes, we saw Betty home and went to the 'Anchor' where we still found Schober, Schubert, Schwind, Derffel and Bauernfeld. Merry. Then home. To bed at 1 o'clock.

(The 'Fritz' who received Franz von Hartmann 'rudely' was his brother, and Haas was one of Schubert's Linz friends. According to Bauernfeld, Vogl on this occasion 'sang Schubert songs with mastery, but not without dandyism'. The 'fifth march' favoured by Hartmann is No. 5 of *Six grandes marches* [D.819].)

On Sunday, 17 December, some of the friends gathered for breakfast at Spaun's, and heard Gahy play some recently published dances for the piano by Schubert which his publisher, to Schubert's annoyance, had entitled '*Hommage aux belles viennoises*' (D.734). Then the assembled company drove off in two carriages to Nussdorf for the day, and after lunch were treated to Schwind and Bauernfeld playing and singing Schubert songs 'quite lamentably'. When all the afternoon guests had gone, 'the old cosiness returned, and Schubert sang splendidly, especially his setting of Lappe's "Der Einsame" [The Solitary Man, D.800] and "Trockne Blumen" [Withered Flowers] from the *Schöne Müllerin* cycle. . . . Then Schubert and Gahy again played enchantingly, whereupon there were general gymnastic and conjuring feats, and at last we parted unwillingly.'

These were the kind of gatherings of which Schwind produced some memorable drawings and sketches. His famous sepia drawing of

1868 is based on the 'big, big Schubertiad' at Spaun's of 15 December 1826. Two such convivial evenings ended the year, and fortunately were recorded in Hartmann's diary:

30 December 1826: We go to the 'Anchor', where Schober, Schwind, Schubert, Bauernfeld and Derffel are. Spaun comes later, and Derffel and Bauernfeld leave. The talk is of chivalric novels, tall stories of the seminary, etc. As we step out of the 'Anchor', all is deeply snowed under. We itch for a game of snowballs, which we carry out immediately, at the point where the Grünangergasse leads into the Singerstrasse. Spaun is on my side, Fritz and Schober on Schwind's. Schober always hits me hard and without fail, and I him or Schwind in particular. Spaun gloriously protects himself against the shots with his open umbrella. Schubert and Haas take no part in the fight. Home, where the house-steward was rude because we rang loudly.

31 December 1826: Towards half-past eight we were due at Schober's, with Enderes, Schwind, Schubert and Bauernfeld, and later on Spaun, which caused general pleasure, since it was thought that he was at Baldacci's and we feared he would not come at all. We are very merry the whole evening, smoke tobacco, and read most amusing letters. Then we sit down to supper in the next room and wait for 12 o'clock to strike. Next, Schober's mother appears from the adjoining room, looking like a ghost. On the stroke of 12, glasses were filled with Tokay, and we drank each other's health for the coming year, Fritz, Spaun and myself not forgetting our dear parents. Then we drank coffee, smoked again, and at 2 o'clock left at last, first Spaun and Enderes, then we others except Schwind, who slept at Schober's. Or rather we waddled off. Parted with Schubert and Bauernfeld in the Singerstrasse.

In February 1827, Schober and his mother moved to a new house, in the street Unter den Tuchlauben, near the Graben. Schubert moved there too, as their guest, and lived with them for most of the remainder of his life. He had two rooms 'and a music closet' in their house, which was more space than he had ever had before. The first works he composed in his new lodgings were two songs on poems by Schober, 'Jägers Liebeslied' (Huntsman's Love Song, D.909) and 'Schiffers Scheidelied' (Boatman's Song of Parting, D.910); later in February he composed the twelve songs which comprise the first part of *Winterreise* (Winter Journey, D.911), his second cycle on poems by Wilhelm Müller. (The second part, the remaining twelve songs, were composed at the Schobers' in October.)

By the end of February, the Schubertians had moved their centre of operations from the *Anker* to another tavern, *Zum Schloss Eisenstadt*

(The Castle of Eisenstadt) in the Naglergasse, near the Graben, and convenient for Schober and Schubert. This was to be their regular haunt for the next six months. 'At the "Castle of Eisenstadt" ', wrote Hartmann on 3 March, 'there were Spaun, Schober, Schubert and Bauernfeld. We talked of the Greeks, the Hungarians and Grillparzer. Quite lively.' The following evening, at Schubert's invitation, Franz and Fritz von Hartmann went to Schober's house. But, although he had invited them and other friends to see his new rooms, Schubert himself failed to put in an appearance, and the party had to be content with Schwind's singing of several early songs by the composer. It was not until later in the evening when they repaired to the 'Castle of Eisenstadt' that they encountered Schubert, with two other drinking companions, Gahy and Enderes.

In February, Beethoven had been given copies of a number of Schubert's songs, among them 'Die junge Nonne' and the *Schöne Müllerin* cycle. According to Anton Schindler, the great composer's devoted friend and first biographer, when he read them through Beethoven exclaimed, 'Truly, there is in Schubert a divine spark!' Early in March, it became known throughout Vienna that Beethoven was on his deathbed. His doctor, who could do no more for him, was brightening his last days by providing the great composer with bottles of his favourite Viennese white wine, Gumpoldskirchner. Friends and admirers, too, sent gifts of food and wine. On 19 March, in company with three or four others, among them the brothers Anselm and Josef Hüttenbrenner, Schubert visited the dying Beethoven. For the first and last time, the two geniuses of music, who had lived in the same city for so many years without meeting, spoke a few words to each other. One week later, on 26 March, Beethoven died. When he was buried in the cemetery at Währing on 29 March, Schubert was one of the thirty-six torch-bearers in the funeral procession, the others including Grillparzer and Raimund. In the evening, Schubert, Schober, Schwind and Fritz von Hartmann repaired to the 'Castle of Eisenstadt', where they remained until almost 1 a.m., drinking and talking of Beethoven.

Schubert was now being promoted by several publishers, among them one new to him, Tobias Haslinger, who published several sets of songs in the first half of 1827, as well as the delightful *Valses nobles* for piano (D.969) and the G major Piano Sonata (D.894) which Schubert had composed the previous October. For some unknown reason, perhaps not unconnected with commercial considerations, Haslinger issued the latter work not as a sonata but under the title 'Fantasie, Andante, Menuetto und Allegretto'. This G major Sonata is less well-known than the final three which were to follow it: unaccountably so, for it is of their stature, a large-scale work lasting nearly forty minutes in performance. Poetry, mystery, delicacy and sheer lyrical beauty are its components: Schumann thought it Schubert's 'most perfect work, both in form and conception'.

Reviews of these newly published works, and of other new pieces by Schubert which were performed at concerts in Vienna, appeared not only in the local press but also in a number of German newspapers and journals. The Leipzig *Allgemeine Musikalische Zeitung* published a long review of the G major Piano Sonata which is a thoughtful and constructive piece of critical writing. The Frankfurt *Allgemeiner Musikalischer Anzeiger*, however, was unimpressed by the *Valses nobles*:

The reviewer is unable to account for the adjective 'noble' in considering these dances. They are not bad, but neither are they more than ordinary. Only some single traits here and there are successful, and do justice to Herr Schubert's favourably familiar manner. For the rest, the reviewer feels that a dance should never consist of two parts only, as is the case here; for its repetition, often for hours on end, must result in unendurable weariness.

There are twelve waltzes in the set of *Valses nobles*, written by Schubert to accompany the dancing at domestic balls. No doubt they would prove tedious if repeated for hours on end, though they are delightful examples of the composer's social manner.

Schubert spent a few weeks in the spring at Dornbach, to the west of the city near the Vienna Woods, staying at the inn *Zur Kaiserin von Österreich* (Empress of Austria), probably with Schober, but making occasional trips into Vienna to meet other friends at the 'Castle of Eisenstadt'. He is known to have composed at Dornbach the delightful spring song 'Das Lied im Grünen' (The Song of Greenery, D.917), and perhaps also some of the eight piano pieces later published as Impromptus (D.899 and D.935). Early in June, Schubert was honoured by the Vienna Gesellschaft der Musikfreunde by being elected as a representative. He accepted, in a communication dated 12 June, addressed to the Society's Executive Committee:

The Executive Committee of the Society of Music Lovers in the Austrian

Empire having found me worthy of election to their representative body, I beg to record my gratification at the honour accorded to me by this election, and my entire readiness to fulfil all obligations connected with the same.

Franz Schubert
Composer

Through a friend, Johann Baptist Jenger, a prominent member of the Styrian Musical Society, Schubert received an invitation for Jenger and himself to spend some weeks in the Styrian capital of Graz, at the home of Dr and Frau Pachler. Marie Leopoldine Pachler (1794–1855), a prominent Graz hostess, was an accomplished pianist who had known Beethoven. Schubert wrote to her on 12 June:

Though I fail to see how I come to deserve such a friendly offer as that which you have made me in your letter to Jenger, and doubt indeed if I shall ever be able to repay it in any way, yet I cannot but accept an invitation which gives me an opportunity, not only of seeing at last the much praised town of Graz, but also of becoming personally acquainted, Madam, with yourself.

Before he went to Graz that summer, Schubert fulfilled a commission by composing one of his most delightful songs for chorus. Anna Fröhlich had asked him to set for female chorus a poem she had been given by Grillparzer. The song was to be performed by her female pupils at the Conservatorium on the occasion of the birthday of one of them, Louise Gosmar. By mistake Schubert first set the poem for contralto solo with male-voice chorus, but when this was pointed out to him he quickly re-wrote the chorus for female voices, and the first performance of this choral 'Ständchen' (Serenade, D.920, version 'b') was given at the home of Louise Gosmar at Döbling on 11 August, with the contralto solo sung by Anna Fröhlich's sister, Josefine. Schubert's setting is magical, its delicate vocal line echoed by the chorus. The first version, however, with its contrast between the solo female voice and the chorus of male voices (D.920, version 'a'), is marginally to be preferred.

Schubert did not attend the Döbling performance, and did not hear the work until the following January, when it was included in a concert of the Gesellschaft der Musikfreunde. He almost missed this performance as well, and had to be brought by Jenger from the 'Oak Tree' (*Zur Eiche*) ale-house. Afterwards, he said to Anna Fröhlich, 'Really, I hadn't realized it was so beautiful a piece.'

That summer, the Schubertians began to patronize yet another ale-house; this one was called *Zum Wolf der den Gänsen predigt* (The Wolf Who Preaches to the Geese) in the Wallnergasse, near the Kohlmarkt. Schubert spent several evenings there in August, though one learns from the diary of the German poet Hoffmann von Fallersleben, who was visiting Vienna, that on 15 August Schubert, without his male friends, was to be found at a wine-garden in Grinzing: 'The old fiddler played Mozart. . . . Schubert with his girl we espied from our seat; he came to join us and did not show himself again. Franz Lachner, the fourth Music Director at the Kärntnertor theatre, also came to see us.'

Schubert and Jenger arrived in Graz on 3 September 1827. There were Schubertiads in the evenings, in which the composer's old friend Anselm Hüttenbrenner, who lived in Graz, participated; and from the 10th to the 12th the entire Pachler house-party went on an excursion to the castle of Wildbach, some twenty miles to the south-west, travelling through beautiful country. A Schubertiad was held in the 'blue room' of the castle, on the first floor, overlooking a fine garden. Schubert enjoyed himself thoroughly, and professed himself delighted with the local Schilcher *vin rosé*.

At most of the Schubertiads in the Pachler house in Graz, Schubert not only played piano duets with Jenger but also sang his own songs, as there was no other singer present. Among the songs he performed was the jaunty 'Der Wanderer an den Mond' (The Wanderer Addresses the Moon, D.870), which he had composed the previous year. On a jocular playbill produced for one of the entertainments, the role of 'Schwammerl' is assigned to Schubert: this appears to have been his nickname at the time. 'Schwammerl', which is Viennese dialect for 'little mushroom', refers probably to the composer's small stature as much as to his chubbiness.

Schubert and Jenger left Graz on 20 September to return to Vienna. They took four days over the coach trip, visiting the towns of Fürstenfeld and Friedberg, and climbing to the top of the Eselberg, before taking the valley road down to Vienna via Schleinz. On the 27th, Schubert wrote to Frau Pachler:

I realize now that my life in Graz was far too pleasant, and I am finding it very hard to settle down in Vienna again. It is big enough, to be sure, but on the other hand it is devoid of open-heartedness and sincerity, of genuine ideas and sensible talk, and, above all, of intellectual accomplishments. There is such a perpetual babble of small-talk here that it is difficult to know if one has a head on one's shoulders or not, and one rarely or never attains to any inward happiness. Though I daresay that, to a great extent, is my own fault, for I take so long to come out of my shell. I soon recognized the unaffected sincerity of social life in Graz, and, had my visit been longer, I should have taken to it even more. In particular I shall never forget the friendly hospitality accorded to me, nor shall I forget your good self or the sturdy 'Pachleros' or little Faust, for with you I spent the happiest days I have known for a long time. Hoping to find yet some adequate way of expressing my gratitude,

I remain,

Yours most sincerely,

Frz. Schubert.

P.S. I hope to be able to send the opera libretto in a few days.

(Even allowing for the hyperbolic language of a 'bread-and-butter' letter, it seems that Schubert felt somewhat unsettled on his return to Vienna. The opera libretto is that of *Alfonso und Estrella*; Schubert later sent the score as well, for Dr Pachler wished to show it to the theatre manager at Graz. It was, however, not performed, and many years later Pachler returned the manuscript to Ferdinand Schubert. 'Pachleros' was a nickname for Dr Pachler, and Faust was the Pachlers' eight-year-old son.)

Schubert had promised to write a piano piece for four hands, for Faust Pachler and his mother to play on Dr Pachler's name-day. On 12 October he sent to Frau Pachler the completed 'Kindermarsch' (Children's March, D.928), with a note:

I enclose herewith, dear Madam, the four-handed piece for little Faust. I am afraid, however, that it may not meet with his approval, for I do not feel that I am exactly made for compositions of this sort. I hope that you, Madam, are enjoying better health than I, for my usual headaches have come back again. I beg to send my heartiest congratulations to Dr Karl for his name-day, and to say that I have not yet been able to get back the libretto of my opera from that sloth, Herr Gottdank, who has kept it to read through for months now.

(Schubert had apparently not yet sent the promised libretto. Why Gottdank, the producer at the Kärntnertor theatre since 1821, should have been reading it unless the opera was being reconsidered is not clear.)

The headaches mentioned by Schubert heralded the beginning of his last, and fatal, illness. In October and November he had to apologize more than once for cancelling social engagements at short notice, presumably because of his headaches. He was, however, very productive during these autumn months of 1827. Amongst other works, he completed the *Deutsche Messe* (German Mass, D.872); the second part of the *Winterreise* song-cycle; the remaining impromptus for piano, as well as the short piano pieces he called, in his faulty French, 'Momens musicals' (D.780); the Piano Trio in E flat (D.929); and the Fantasy in C for piano and violin (D.934). In the weeks he had spent in Graz in September, he composed two songs in addition to the piano dances known as the *12 Grazer Walzer* (D.924) and the *Grazer Galopp* (D.925). Between 1812 (when he was fifteen) and 1827, Schubert composed more than 400 dances for the piano, about 130 of them waltzes. Though these are minor pieces, many of them are works of great charm, melodic wealth and harmonic invention. After the Graz waltzes and galop he seems to have written no more of these delightful miniatures. Life was now increasingly serious.

The German Mass, the result of a commission from a professor at the Polytechnic Institute of Vienna, is a setting not of the traditional Latin text of the Mass but of hymns by Johann Philipp Neumann, professor of physics at the Institute. Its exact title is 'Songs for the Celebration of the Holy Sacrament of Mass, together with an appendix containing the Lord's Prayer'. Intended to be sung by the congregation in Catholic churches, the work was in fact admitted for church use only in the second half of the nineteenth century. Its simple hymn tunes, accompanied by wind instruments and organ, are too dull to be suitable for concert performance.

Some of the other works of that autumn are masterpieces. The six lyrical *Moments musicaux* and the four Impromptus (D.935) contain some of Schubert's most individual and poetic writing for the piano. The Trio for piano, violin and cello in E flat, like its companion piece in B flat early the following year, is a great classic of chamber music, its slow movement one of the most affecting Schubert ever wrote.

The Fantasy in C for piano and violin, written for the Bohemian virtuoso violinist Josef Slavik, is often dismissed as an unsatisfactory and uncharacteristic display piece; but it is really a fascinating, large-scale work lasting more than twenty minutes, with the stature of a sonata though it is in one continuous movement. The element of technical display is secondary to the exalted, poetic mood of the Fantasy, which begins with a most beautiful and reflective melody for the violin, and later contains variations on a reminiscence, introduced by the piano, of Schubert's song 'Sei mir gegrüsst'. This C major Fantasy for violin and piano deserves to be much better known.

The major work of the autumn was Schubert's completion of his *Winterreise* song-cycle. The wanderer of this cycle is not the comparatively healthy young man of *Die schöne Müllerin*, but a saddened, disillusioned figure of despair. In *Winterreise* one does not find the spring-sadness of the earlier cycle but the chronic melancholy and deep resignation of a mind at the end of its tether. Spaun left an account of the first performance of *Winterreise*, which was given by the composer to an audience of his friends towards the end of 1827:

For a time Schubert's mood became more gloomy, and he seemed upset. When I asked him what was the matter he merely said to me, 'Well, you will soon hear it and understand.' One day he said to me, 'Come to Schober's today, I will sing you a cycle of awe-inspiring songs. I am anxious to know what you will say about them. They have affected me more than has been the case with any other songs.' So, in a voice wrought with emotion, he sang the whole of *Winterreise* through to us. We were quite dumbfounded by the gloomy mood of these songs, and Schober said he had only liked one song, 'Der Lindenbaum'. To which Schubert only said, 'I like these songs more than all the others, and you will get to like them too.' He was right. Soon we were enthusiastic over the effect of these melancholy songs, which Vogl performed in a masterly way.

To be fair to Spaun, Schober and the others, one should say that they probably did not get a proper impression of the songs from Schubert's *voix de compositeur*. But when Vogl sang the cycle to them, its greatness was made manifest. Some months later, after the publication of the first part of the cycle, the critic of the *Wiener Allgemeine Theaterzeitung* wrote: 'Schubert has understood his poet with the kind of genius that is his own. His music is as naïve as the poet's expression; the emotions contained in the poems are as deeply reflected in the composer's own feelings, and these are so brought out in sound that none can sing or hear them without being touched to the heart.'

Johann Friedrich Rochlitz, to whom, five years earlier, Schubert had pointed out Beethoven at an inn, wrote in November to urge Schubert to set his poem 'Der erste Ton' (The First Sound) to music. Rochlitz's letter is a model of how not to persuade a composer to set one's poem:

I will set down here how I imagine the music for it; but do not by any means think that I wish to dictate in any way. . . . Overture: a single, short, plucked chord, *ff*, and then a note sustained as long as possible, < > for clarinet or horn, with a pause. Now a soft opening darkly intertwined, harmonically rather than melodically – a kind of chaos which only gradually grows clearer and lighter. Whether the overture is to close here or to be followed by an allegro I will not decide; if the latter is chosen, let the allegro be serious, but very forceful and brilliant, yet dying down on a close derived from the first movement. At this point, declamation without music up to the words 'Wirken gegeben'.

Not surprisingly, Schubert did not rise to the bait of 'Der erste Ton'. He replied to Rochlitz:

I was much honoured by your letter, in as much as it was a means of bringing me into closer touch with a most distinguished man.

I have given considerable thought to your proposal regarding the poem, 'Der erste Ton', and I feel that your suggested treatment of it might indeed produce a very fine effect. However, as it is more of a melodrama than an oratorio or cantata, and the former (perhaps rightly) is no longer popular, I must frankly confess that I should greatly prefer a poetical work that could be treated as an oratorio, partly because it is not always possible to find a man like Anschütz to declaim, but also because it is my greatest wish to produce a musical work with no other aid than the inspiration of a long poem of a type that essentially lends itself to a musical setting. I need hardly say that I recognize you to be the poet for such a work, and certainly I would do my best to set it to music.

'Der este Ton' is in any case a splendid poem, and should you really wish me to set it to music, I would endeavour to do so; though, with your consent, I would arrange for the music (the actual song, that is) to begin at the words 'Da vernahm'.

That was the end of the matter. Schubert was clearly not interested in melodrama or spoken declamation against a musical accompaniment, though he had, in fact in 1826, composed one not very interesting piece in this genre: 'Abschied von der Erde' (Farewell to the Earth, D.829), for piano and speaking voice. The genre was particularly popular in Vienna, though not with Schubert.

The advent of the new year, 1828, was celebrated at Schober's with a party on New Year's Eve. Schubert, Schober, Spaun, Schwind, Bauernfeld, Gahy and the Hartmann brothers were all present, and Bauernfeld read his poem 'On New Year's Eve 1828', which was published the following week in the *Wiener Zeitschrift für Kunst*. Its theme is the passing of time and of youth, and among its ten stanzas is one which, with hindsight, one could read as prophesying Schubert's death later in the year:

> The spells of the poet, the pleasures of singing,
> They too will be gone, be they true as they may;
> No longer will songs in our party be ringing,
> For the singer too will be called away.
> The waters from source to the sea must throng,
> The singer at last will be lost in his song.

Schubert was not to see the year out, yet in the months left to him he composed more of his finest works than in any previous year. It was as though he knew he was fighting against time to set down on paper all the musical ideas that came to his mind. One of the earliest of the masterpieces of 1828 is the second of his trios for piano, violin and cello, the Piano Trio in B flat (D.898). Like its predecessor in E flat (D.929), this is one of the best-known and most loved works in the chamber music repertoire. As Robert Schumann wrote of both trios, 'One glance at Schubert's Trio [D.898] and all the troubles of human existence disappear, and all the world is fresh and bright again . . . the Trio in E flat major [D.929] is active, masculine, dramatic, while the one in B flat major [D.898] is passive, feminine, lyrical.'

The Trio in B flat was given its first performance on 28th January, in the last Schubertiad to be held at Spaun's house, which was a gathering in celebration of his engagement. The trio was played by Karl Maria von Bocklet (pianist), Ignaz Schuppanzigh (violinist) and Josef Linke (cellist), and Bocklet is said to have kissed the composer after the performance. Earlier in January, the Schubert circle's reading parties had recommenced at Schober's, having been in abeyance for nearly four years. It was at the reading on 12 January that Schubert first heard the poems of Heine's *Buch der Lieder* (Book of Songs), which had been published some months earlier. This resulted in his setting six of the poems. They were published posthumously in 1829 as part of the collection, *Schwanengesang* (Swansong, D.957).

Schubert's Heine songs are all such masterpieces that one cannot help regretting that he did not have the opportunity to compose many more of them. Heine's sentiment, tempered with irony, has been beautifully translated into music in these songs. 'Der Atlas' (Atlas) is powerful and bitter, compressed yet implacable; 'Ihr Bild' (Her

Portrait) is a gentle portrayal of grief; 'Das Fischermädchen' (The Fisher Girl') a charming barcarolle which perhaps ignores the note of sophistication in Heine's poem – if so, it is Schubert's only lapse in complete understanding throughout this group; 'Die Stadt' (The City), a masterly impressionistic landscape; and 'Am Meer' (By the Sea), one of Schubert's extraordinary seascapes, in which nature's moods mirror the emotions suffered by humans, in ineffably sad music. The final Heine song, 'Der Doppelgänger' (The Phantom Double), is the greatest of all, written throughout in a kind of heightened recitative or arioso, the drama presented as much by the piano as by the voice, the total effect intensely dramatic and affecting.

On 18 January 1828, Schubert wrote to Anselm Hüttenbrenner in Graz, for the last time:

My dear old Hüttenbrenner!!!
Are you surprised at my writing after all this time? I am, too! But there is a good reason for it now. So listen! At your end in Graz a drawing-master's post has fallen vacant, and candidates for the same have already been requested to put in their applications. My brother Karl, whom I think you also know, wants to obtain this post. He is highly skilled, both as a landscape painter and also as a draughtsman. If you could manage to do something for him in this affair, I should be infinitely grateful. You are an influential man in Graz, and maybe you know someone either in the Government or elsewhere who has a voice in the matter. My brother is married and has children, and he would be very glad, therefore, to find himself in an assured position. I hope that all goes well with you, and with your dear family and brothers too. My warmest greetings to them all. A trio of mine for pianoforte, violin and violoncello was performed at Schuppanzigh's house the other day, and pleased everyone very much. Bocklet, Schuppanzigh and Linke played it admirably. Have you written nothing new? Apropos, why doesn't Greiner, or whatever his name is, publish the two songs? What the devil is the meaning of it?

I repeat my request made above. Remember that whatever you do for my brother you are doing for me.

Hoping for a favourable reply,
I remain
until death
your faithful friend
Frz. Schubert.

(The two songs Schubert was enquiring after were 'Im Walde' [In the Forest, D.834] and 'Auf der Bruck' [At Die Bruck, D.853]. The title of the second song is sometimes mistranslated as 'On the Bridge'. 'Die Brücke' means 'the bridge' but Die Bruck is a holiday resort near Göttingen. Both songs were published in Graz at the end of May. Karl Schubert did not obtain the post of drawing-master at the training-school at Graz.)

In January there was a public performance of the C major Fantasy for violin and piano, which Josef Slavik and Karl Maria von Bocklet played at Slavik's concert in the County Hall. The concert took place at midday, and the critic of the *Sammler* somewhat unfairly wrote that the Fantasy 'occupied rather too much of the time a Viennese is prepared to devote to pleasures of the mind'. Several members of the audience appear to have agreed with him, for he continued, 'The hall emptied gradually, and the writer confesses that he too is unable to say anything about the conclusion of this piece of music.' The Leipzig *Allgemeine Musikalische Zeitung* said that the favourite composer of the Viennese 'has in this case positively miscomposed', but the London *Harmonicon* considered that the Fantasy possessed 'merit far above the common order'.

Resolving never to go to their current regular tavern again after a fracas on 2 February with 'the unmannerly hostess and therefore also with her husband', the Schubertians now made the *Rebhuhn* in the Goldschmiedgasse their habitual haunt. (It still exists as the *Café Rebhuhn*.)

On the same day in February, two foreign publishers wrote to Schubert hoping to acquire some of his works. They were H. A. Probst in Leipzig, and B. Schott's Sons in Mainz. Probst's letter was delayed, having been first delivered to a Josef Schubert at the Theater an der Wien: Schubert replied to the firm of Schott on 21 February:

I am much honoured by your letter of February 8th, and am very pleased to enter into closer association with a firm of such repute, and one that is in a position to give publicity to my works abroad.

I have the following compositions on hand:

(*a*) Trio for pianoforte, violin and violoncello, which was performed with great success here.

(*b*) Two string quartets (in G major and D minor).

(*c*) Four impromptus for pianoforte solo, which could be published either separately or together.

(*d*) Fantasy for pianoforte, four hands, dedicated to the Countess Caroline Esterházy.

(*e*) Fantasy for pianoforte and violin.

(*f*) Songs for one voice with pianoforte accompaniment, the poems by Schiller, Goethe, Klopstock, etc., etc., and Seidl, Schober, Leitner, Schulz, etc., etc.

(*g*) Four-part choruses for both male and female voices with pianoforte accompaniment, of which two contain solo parts, the poems by Grillparzer and Seidl.

(*h*) A five-part song for male voices, poem by Schober.

(*i*) 'Schlachtlied' [Battle Song] by Klopstock, a double chorus for eight male voices.

(*j*) Comic Trio, 'Der Hochzeitsbraten' [The Wedding Breakfast], by Schober, for soprano, tenor and bass, which has already been performed with success.

This completes the list of my finished compositions: in addition I have written three operas, a Mass and a symphony. I only mention these last, however, in order to make known to you my efforts in the highest forms of musical art.

Should you care to consider for publication anything from the above list I should be pleased to send it in return for a moderate remuneration.

B. Schott's Sons replied, expressing a desire to publish 'by degrees and as soon as possible' everything except the string quartets and the songs. Now busy with preparations for a public concert of his works in Vienna, Schubert did not respond for several weeks. The plan to give a public concert consisting entirely of his own compositions had been in his mind for a long time. It was now finally put into effect, and the following announcement appeared in the *Theaterzeitung*:

Among the manifold exhibitions of the art of music which have been offered us in the course of this season, and still await us, one should attract general attention the more because it offers enjoyment both new and surprising by the novelty and sterling value of the compositions and the attractive variety among the musical items as well as the sympathetic collaboration of the most celebrated local artists.

Franz Schubert, whose powerfully intellectual, enchantingly lovely and original compositions have made him the favourite of the entire musical public, works which may well secure their creator a more than ephemeral, indeed an imperishable, name by their genuine artistic value, will perform on 26 March, at a private concert (in the Austrian Society of Music Lovers' hall) a series of the latest products of his mind, according to the following programme:

1. First movement from a new string quartet [probably the G major, D.887], performed by Messrs Böhm, Holz, Weiss and Linke.

2. Four new songs, performed by Herr Vogl, retired Imperial and Royal Court Opera singer [Vogl was accompanied by Schubert, and the songs were 'Der Kreuzzug' (The Crusade, D.932), 'Die Sterne' (The Stars, D.939), 'Fischerweise' (Fisherman's Song, D.881) and 'Fragment aus dem Aischylos' (Fragment from Aeschylus, D.450)].

3. 'Ständchen' [Serenade, D.920], poem by Grillparzer, performed by Mlle Josefine Fröhlich and the lady pupils of the Conservatorium.

4. New trio for pianoforte, violin and violoncello [in E flat, D.929], performed by Messrs K. M. von Bocklet, Böhm and Linke.

5. 'Auf dem Strom' [On the River, D.943], song with horn and pianoforte accompaniment, performed by Messrs Tietze and Lewy.

6. 'Die Allmacht' [The Almighty, D.852], poem by Ladislaus von Pyrker, sung by Herr Vogl.

7. 'Schlachtlied' [Battle Song, D.912], poem by Klopstock, double chorus for male voices.

May the glorious German-language composer, then, be granted an attendance such as his modesty and unobtrusiveness would alone deserve, quite apart from his artistic eminence and the rare and great musical enjoyment which is to be expected.

Tickets, at 3 florins [Viennese Currency], are to be had at the music establishments of Messrs Diabelli, Haslinger and Leidesdorf.

'Auf dem Strom' was written specially for the concert, and most of the other works performed were comparatively recent. The concert, which took place in a small hall in the house *Zum roten Igel* (The Red Hedgehog) belonging to the Gesellschaft der Musikfreunde, was completely sold out. As the takings amounted to the considerable sum of around 800 florins, the audience must have numbered between 250 and 300. The concert began at 7 p.m., and probably ended no later than 9 p.m. (The programme would have taken one and a half hours to perform.) Afterwards, the Schubertians repaired to the *Schnecke* (The Snail), a tavern on the Petersplatz where they 'rejoiced until midnight'.

Schubert's concert received very little attention from the Viennese press, probably because of local excitement over the violinist Paganini who had arrived in Vienna on 16 March. Paganini gave his first concert on the 29th, and remained in Vienna for four months, during which time he gave fourteen concerts. (His admission prices made such a sensation that, for some time thereafter, Viennese cab-drivers referred to the five-florin note as a *Paganinerl*.) However, Schubert's concert was reviewed by a number of foreign journals, and for the most part favourably, though the correspondent of the Dresden *Abendzeitung*, while conceding that 'there was unquestionably much that was good among it all', thought that 'the minor stars paled before the radiance of this comet in the musical heavens [Paganini]'.

By March, Schubert had completed the large-scale symphony on which he had been working for some time, most of which had probably been written in the summer of 1825 at Gmunden and Gastein. This was the Symphony in C major, now called the 'Great' C major Symphony, No. 9 (D.944), not only on account of its stature and length but also to distinguish it from the earlier C major Symphony, No. 6 (D.589). Schubert presented the new symphony to the Society of Music Lovers for performance, but when it was declined as being too long and too difficult, he withdrew it and substituted the earlier C major Symphony (which the Society performed one month after its composer's death).

The 'Great' C major Symphony is generally agreed to be the peak of Schubert's achievement in symphonic music, and one of the great Viennese classical symphonies, along with Mozart's final three and Beethoven's odd-numbered symphonies. It is a work which miraculously combines authority with sweetness, lyricism with strength, classicism with romanticism, and grandeur with human warmth. It is a long work (Schumann commented on the 'heavenly length' of its last movement), but so majestic in conception that no one who loves the music of Schubert feels that it could be shortened by a single bar. There are magical touches in each movement, and the slow movement is the essential, poetic heart of Schubert. The symphony was not performed during Schubert's lifetime: it is distressing to think that the composer never actually heard the work. It was rescued from oblivion by Schumann, who discovered it amongst a number of Franz Schubert's manuscripts shown to him in 1838 by Ferdinand Schubert.

After his successful concert on 26 March 1828, Schubert turned again to negotiating with those publishers who had approached him. On 10 April he wrote both to Schott and to Probst. To Schott he offered the Trio in E flat (D.929) and other works:

The arrangements and preparation connected with my concert – which consisted entirely of my own compositions – were responsible for this long delay in replying to your letter. In the meantime I have had copies made of the trio for which you asked – this was received by a crowded house with such extraordinary enthusiasm that I have been asked to repeat the concert – and also of the impromptus and the five-part male chorus. If you agree to the price of 100 florins, Assimilated Currency, for this trio, and 60 florins for the other two works together, I can send them off at once. I would beg you, though, to have them published as soon as possible.

A letter was despatched on the same day to Probst, in Leipzig, in reply to the publisher's initial enquiry:

You have honoured me with a letter which has been left unanswered until now by reason of the arrangements connected with my concert. It may perhaps interest you to hear that this concert, at which only my own compositions were performed, was given before a crowded audience, and that I myself received an extraordinarily enthusiastic reception. A trio for pianoforte, violin and violoncello roused such widespread interest that I have been invited to give a second concert (which will be a repetition, more or less, of the first). I shall, by the way, be very glad to let you have some of my compositions if you are prepared to pay the moderate sum of 60 florins, Assimilated Currency, for a good selection of the same. It is hardly necessary to assure you that I shall only submit what I consider to be really successful compositions – in so far as the composer himself and various select groups of friends are able to judge – for it is naturally a matter of the first importance to myself to send nothing but really fine work into foreign countries.

The Mainz firm, Schott's, replied that the trio was probably a long work, and that as they had recently published several trios they would content themselves with taking the set of impromptus (D.935) and the five-part male chorus ('Mondenschein'; Moonlight, D.875) for 60 florins. Schubert sent these, with a short covering letter, on 23 May. By 2 October he had not received even an acknowledgement that the compositions had arrived, so he wrote again:

A considerable time has elapsed since your last letter, and I should be very glad to know if you have duly received the compositions which I despatched through Haslinger, namely four impromptus and a five-part male chorus. Will you kindly let me have an answer about this? I am especially anxious that these compositions should be published as soon as possible. The opus number for the impromptus is 101 and that for the five-part chorus is 102. I hope for a quick and favourable reply.

B. Schott's Sons replied that they had sent the impromptus on to their Paris establishment for their opinion, which they had only now received. The works were thought by the Paris office to be 'too difficult for small pieces' and not likely to sell well in France. 'If at any time', Schott's continued, 'you should write something less difficult and yet brilliant in an easier key, please send it to us without more ado.' Meanwhile, they enclosed thirty florins for the male chorus alone. (When the second set of impromptus was eventually published, eleven years after Schubert's death, it was not as opus 101 but as opus 142.)

The other publisher, Probst, accepted promptly the offer of a trio and sent sixty florins to Schubert before receiving the manuscript. 'I still hope', Probst wrote, 'that you will shortly accede to my request to send me very soon some selected small pieces for the voice or for four hands, a trio being as a rule merely a prestige piece and rarely capable of bringing in anything.' Schubert replied on 10 May:

I beg to send you herewith the trio for which you ask, although the suggested price of 60 florins, Assimilated Currency, was intended for a volume of songs or of pianoforte pieces – not for a trio which has six times as much work in it. However, in order at length to make a start, I beg you to hurry on with the publication as soon as possible, and to send me six copies. The cuts indicated in the last movement are to be most scrupulously observed. See that really capable players are found for the first performance, and above all see that, at the changes of the time-signature in the last movement, the tempo is not lost. The minuet at a moderate pace, and *piano* throughout; the trio, on the other hand, to be played vigorously except where *p* and *pp* are marked.

For some reason, Schubert's letter took more than two months, instead of the usual few days, to reach Leipzig. Probst wrote to Schubert on the day he received it, 18 July, warning the composer not to be surprised if, as a result, the trio was to be published later than perhaps he had expected. He assured Schubert that it would be ready in six weeks, and asked for details of title, dedication and opus number, Schubert replied on 1 August:

The trio is opus 100. I beg you to make sure that the edition is free from errors. I am ardently looking forward to its publication. This work will not be dedicated to any one person, but rather to all who find pleasure in it. That is the most profitable form of dedication.

More than six weeks went by, but the trio did not appear. Schubert wrote again on 2 October:

I am wondering if the trio will ever appear. Are you still without its number? It is opus 100. I am anxiously awaiting its publication. I have composed among other things three sonatas for pianoforte alone, which I want to dedicate to Hummel. I have also set to music several lyrics by Heine, of Hamburg, which have had an extraordinarily good reception here, and finally I have written a quintet for two violins, one viola, and two violoncelli. I have played the sonatas in several places with great success, but the quintet will be tried out only in the next few days. Should any of these compositions by any chance commend themselves to you, please let me know.

The Trio in E flat, opus 100 (D.929), was published during October, but by the time copies reached Vienna its composer was no longer alive.

In March, the month in which he had completed the 'Great' C major Symphony, Schubert also composed 'Mirjams Siegesgesang' (Miriam's Song of Triumph, D.942), an attractive setting for soprano solo and chorus with piano accompaniment of a poem by Grillparzer on the Old Testament story of the escape of the Jews from Egypt. This may have been composed with the 26 March concert in mind, but in the event it was not included. Schubert planned eventually to write an orchestral accompaniment for the work, which takes about seventeen minutes to perform, but did not do so. In April he completed the most poetic of his works for piano duet, the superb Fantasy in F minor (D.940). He had begun to sketch it in January, and it must have been finished in draft by 21 February for Schubert included the Fantasy in the list of works he offered to Schott on that day. But it was not until April that he put the finishing touches to it, and wrote out a fair copy. It was played by Schubert and Franz Lachner on 9 May to an audience of one, Bauernfeld, who confided to his diary: 'Today Schubert (with Lachner) played his new, wonderful four-hand Fantasy to me.' The Fantasy is the only work which Schubert dedicated to the Countess Caroline Esterházy, though it is said that he once told her that such dedications were unnecessary, as all his work was dedicated to her.

Several fine pieces, mostly for piano, were composed during May and June. The three 'Klavierstücke' (Piano Pieces, D.946) may have been intended as part of a third set of impromptus. They are certainly no less delightful than the impromptus, which they resemble in style. Two piano duets, the lively Allegro in A minor (D.947), to which Schubert's publisher gave the title 'Lebensstürme' (Life's Storms), and the beautifully lyrical Rondo in A major (D.951), are both characteristic of Schubert's mature piano style. However, the 'Notturno' in E flat (D.897), perhaps intended as the slow movement of a trio for piano, violin and cello, is disappointingly weak. (Its date of composition is uncertain: it may be a much earlier work.)

In the summer, Schubert received invitations to Graz from the Pachlers, and to Gmunden, the lakeside town on Traunsee, from Ferdinand Traweger, with whom he and Vogl had stayed in happier days. Unfortunately, he was able to accept neither invitation, for his finances were now in such a state that he was unable to muster sufficient money for his travel expenses. The proceeds of his concert had, it seems, already been dissipated: perhaps he had taken the opportunity to repay a number of debts. He managed to get away from Vienna only for three or four days at the beginning of June, with Franz Lachner and another friend. They went to the nearby spa of Baden, whence they made an excursion on 4 June to the twelfth-century Cistercian Abbey at Heiligenkreuz. There Lachner and Schubert played on the organ a fugue for four hands (D.952) which Schubert had written the previous day. This was his only work for organ alone.

A rather mundane setting of the first eight verses of Psalm 92, 'Lied für den Sabbath' (Song for the Sabbath, D.953) in the original Hebrew, which Schubert composed in July for the City Synagogue, was performed there during the summer with the Cantor Salomon Sulzer as chief soloist.

During June, Schubert began work on a new Mass in E flat, which he completed in August but which did not receive its first performance until a year after his death. The last of Schubert's Masses, a series of joyous and humane works which inspire affection rather than religious awe, the E flat Mass (D.950) is also his finest, a personal and deeply felt work imbued with something of the sadness which found its way into almost everything he composed in these last months of his life. Schubert intended this Mass to be first performed in the autumn at the Holy Trinity church in the Alserstrasse (the church in which Beethoven's funeral service had been held), but the performance did not take place until a year later, when the Mass was conducted by Ferdinand Schubert.

Until the end of August, there are still to be found references in Franz von Hartmann's diaries to evenings in taverns and cafés when the assembled company was 'most merry' with Schubert, Schwind, Schober and others. On 26 August they were at the 'Oak Tree' on the

Brandstätte square, where the music was provided by the twenty-four-year-old Johann Strauss (senior) and his orchestra. But on 1 September, on the advice of his doctor, Ernst Rinna, Schubert moved from Schober's to his brother Ferdinand's house in the Neue Wieden suburb. He had complained of fits of giddiness, and the doctor thought that the air outside the city would do him good. Schubert did not consider the move to be a permanent one, for he left most of his music manuscripts in a cupboard at Schober's. His brother's house, unfortunately, was extremely damp, and must have had anything but a beneficial effect on his condition. (Today the house, Kettenbrückengasse 6, is part of a closely built-up area; in Schubert's time the street had no proper name, was referred to simply as the 'newly opened street near the archepiscopal barn', and was in semi-rural surroundings.)

On 5 September, Schubert was well enough to attend the first performance at the theatre in the Hofburg of a comedy, *Die Brautwerber* (The Suitors), by his friend Bauernfeld. Together with Grillparzer, Schwind and Schober, he went afterwards to the inn where the author was expected to join them. However, Bauernfeld did not appear: he was walking the streets in despair at the poor reception his play had received.

August had been a productive month for Schubert. As well as completing his Mass in E flat, he had composed seven songs to poems by the Berlin critic and poet Ludwig Rellstab (1799–1860). The six settings of Heine, whose poems Schubert had encountered at one of Schober's readings in January, were probably also completed during August. The Rellstab songs include the amiable 'Liebesbotschaft' (Love's Message); the romantic 'Ständchen' (Serenade), which is undoubtedly the most widely known Schubert song, played in countless transcriptions and arrangements; an outburst of wrathful despair, 'Aufenthalt' (Resting Place); and the warmly exhilarating 'Abschied' (Farewell). Together with 'Die Taubenpost' (The Pigeon Post), a setting of a poem by Johann Gabriel Seidl which Schubert composed two months later, these Heine and Rellstab settings were issued by the Viennese publisher Haslinger in May 1829, six months after their composer's death, as a cycle of fourteen songs with the romantic title of *Schwanengesang* (Swansong, D.957). As they are the last songs for solo voice and piano that Schubert wrote, the title is not inappropriate, though he did not choose it. In no sense a real cycle, this collection of fourteen individual songs includes some of Schubert's finest Lieder.

On 25 September, Schubert wrote to one of his friends, Johann Baptist Jenger:

I have already handed to Haslinger the second part of *Winterreise*. Nothing will come of the journey to Graz this year, as money and weather are wholly unfavourable. The invitation to Dr Menz's I accept with pleasure, for I always very much like to hear Baron Schönstein sing. You may meet me on Saturday afternoon at Bogner's coffee-house, Singerstrasse, between 4 and 5 o'clock.

The party at Dr Ignaz Menz's was on Saturday, 27 September. Baron Schönstein sang Schubert songs, and the composer himself played all three of the new piano sonatas he had composed during the month. The last one, in B flat, he had completed only the previous day. Also in September he had composed his final piece of chamber music, the great C major String Quintet (D.956).

These three late piano sonatas represent the peak of Schubert's achievement in the genre. The first, in C minor (D.958), is, in style, perhaps the most Beethovenian of his piano works, yet its personal utterance, its individual tone, is very much that of Schubert. The A major Sonata (D.959) ranges widely in mood, its wealth of melody spontaneous and seemingly inexhaustible. The last of the three, the Sonata in B flat (D.960), is a favourite with lovers of Schubert's music: from the calm serenity of its opening, through the wistful sadness of its andante and the brilliant yet delicate scherzo, to the brave gaiety of the finale, there is hardly a bar of this work which does not carry the imprint of Schubert's creative personality. He does not seek Beethoven's concentration, but exploits his own more leisurely feeling for structure in this expansive, warm and lovable sonata, surely the finest he composed.

Schubert's final chamber music work, the String Quintet in C (D.956), also composed in September 1828, is one of the greatest works of its kind ever written. Benjamin Britten once wrote: 'It is arguable that the richest and most productive eighteen months in our music history is the time when Beethoven had just died, when the other nineteenth-century giants, Wagner, Verdi and Brahms, had not begun; I mean the period in which Franz Schubert wrote the *Winterreise*, and C major Symphony, his last three Piano Sonatas, the C major String Quintet, as well as a dozen other glorious pieces.' Of all these works of Schubert's last months, none is valued more highly than the Quintet, scored for two violins, viola, and two cellos. At the heart of the work is the extraordinarily eloquent and consolatory second movement, an adagio of elegiac beauty which affects the true Schubertian more deeply than almost any other music. Sentimental though the observation may be, it is difficult not to feel that here one is overhearing Schubert's farewell to the world.

With his brother Ferdinand and two friends, Schubert went on a three-day walking tour at the beginning of October. They first walked south from Vienna for about fifteen miles to Unter-Walters-dorf in Lower Austria, and on seven miles further to Eisenstadt (then in Hungary, now in the Burgenland province of Austria), where they visited Haydn's grave. On his return to Vienna, Schubert received a letter from Anton Schindler, Beethoven's old friend and factotum who was now living in Budapest, inviting him to attend the first performance there of Lachner's opera *Die Bürgschaft* (The Pledge), and to stay with Schindler as his guest, and also suggesting that, while there, Schubert should give a concert of his songs:

This promises a good success, and since it is well known that your timidity and easy-going ways will keep you from lending much of a hand in such an undertaking, I advise and inform you that you will find people here who will most readily support you, heavy as you are. . . . There is a young amateur here who sings your songs with a fine tenor voice well, really quite well, and he is with us; the gentlemen of the theatre ditto; my sister ditto; in this way you need only deposit your fat carcass here and accompany whatever is performed. Songs for several voices cannot fail to make their effect either. Some of them are known here. Write nothing new: it is not necessary!

But it was too late. Schubert's health would no longer allow him to undertake the twenty-eight-hour stage-coach journey from Vienna to Budapest. He apparently did not even reply to Schindler's invitation. He was well enough to continue composing during October and completed three short but beautiful pieces of church music for soloists, chorus and orchestra: a new 'Benedictus' (D.961) for his C major Mass of 1816 (D.452); a 'Tantum ergo' (D.962); and an 'Offertorium' (D.963). He also wrote his last two songs, the engaging 'Die Taubenpost', which was included with the Rellstab and Heine settings of earlier in the year in *Schwanengesang* (D.957), and 'Der Hirt auf dem Felsen' (The Shepherd on the Cliffs, D.965), a delightful song for soprano, clarinet and piano, which had been commissioned by the soprano Anna Milder-Hauptmann. It is not known which of the two is the very last song Schubert composed.

Until recently, it was thought that the 'Great' C major was Schubert's final symphony. But, in 1978, examination of several Schubert manuscripts in the Vienna Municipal Library revealed that, among sketches for a number of symphonic movements composed at various times, there lay the drafts of three movements of a symphony composed in the last weeks of Schubert's life, in October and early November 1828. Several musicologists have worked on the sketches, and a version of what can now confidently be referred to as Schubert's Tenth Symphony in D major has been edited for performance by Brian Newbould. Further editorial work was undertaken by the Belgian composer and conductor Pierre Bartholomée, and the Newbould-Bartholomée Schubert Tenth Symphony has been recorded for the gramophone. As the 1828 drafts lacked a scherzo, Newbould has used one (D.780a) dating from the spring of 1821 which Schubert may have intended inserting into the 1828 work, which consists of an allegro, an andante and a final allegro. The resulting Symphony No. 10 (D.936a/780a) is a major work, authentically Schubertian in sound and musical character, and with a remarkable slow movement, written in the last weeks of Schubert's life, which in its desolate harmonies anticipates Mahler's Ninth Symphony of more than eighty years later.

Towards the end of October, the circle of Schubertians lost a member, and Schubert the companionship of a dear friend, when Schwind moved to Munich to join the Art Academy there. At the end of the month, Schubert's condition began seriously to deteriorate. On 31 October he and Ferdinand had a meal together at the *Rotes Kreuz* tavern in the Himmelpfortgrund, which had been an old Schubert family haunt. Here Schubert was nauseated by the fish he tried to eat, and from then on until his death he appears to have eaten very little. Three days later, again with Ferdinand, he visited the parish church at Hernals to hear a Requiem composed by his brother, and afterwards went for a three-hour walk with Ferdinand and the church's choir-master, Josef Mayssen.

Having been studying a number of Handel scores, Schubert had come to the conclusion that he ought to learn more about the art of composing fugues. Together with Josef Lanz, a fellow-composer eleven days his senior, he enrolled in the class of Simon Sechter (1788–1867), the foremost master of music theory in Vienna. Schubert and Lanz had their first lesson on 4 November, but a week later, on the 11th, Schubert took permanently to his bed in Ferdinand's small apartment. Here he was looked after by Ferdinand, his wife Anna, and their twelve-year-old daughter, Therese, and also by his and Ferdinand's thirteen-year-old step-sister, Josefa, whom Spaun later described as a 'loving nurse'.

On 12 November, Schubert wrote his last letter:

Dear Schober,

I am ill. I have had nothing to eat or drink for eleven days now, and can only wander feebly and uncertainly between my armchair and my bed. Rinna is treating me. If I take any food, I bring it up again at once.

Please be so good, then, as to come to my aid in this desperate condition with something to read. I have read Cooper's *The Last of the Mohicans, The Spy, The Pilot* and *The Pioneers*. If by chance you have anything else of his, I beg you to leave it for me at the coffee-house with Frau von Bogner. My brother, who is conscientiousness itself, will bring it over to me without fail. Or indeed anything else.

Your friend,
Schubert

Schober sent his friend some volumes of Fenimore Cooper, but did not visit him for fear of infection. Spaun came, however, and Schubert's last visitors were Bauernfeld and Franz Lachner, on 17 November. (From Spaun we learn that, in his last lucid moments, Schubert busied himself correcting the proofs of part two of *Winterreise*.) The previous day, two doctors had held a conference at Schubert's sick-bed. One of them, Josef von Vering (a friend of Schubert's regular doctor, Rinna, who was then ill), was a specialist in venereal diseases. Vering and his colleague Wisgrill diagnosed typhoid fever, and prescribed a change in treatment. A professional nurse had already been engaged, and she was now joined by a male nurse. Medicine was administered to Schubert at regular intervals, but on the evening of the 17th he became violently and continuously delirious, and remained in a state of delirium throughout the 18th. He lapsed from delirium into unconsciousness on the next day, Wednesday, 19 November, and at three in the afternoon turned to the wall with the words, 'Here, here is my end', and died. He had lived for thirty-one years, nine months, and nineteen days. The cause of his death was officially described as 'nervous fever', which, in those days, meant virtually anything which perplexed the physicians.

The funeral took place on 21 November. At 6 a.m. on the morning of that day, Ferdinand wrote to his father:

Very many are expressing the wish that the body of our good Franz should be buried in the Währing churchyard. Among those many am I too, believing myself to be induced thereto by Franz himself. On the evening before his death, though only half conscious, he still said to me: 'I implore you to transfer me to my room, do not leave me here, in this corner under the earth; do I then deserve no place above the earth?' I answered him: 'Dear Franz, rest assured, believe your brother Ferdinand, whom you have always trusted, and who loves you so much. You are in the room in which you have always been so far, and lie in your bed!' And Franz said: 'No, it is not true. Beethoven does not lie here.' Could this be anything but an indication of his inmost wish to repose by the side of Beethoven, whom he so greatly revered?

Schubert's coffin was carried by a group of young students, followed by friends and admirers of the composer, to St Joseph's church in the Margareten suburb. After a service, which included the performance of an arrangement for chorus and wind instruments of Schubert's 1817 song 'Pax vobiscum' (D.551), with new words by Schober, who had written the text of the original song, the coffin was conducted to the church at Währing and interred in the Währing cemetery, close to the grave of Beethoven. Two years later, a monument was placed above Schubert's grave, inscribed with an epitaph written by Grillparzer: 'Die Tonkunst begrub hier einen reichen Besitz aber noch viel schönere Hoffnungen' (The art of music here interred a rich possession but even fairer hopes). In 1888 the remains of Beethoven and Schubert were transferred to the Central Cemetery of Vienna, where so many of the great Viennese composers lie buried.

That Schubert received little or no recognition during his lifetime is untrue. Approximately seventy of his works were given their first performances in Vienna soon after they were composed, and Schubert himself appeared in public on several occasions as pianist or conductor. He was only thirty-one when he died, and on the threshold of his career, but 478 of his compositions had already been published, most of them in Vienna. His greatest success was with his songs, of course, but he composed so many that the market could not keep pace with them. He earned from his music the equivalent of about £10,000 today, which seems pitifully little to an age whose practitioners of music are not considered successful unless they have earned their first million while still in their teens. But if Beethoven, who at his death was rightly considered the greatest composer of his time, had died a quarter of a century earlier at the age of thirty-one, he too would have been no further advanced along the path to material success than his younger contemporary whose life ended at that age. Schubert may occasionally have lived in a garret: he never starved in one.

For many years it was only his reputation as a composer of songs that kept the name of Franz Schubert alive. Liszt, who called Schubert 'the most poetic musician' of all, made brilliant transcriptions for the piano of many songs as well as arrangements of much of the dance music. As the nineteenth century progressed, the symphonies became known, but it was not until the twentieth century that the sonatas and chamber music became popular, and Schubert's real stature began to be recognized. Today, he is no longer considered merely the junior contemporary of Beethoven, pouring his full heart, like Shelley's skylark, 'in profuse strains of unpremeditated art'. Schubert's art, for all its appearance of spontaneity, was not unpremeditated but highly conscious, and his stature is that of one of the immortals of music. The words addressed to the art of music in Schubert's song 'An die Musik' can fairly be applied to the music of Schubert himself:

> Du holde Kunst, in wieviel grauen Stunden,
> Wo mich des Lebens wilder Kreis umstrickt,
> Hast du mein Herz zu warmer Lieb'entzunden,
> Hast mich in eine bessre Welt entrückt!

> Oft hat ein Seufzer, deiner Harf'entflossen,
> Ein süsser, heiliger Akkord von dir
> Den Himmel bessrer Zeiten mir erschlossen,
> Du holde Kunst, ich danke dir dafür!

> (Thou dearest art, how oft in gloomy hours,
> When life's wild coils were holding me enmeshed,
> Have I been warmed at heart by your great powers,
> And borne to a far better world, refreshed!

Oft has a sigh that your harp-strings have uttered,
A sweet and holy chord of sheerest bliss,
The heaven of better times for me unshuttered.
Thou dearest art, my thanks to thee for this!)

CHAPTER EIGHT

Genius Observed

Many of Schubert's friends left written accounts of him: memories, anecdotes, descriptions of his personal appearance, his personality, his habits. Commenting on a biography of Schubert by Heinrich Kreissle von Hellborn in 1864, Josef von Spaun, who was by then 76 years old, quarrelled with the biographer's description of the composer: 'Schubert is not described correctly,' wrote Spaun,

either from a physical or from an intellectual standpoint. His face is portrayed as almost ugly and negroid; but anyone who knew him well will be forced to contradict that. The portrait of Schubert painted by Rieder, and engraved, is extraordinarily like him. Looking at it, one can judge for oneself whether the face is ugly and negroid. Just as little can one say that Schubert was handsome; but he was well formed and when he spoke pleasantly, or smiled, his features were full of charm, and when he was working, full of enthusiasm and burning with zeal, his features appeared transformed and almost beautiful.

So far as his body is concerned, one might imagine him as a fat lump, from the descriptions in the biography. But that is entirely incorrect. Schubert had a solidly built, thick-set body but there was no question of his being fat or of having a paunch. His very youthful friend, Moritz Schwind, exceeded him in girth even in those days.

Spaun's comment on Schwind does not ring true, for most contemporary descriptions of the young artist refer to his slim, almost girlish figure. But, in later life, these Schubertians could be astonishingly rude about one another. A Viennese journalist, in an article in *Die Neue Freie Presse* in 1866, wrote: 'Schwind, asked by a Viennese lady what Schubert looked like, answered in his devastating way, "Like a drunken cabby!" ' A more considered description of the composer was provided by Leopold von Sonnleithner, writing in 1857:

The lithograph portrait of Schubert at Diabelli & Co. in Vienna is the best likeness, except that the body is much too heavy and broad; the big plaster bust is also a very good likeness, especially in the lines of the mouth. Schubert was below average height, with a round, fat face, short neck, a not very high forehead, and thick, brown, naturally curly hair; back and shoulders rounded, arms and hands fleshy, short fingers, plump hands; his eyes (if I am not mistaken) grey-blue, eyebrows bushy, nose stubby and broad, lips thick; the face somewhat negroid. The colour of his skin was fair rather than dark, but it was inclined to break out into little pimples and was somewhat darker because of this. His head sat somewhat squeezed between his shoulders, inclining rather forward.

Schubert always wore spectacles. In repose, his expression appeared dull rather than vivacious, sullen rather than cheerful; one could have taken him for an Austrian (or even a Bavarian) peasant. Only if one observed him more closely did his features become slightly animated among intimate friends, when there was wine or beer; but even then he never laughed freely and openly, but only managed a chuckle which sounded toneless rather than bright. Shy and taciturn, especially in smart society, which he only frequented in order to accompany his songs, more or less as a favour. Whilst doing this his face wore the most serious expression, and as soon as it was over he withdrew into a neighbouring room. Indifferent to praise and applause, he shunned compliments and was content if his intimate friends gave him evidence of their satisfaction. He sometimes went to private balls at the houses of families he was intimate with; he never danced, but was always ready to sit down at the piano, where for hours he improvised the most beautiful waltzes; those he liked he repeated, in order to remember them and write them out afterwards.

Eduard von Bauernfeld, writing at various times, described his friend's personality rather than his outward appearance. In 1857, nearly thirty years after the composer's death, Bauernfeld wrote:

Schubert's outward life was, by the way, of the utmost simplicity; at first it was spent in the poor circumstances of a school teacher and later in those of an Austrian genius; he was an example unique in this country and one who, here especially, even though it may have been the same everywhere, had to fight against want and stupidity. But the inner life he shared with friends and those who were congenial to him offers just as little in the way of tangible biographical features and could be portrayed only in some form of poetic description. Schubert had, so to speak, a double nature, the Viennese gaiety being interwoven and ennobled by a trait of deep melancholy. Inwardly a poet and outwardly a kind of hedonist, it was only natural that, as a person, he was judged according to the outward appearance and this, moreover,

was a bitter task for him. In the morning he felt the urge to compose, and in the afternoon he wanted to rest and, in summer, go out of doors. There was only one piano lesson which afforded him pleasure. The young Countess Marie Esterházy delighted him by her feelings for music and by her amiability. His association with the Esterházy family also resulted in an invitation for several months to Zseliz, in Hungary, where Schubert felt very much at home.

Spaun, too, refutes the suggestion that Schubert was a habitual drunkard:

Schubert was always cheerful, talkative and often witty too. The summer drew him out of doors and then it sometimes happened that, owing to a beautiful evening or because of congenial company, he forgot an invitation, often even one in aristocratic society. This caused annoyance, but it hardly bothered him at all.

Because he liked to go into the country and often drank a glass of wine there in pleasant company, spiteful voices labelled him as a glutton, as a drunkard; but nothing is further from the truth than this miserable gossip; on the contrary, he was very temperate, and even at times of the greatest gaiety he never exceeded a reasonable amount.

Anselm Hüttenbrenner, encouraged by Franz Liszt in 1854 to write down his recollections of Schubert, supports what others have reported of Schubert's personality and his working habits:

Schubert never composed in the afternoon; after lunch he went to a coffee-house, drank a small portion of black coffee, smoked for an hour or two and read the newspapers at the same time. In the evening he went to one or other of the theatres. . . . He foresaw clearly that Rossini's works would do great harm to German-language opera, but consoled himself with the thought that, in the long run, they would not be able to endure, because of their lack of intrinsic worth, and that eventually people would recover their senses again and seek out *Don Giovanni*, *Die Zauberflöte* and *Fidelio*. However, he did not entirely reject Rossini's works; he praised in this prolific writer the refined taste in instrumentation and the novelty and charm of many of his melodies. He would certainly have given his approval to *Guillaume Tell*, had he lived to hear it. . . . Meyerbeer's *Crociato*, which Schubert heard with me at the theatre at Graz with a good cast, made an unfavourable impression on him. After the first act he said to me: 'Look here, I can't stand any more of this; let's go outside!'

About himself and his works Schubert seldom spoke and when he did it was only a few words. His favourite topics of conversation revolved around Handel, Mozart and Beethoven. He also thought very highly of the two

Haydns; but their work provided his spirit with too little nourishment and stimulus. With Bach's compositions, which in my old age I now play assiduously, Schubert was only slightly conversant; but to judge by his taste, he too, at a more advanced age, would have found a lively interest in the extremely original compositions of this great master of music. It was Beethoven's Mass in C which, most of all, moved him to devotion.

When the merry musical brotherhood, of whom there were often ten, met together intimately anywhere, each had his own nickname. . . .

A slightly different flavour of the good old times is suggested by Leopold von Sonnleithner in 1857, though he too confirms Schubert's industriousness:

Unfortunately Schubert, who lacked all sense of money matters, was always in difficulties, so that, when he was short of cash, the publishers bought his works for a trifling sum and gained a hundredfold thereby. Schubert was extraordinarily fertile and industrious in composing. For everything else that goes by the name of *work* he had no use. Seldom going to the theatre or into fashionable society, he loved to spend an evening at an inn, in the company of gay friends, and on such occasions midnight often passed unnoticed and pleasure was indulged to excess. As a result of this he acquired the habit of staying in bed in the morning until 10 or 11 o'clock; and as this was the time when he felt the greatest urge to compose, the morning hours passed in this way, and the best time for earning some money by teaching was thus lost. . . . Unfortunately I must confess that I saw him in a drunken state several times. On one occasion I was with him at a party, in one of the suburbs, where there was a great deal of music-making and feasting. I went home at about 2 o'clock in the morning; Schubert remained still longer and the next day I learnt that he had had to sleep there as he was incapable of going home. This happened in a house where he had not long been known and where he had only been introduced a short time previously.

One can hardly live simultaneously a life of profligacy and that of an industrious and prolific composer. Schubert's dedication was to his work, not to drunken carousing. That he occasionally over-indulged in alcohol can hardly be denied, but the mental image of Schubert as a near-alcoholic who occasionally dashed off a beautiful song resolutely fails to come to mind. What does is a completely different image, the one suggested by Albert Stadler, writing in 1858 (see p. 11).

Several anecdotes concerning individual incidents were recalled by Schubert's friends and acquaintances. Max Löwenthal, who first knew the composer as a fellow-pupil at the *Gymnasium*, noted in his diary in 1838, ten years after Schubert's death: 'Some gay sparks, among them Schubert, Bauernfeld and Schober, were on their way home one night after a celebration. They came to a building site on which even the foundations had scarcely been laid. They gathered round and sang a full-throated serenade to the future occupiers of the building to be.'

This occasion was also commemorated years later on a section of 'Die Lachnerrolle' (The Lachner Roll), a long roll of water-colour sketches produced by Schwind in 1862 in honour of Franz Lachner. Schubert, Lachner, Schwind (not Schober) and Bauernfeld are shown serenading an unknown lady in front of the scaffolding of a house under construction.

Another fascinating vignette, a sudden, lively glimpse of Schubert, is offered by Leopold Kupelwieser, who, in conversation with the composer's biographer Kreissle, around 1860, said that once, when Schubert was playing his 'Wanderer' Fantasy to a circle of friends, he broke down in the last movement, his technique not being up to it, and sprang up from the piano with the words: 'Let the devil play the stuff!'

One story which did not reach print until 1887, but which was handed down orally, originated with a proof-reader at the publishing house of Diabelli. The proof-reader, Josef Fahrbach (who was later to become well known as a flautist), was in Diabelli's shop one day when a young man with a roll of music manuscript in his hand appeared shyly in the doorway. Diabelli waved him away briskly with the words, 'Nothing doing today!', whereupon the young man made a bow and departed. 'He comes here every week with new compositions,' Diabelli explained to his proof-reader, who only later discovered that it was Franz Schubert who had been thus dismissed.

Two Schubert stories, given to him by Schwind, were told by the Viennese music critic Eduard Hanslick in his memoirs in 1863:

One morning Schwind turned up at Schubert's to take him on an excursion. Schubert hurried to finish his dressing and was rummaging in his chest of drawers for a pair of socks. But, however much he rummaged, every pair turned out to be hopelessly torn to pieces. 'Schwind,' said Schubert, with superstitious seriousness, at the end of this forlorn inspection, 'Schwind, now I really do believe that whole ones are not knitted any more.'

Of Schubert's amazing facility in writing, Schwind had a number of little anecdotes from his own observation. He had once put Schubert up for the night in his modest summer lodgings at Heiligenstadt. The following morning dawned to the accompaniment of heavy rain and put any idea of a walk out of the question. Schubert paced irritably up and down the room. 'Schubert! For heaven's sake do something!' Schwind ordered him after a while. 'Compose a song!' 'How can I do that here,' replied the bored guest, 'here, where I have neither piano, manuscript paper nor words to set?' 'I will take care of that,' Schwind assured him. No sooner did he say it than, with pen and ruler, he transformed several sheets of sketching-paper into faultless three-stave manuscript paper. Then he ferreted out an old anthology of verse from his small collection of books, and pointed out five or six poems in it as being suitable for setting to music. Schubert had hardly read them before his pen was gliding merrily over the paper. Even before meal-time came, the songs were composed, and so beautifully composed that, to this day, Schwind maintains those music lines were not the least valuable lines he ever drew.

The composer Franz Lachner published his memoirs of Schubert in the Vienna *Presse* in 1881:

It was on a beautiful autumn day in the year 1822 that . . . as a nineteen-year-old youth . . . I went to Vienna.

My mid-day meal I took as a rule at Haidvogel's, at that time a very well-known eating-house in the Stefansplatz, which was pulled down some years ago. There, too, was frequently to be seen a young man of unusual appearance, apparently some years older than myself. There was something singular in his bearing. A round, fat, somewhat puffy face, an arched forehead, pursed-up lips, a snub nose and curly though rather scanty hair gave his head an original appearance. His height was below the average, his back and shoulders rounded. His facial expression was not uninteresting. Since he always wore spectacles, he had a rather fixed look. But if the conversation turned to music, his eyes began to light up and his features became animated.

Gradually the daily meeting, and the fact that I happened to sit next to this young man at a concert and was interested by his remarks on the musical interpretations, brought about our acquaintance. From this, as the similarity of our interests became apparent, there arose, by degrees, an uninterrupted, almost daily, association and a warm friendship.

The young man was Franz Schubert, a name then known only to a small circle of people but which ten years later attracted the attention of the entire musical world, when he was numbered among the stars of the first magnitude, not only as a song composer but in the sphere of instrumental music as well.

Through him, in due course, I also got to know his friends Bauernfeld,

Schwind, Randhartinger, Lenau, Anastasius Grün, Grillparzer, Castelli, Karajan, Dessauer, Feuchtersleben and others, with whom there arose a mutual daily association. We frequently foregathered at the inn *Zum Stern* [The Star], on the Brandstätte; there the poets read aloud their latest creations, as did Bauernfeld his comedies, a large proportion of which are still to be found in the theatre repertoires. And individual members of the company supplied us composers with the poems for both large and small musical creations. . . .

We both shared with one another, Schubert and I, the projects for our works and frequently went for walks, sometimes long and sometimes short, in the charming surroundings of Vienna, to Hietzing, Dornbach, Klosterneuburg, on the Kahlenberg and the Leopoldsberg, etc., when Schwind and Bauernfeld frequently joined us. Schubert was often in my apartment, which, at that time, was in a house giving on to a garden behind the hospital for disabled soldiers. There we played for the first time his glorious Fantasy in F minor, for pianoforte duet, and many of the other works written at that time.

Another story involving Schubert and Lachner was told by Lachner to a friend who published it in a special Schubert number of the Stuttgart *Neue Musik-Zeitung* in 1889:

In the afternoons Schubert and Lachner, both enthusiastic nature-lovers, used to go for walks in the vicinity of Vienna. On one occasion there attached himself to them a rather importunate fellow by the name of Siebert, a bass, deeply convinced of his own pre-eminence as a singer and, in fact, famous in Vienna at that time.

The two composers could not get rid of this individual, who was as insufferable as he was famous, and decided to have recourse to a sly attack on his vanity.

No sooner said than done. The two friends were in the habit of wandering alone though the woods on the outskirts of Vienna and of climbing up the hills for the views. Siebert did not budge from their side. So the two composers led him up a rather high eminence, the slopes of which were wooded. On reaching the top, Lachner and Schubert asked the bass, Siebert, if he would be good enough to sing them some songs and dramatic arias with that wonderful, silvery voice of his. Siebert was very flattered and consented at once. But the two gentlemen asked if they might listen to Siebert's songs and arias in the wood, where the dying away of his voice would produce an absolutely magical effect. Delighted, Siebert gave his consent.

For half an hour the vain singer sang to nature from the hilltop. The two composers departed quickly through the wood and for a long, long time continued to hear his vocal performances growing ever fainter until the voice of the abandoned singer reached them no longer. They were saved.

A charming, child's-eye view of Schubert is provided by Eduard Traweger, who was only four years of age when the composer and Vogl stayed with the Traweger family in Gmunden in the summer of 1825. At the age of thirty-eight, Eduard Traweger recalled those days:

I was laid up with croup; the doctor ordered leeches but no one could persuade me to undergo the operation. Vogl and Schubert encouraged me. Finally the unbounded respect for Schubert which my father instilled into us had its effect. In tears I asked Schubert if he would apply the leeches and this he did, under the doctor's instructions. As the blood-suckers hung on my neck Schubert gave me a silver pencil as a keepsake. I still remember this scene as though it were today.

When Vogl sang and Schubert accompanied on the pianoforte, I was always allowed to listen. On these enjoyable occasions relations and friends were often invited. With such compositions performed liked this, it was inevitable that feelings should find expression, and when the song was over it was not an uncommon occurrence for the men to throw themselves into each other's arms, and the excess of emotion overflowed into tears. How often have I told of such occasions afterwards! Hardly was I awake in the morning when, still in my nightshirt, I used to rush in to Schubert. I no longer paid morning visits to Vogl because once or twice, when I disturbed him in his sleep, he had chased me out as a 'bad boy'. Schubert, in his dressing-gown, with his long pipe, used to take me on his knee, puffed smoke at me, put his spectacles on me, rubbed his beard against me and let me rumple up his curly hair, and was so kind that even we children could not be without him. From a certain Albrecht, who is now said to be a school teacher in Haslach in Upper Austria and who might know something about those days because, as music master, he was often at our house, I learned the first steps in writing, and when I showed Schubert my first hieroglyphs he gave me a lead inkstand from his table, which was heavily laden with music, and this I preserve to this day as a sacred relic. This inkstand was always kept under glass until, when I became a student, I took it with me. With much trouble Schubert now taught me the song 'Guten Morgen, schöne Müllerin' and to this day I can still hear how he used to call to me: 'Come along, Eduardl, sing "Guten Morgen" and you will get a lovely *Kreutzer*' (generally a silver *Groschen*) – and I squeaked as well as I could. If friends were present it was more difficult to induce me to do it; but if Schubert took me between his knees and accompanied me like that, I managed it nevertheless.

Perhaps the most lively and most convincing of the elderly Schubertians' written recollections of the friend of their youth was Bauernfeld's. He, Schwind and Schober had been closer to Schubert than the other members of the circle:

In the winter of 1824–25, as a law student in my fourth year, I was up to my eyes in work with the Vienna Edition of Shakespeare as well as with my own writings. . . . At that time I also spent nearly all my evenings in my solitary room.

I was sitting thus in my den one evening in February 1825 when my boyhood friend Schwind arrived, bringing with him Schubert, who meanwhile had already become famous, or, at least, well known. We were soon on intimate terms with one another. At Schwind's request I had to recite some crazy youthful poems of mine; we then went to the piano, where Schubert sang and we also played duets, and later went to an inn till far into the night. The bond was sealed, the three friends remained inseparable from that day on. But others, too, grouped themselves around us, mostly painters and musicians, a circle of people, with a zest for life and with similar aims and ideas, who shared together their joys and sorrows; foremost among these was the excellent Schober, who finally arrived in Vienna in the summer of 1825.

In old age one gets loquacious now and again but it is only in youth that one really has something to impart and never runs out of things to say.

And thus it was with us. How often did we three wander about until the small hours, accompanying one another home – but as we could not bring ourselves to part, it was not uncommon for us all to spend the night together, at one or the other's lodgings. We were not very particular about comfort on these occasions! If necessary, friend Moritz would throw himself down on the bare floor boards, wrapped only in a leather coverlet, and once, when I did not have one, he carved Schubert's spectacle-case into a pipe for me. In the matter of property the communistic viewpoint prevailed; hats, boots, neckerchiefs, even coats and certain other articles of clothing too, if they but chanced to fit, were common property; but gradually, through manifold use, as a result of which a certain partiality for the object always ensues, they passed into undisputed private possession. Whoever was flush at the moment paid for the other, or for the others. Now it happened from time to time that two had no money and the third – not a penny! Naturally, among the three of us, it was Schubert who played the part of a Croesus and who, off and on, used to be swimming in money, if he had happened to dispose of a few songs or even of a whole cycle, as in the case of the Walter Scott songs, for which Artaria or Diabelli paid him 500 Viennese florins – a fee with which he was highly satisfied and which he wanted to use sparingly, though this, as always hitherto, remained merely a good intention. To begin with, there would be high living and entertaining, with money being spent right and left – then we were on short commons again! In short, we alternated between want and plenty.

To one such time of plenty I am indebted for having heard Paganini. The five gulden which this concert pirate demanded were beyond my means; that Schubert had to hear him went without saying, but he simply would not hear him again without me; he was seriously annoyed when I hesitated to accept the ticket from him. 'Don't be an idiot,' he cried. 'I have already heard him once and was annoyed you weren't there! I tell you, we shall never see this fellow's like again! And I have stacks of money now – so come on!' With that he dragged me off.

The picture of Schubert that emerges from the recollections of his friends may appear, on the surface, to have contradictory elements in it. One man's near-alcoholic, after all, is another man's good company. But the composite portrait of the composer which lived in the memories of his dearest friends is, surely, an attractive and amiable one. It is the portrait of someone with a gift for friendship, and a love of nature, whose purpose in life was to write music. It is also the portrait of someone who, though his music has proved to be able to transcend time and place, is nevertheless himself very much of his time and place, a typical Viennese in his love of his native city, and his delight in its parks, its alleyways, its churches and theatres, and its surrounding countryside. Surely to no other Viennese artist can one more aptly apply the lines of Grillparzer:

> Hast du vom Kahlenberg das Land dir rings besehen,
> So wirst du, was ich schrieb und was ich bin verstehen.

(If from Kahlenberg you have looked at the country around you,/you will have understood what I write and what I am.)

What one sees from the hill of Kahlenberg is Schubert's city of Vienna with its outlying woods and vineyards, and the winding Danube. This is the landscape from which the composer derived much of his inspiration. Looking down at it, one calls to mind the words Schubert wrote in his diary at the age of nineteen: 'There is hardly anything more agreeable than to get out into the green countryside at the end of a hot summer's day: and for this purpose the fields between Währing and Döbling seem to have been especially created. In the mysterious twilight and with my brother Karl for company, I felt so happy and contented. "How beautiful," I thought, and exclaimed aloud, standing still with enchantment.'

Appendix

Schubert wrote the following description of his travels in Austria for his brother Ferdinand. The letter was begun on 12 September 1825 (see p. 130).

Dear Brother,
Since you have asked me to do so, of course I should like to give you a detailed account of our journey to Salzburg and Gastein, though you know what a poor hand I am at relating and describing things. However, as I should have to do this in any case on getting back to Vienna, I would prefer to give you in writing now rather than in words later a faint idea of all this extraordinary beauty, for I feel this way is likely to be more successful than the other.

We set out from Steyr, then, about the middle of August, and went by way of Kremsmünster, which indeed I had often seen before, but which, on account of its fine position, I can never pass by. You look right over a very lovely valley, broken here and there by gentle little hills, to the right of which rises a fair-sized mountain; from the road that leads down from it, over a brook running in the contrary direction, you have a magnificent view of the great monastery spread out along the hill's crest, and of the extremely picturesque mathematical tower. We met with a very friendly reception, being already well known here, especially Herr von Vogl, who was educated at the monastery. We did not stop, however, but continued our journey, which does not call for any particular comment, as far as Vöcklabruck, which we reached that night: a dismal little hole. Next morning we came by way of Strasswalchen and Frankenmarkt to Neumarkt, where we had lunch. These villages, which lie in the county of Salzburg, are remarkable for the peculiar construction of their houses. Nearly everything is of wood. The wooden kitchen utensils rest on wooden stands, and these are placed outside the houses, round which run wooden balconies. Old targets, too, pierced through and through, are to be found hanging up everywhere outside the houses. These are preserved as trophies of victory from a long time past: the dates 1600 and 1500 are frequently to be found on them. Bavarian money begins to be used here too. From Neumarkt, the last postal stage before

Salzburg, mountain peaks with fresh snow upon them were already visible, rising out of the Salzburg valley. About an hour or so from Neumarkt, the country becomes really fine. The Wallersee's clear blue-green stretch of water gives a vivid touch of colour to this completely charming landscape. The land here lies very high, and from this point the road drops steadily down as far as Salzburg. The mountains rise up ever higher, in particular the Untersberg, which stands out, fantastic and wonderful, above the rest. The villages show traces of former prosperity. Marble window-frames and door-posts are to be found everywhere, even in the poorest farmhouses, and sometimes staircases of red marble too. The sun grows dim, and heavy clouds float over the black mountains like nebulous spirits. Yet they do not touch the summit of the Untersberg, but creep past it as though terrified of its dreadful interior. The broad valley, with its sprinkling of solitary castles, churches and farmyards, slowly unfolds itself before our spellbound eyes. Towers and palaces gradually appear, and at last we pass the Kapuzinerberg, whose vast wall of rock rises sheer up from the roadway, and frowns menacingly down upon the traveller below. The Untersberg and its attendant mountains assume gigantic proportions, as though they would crush us with their magnitude. And now the road leads by way of some very fine avenues into the town itself. This famous seat of the former Electors is surrounded by fortresses built of great rocks of rough-hewn stone. The inscriptions on the city gates bear witness to the vanished power of the church. The moderately broad streets are filled with houses all five or six storeys high, and our way now lies, past the quaintly decorated house of Theophrastus Paracelsus, over the bridge which spans the dark and foaming torrent of the Salzach. The town itself made rather a gloomy impression upon me, for the bad weather caused the ancient buildings to look more sombre still, and the fortress which stands on the highest peak of the Mönchsberg seems to send its ghostly greeting down through every street. Unfortunately, just after our arrival the rain set in – no rare event here – and our sight-seeing in consequence was confined to the many palaces and splendid churches which we had already glimpsed in driving past. Through Herr Pauernfeind, a merchant known to Herr von Vogl, we obtained an introduction to Count von Platz, president of the assizes, by whose family we were most kindly received, our names being already known to them. Vogl sang some of my songs, whereupon we received a pressing invitation to perform the same items again before a specially invited audience on the following evening. On this occasion the 'Ave Maria' mentioned in my first letter met with particular favour and touched all hearts. The way in which Vogl sings and I accompany him, so that we seem to be fused for the moment into a single being, is something entirely new and unknown to these people. Next morning, after climbing the Mönchsberg, from which there is a view over the greater part of the town, I was really astonished at the profusion of splendid buildings, palaces and churches. Yet the number of inhabitants here is small: many of the buildings stand empty, several are occupied only by one family, or at the most two or three. In the many beautiful squares grass grows between the paving-stones, so little are they frequented. The cathedral is a heavenly building, on the pattern of St Peter's in Rome, but of course on a smaller scale. The church is in the form of a cross, and is surrounded by four vast courtyards, each of which forms in itself a public square. Colossal figures of the apostles, carved in stone, stand at the entrance doors. The interior of the church is supported by a number of marble pillars, is adorned with portraits of the Electors, and is really beautiful in every detail. The light, which shines in through the cupola, illuminates every corner. The effect produced by this extraordinary clarity is most wonderful, and all other churches would do well to imitate it. In the four courtyards surrounding the church there are great fountains, and these are decorated with the finest and most daring figures imaginable. From here we went into St Peter's monastery, where Michael Haydn once lived. This church is wonderful too. Here too, as you know, is M. Haydn's monument. It is quite attractive, but badly placed in a remote corner, and the scraps of music-paper carved round it make a rather silly effect. The urn contains his head. I thought to myself: may your calm, clear spirit, good Haydn, rest upon me, and though I cannot ever be so tranquil and so clear, yet certainly no one on earth reveres you more than I. (A heavy tear fell from my eye, and we moved on further.) We had lunch at Herr Pauernfeind's, and in the afternoon, as the weather allowed us to go out, we climbed the Nonnenberg, which, though not very high, has the most beautiful view of all. You see right over the inner Salzburg valley from there. It is almost impossible to give you any idea of the loveliness of this valley. You must imagine to yourself a garden, many miles in circumference, in which innumerable castles and estates peer out through or above the trees. Imagine a river too, winding its serpentine course through the landscape; imagine meadows and fields like so many exquisitely coloured carpets; imagine excellent roads which twist ribbon-like about them; and finally vast avenues of gigantic trees, all this surrounded by an immense range of mountains, as though they were the guardians of this heavenly valley. Imagine all this and you will have a faint idea of its inexpressible beauty. The rest of our sight-seeing in Salzburg will not be done until the return journey, and I will leave it till then, for I want to continue my description in the right chronological order.

Steyr, 21 September

From the date above, you will see that several days have slipped by between these lines and my last, and that we have moved, alas, from Gmunden to Steyr. So, to continue my account (which I may say I now regret ever having begun, since it runs away with so much of my time), I follow the following-up as follows: the following morning, that is to say, was the finest day in the whole world. The Untersberg [literally 'lower mountain'], or rather the highest mountain, with its own squadron and the rest of the mountainous mob, shone and sparkled magnificently in – or rather next to – the sun. We drove through the valley already described as through Elysium, though our paradise had this advantage over the other, that we were seated in a delightfully comfortable carriage, a luxury unknown to Adam and Eve. Instead of encountering wild beasts, we met with many a charming girl. . . . It is really not right to make such feeble jokes in such beautiful surroundings, but I simply cannot be serious today. Thus, sunk in bliss, we steered our easy course through the lovely day and still lovelier country, until our attention was caught by an attractive building known as Monat-Schlösschen [Month's Little Castle] because an Elector had it built in a single month for a fair lady. Everyone here knows this, but no one is shocked. What enchanting tolerance! The charm of this little building certainly adds to the beauty of the valley. A few hours later we came into the remarkable but extremely dirty and dismal town of Hallein. The inhabitants all look like ghosts: pale, hollow-eyed, and thin as sticks. The dreadful contrast between this rathole and the surrounding valley made the gloomiest impression upon me. It was like falling from heaven on to a dung-heap, or hearing, after the music of Mozart, some piece by the immortal A. There was no inducing Vogl to see either the salt mountain or the salt-mines, for his great soul, harried by gout, urged him on to Gastein, like a traveller in the dark yearning for a ray of light. So we drove on further, past Golling, where the first huge, impassable mountains came into view, whose fearful gorges are crossed by the Lueg pass. After we had crawled slowly up the side of one great mountain, with other terrible ones to either side and immediately in front of us, as though the whole world were boarded up here with no possible way through, having reached the highest point we looked suddenly straight down into a terrifying ravine, and my heart leapt into my throat. After we had recovered a little from the first shock, we were able to look at the fantastically high walls of rock which seemed to end some distance away in a blind alley with no visible outlet. In the midst of these fearful works of nature, man has striven to immortalize his still more fearful bestiality. For here, where far, far below, the Salzach river foams and thunders over its rocky bed, there took place that fearful massacre of the Bavarians on one side of the river by the Tyrolese on the other. The Tyrolese, concealed on the rocky heights, fired down with fiendish and triumphant yells on the Bavarians, who were trying to gain the pass, and those who were hit were precipitated into the abyss, without so much as seeing whence the shots came. A chapel was erected on the Bavarian side, and a rough cross set up in the rocks on the Tyrolean side, partly to commemorate this extremely shameful outbreak which continued for several days and weeks, and partly as an act of expiation. O glorious Christ, to how many deeds of shame must thou lend thine image! They set up thy likeness, who art thyself the most terrible monument of all to man's fallen state, as though to say 'Behold! We have trampled with impious feet upon almighty God's most perfect creation. Why should it cost us pains to destroy with a light heart the remaining vermin, called Man?' But let us turn away our eyes from such melancholy sights, and apply ourselves rather to finding a way out of this hole. After a longish descent, with both walls of rock drawing ever closer together, and the road and stream narrowing down to a total breadth of 2 fathoms, the road turns here, where you least expect it, below an overhanging rock where the constrained Salzach rages furiously, to the traveller's pleasant surprise. Though still shut in by mountains as high as the sky, the road now continued broad and level. In the afternoon we came to Werfen, a market town with an important fortress that was built by the Electors of Salzburg and is now being restored by the Emperor. On the way back we climbed up to it. It is d——d high, but offers a splendid view over the valley, which is bounded on one side by the immense range of the Werfen mountains. These are visible as far as Gastein. Heavens! Hell! Describing a journey is a terrible business. I simply cannot do any more. As I shall be coming back to Vienna in any case at the beginning of October, I will hand over this scrawl to you myself, and tell you the rest in person.

(The 'mathematical tower' is an eighteenth-century observatory which contains a collection of mathematical and astronomical instruments. The Electors mentioned by Schubert are the Archbishops of Salzburg, who, as well as being primates of the Catholic Church, were also secular princes and, as such, Electors of the Empire. The house in Salzburg where the famous physician Paracelsus died in 1541 is still standing on the 'Platzl', near the main bridge across the Salzach. The composer Michael Haydn was the younger brother of the more famous Joseph. The composer 'A', contrasted so unfavourably with Mozart, may be Johann Georg Albrechtsberger [1736–1809], a minor Viennese organist, composer and teacher, with whom the young Beethoven studied for fifteen months.)

Select List
of Books in English

(An exhaustive bibliography is to be found at the end of the Schubert article in *The New Grove Dictionary of Music and Musicians*, London, 1980.)

Gerald Abraham (Ed.), *Schubert: A Symposium* (London, 1946)
Maurice J. E. Brown, *Schubert: A Critical Biography* (London, 1958)
Maurice J. E. Brown, *Schubert Songs* (London, 1967)
Maurice J. E. Brown, with Eric Sams, *The New Grove Schubert* (London, 1982)
Richard Capell, *Schubert's Songs* (Second edition, London, 1957)
Otto Erich Deutsch, *Schubert: A Documentary Biography* (London, 1946)
Otto Erich Deutsch, *Schubert: Memoirs by His Friends* (London, 1958)
Alfred Einstein, *Schubert* (London, 1951)
John Reed, *Schubert: The Final Years* (London, 1972)
Joseph Wechsberg, *Schubert: His Life, His Work, His Time* (London, 1977)

Index

General Index

Index of Works by Schubert
Referred to in the Text

A NOTE ON THE TYPE

The text of this book was set in a digitized version of Bembo, a well-known Monotype face. Named for Pietro Bembo, the celebrated Renaissance writer and humanist scholar who was made a cardinal and served as secretary to Pope Leo X, the original cutting of Bembo was made by Francesco Griffo of Bologna only a few years after Columbus discovered America.
Sturdy, well balanced, and finely proportioned, Bembo is a face of rare beauty, and is extremely legible in all of its sizes.

Composed in Great Britain.

Printed and bound by the Haddon Craftsmen, Inc.,
Scranton, Pennsylvania.

Display and binding design by Marysarah Quinn.